LANGUAGE

AND INFORMAL LOGIC

LANGUAGE

AND INFORMAL LOGIC

ROBERT T. HARRIS

Bradley University

AND

JAMES L. JARRETT

Great Books Foundation

and

Columbia University

❧

LONGMANS, GREEN AND CO.

NEW YORK • LONDON • TORONTO

LONGMANS, GREEN AND CO., INC.
55 FIFTH AVENUE, NEW YORK 3

LONGMANS, GREEN AND CO., Ltd.
6 & 7 CLIFFORD STREET, LONDON W 1

LONGMANS, GREEN AND CO.
20 CRANFIELD ROAD, TORONTO 16

LANGUAGE AND INFORMAL LOGIC

PUBLISHED SIMULTANEOUSLY IN THE DOMINION OF CANADA
BY LONGMANS, GREEN AND CO., TORONTO

FIRST EDITION APRIL 1956
REPRINTED JANUARY 1957
AUGUST 1958

LIBRARY OF CONGRESS CATALOG CARD NUMBER 56-6217

Printed in the United States of America

VAN REES PRESS • NEW YORK

To

PAUL ✓ PETER ✓ EUGENE ✓ JOHN

✦

To

DENNIS ✓ BRENT ✓ JULIE

PREFACE

This book is about communication among men. Its chief aim is to increase the reader's skill in interpretation and expression of meaning. The authors have tried to give a simple but accurate picture of what languages are and do, and to discuss various kinds of meaning and the linguistic vehicles that convey them. It is not their intention to teach composition, rhetoric, or speech but rather to forward learning in those subjects by a general discussion of language and informal logic.

We have made abundant use of studies in many fields: linguistics, anthropology, sociology, psychology, and physiology; logic, semantics, and communication theory; lexicography and grammar; speech, rhetoric, composition, poetry, and literary criticism.

Although no effort has been spared to keep our book elementary and readable we have attempted to avoid misleading and annoying oversimplification. Readers do not deserve to be "talked down" to, and they should be spared anything that might later have to be unlearned. With this in mind, we have tried to maintain a cautious attitude toward undue rigidity in distinctions like Meaningful vs. Meaningless, Fact vs. Value, Emotive vs. Referential—all of them popular distinctions, to be sure, but sometimes misleading ones.

This is a book based on the conviction that poetry at its best is not less meaningful than physics at its best, and that any theory which denies this needs a new definition of "meaning." Nor are political, economic, and psychological realities denied just because they are intangible. "It is very simple," as Kant once said, "to make a popular presentation by merely renouncing all thorough insight." In its support of these high-level realities, as in its determined avoidance of a too easy consistency, the book is not less, but more, empirical.

A major pedagogical assumption back of the book is that mere reading is not enough; it is no substitute for discussion, mental exercise, writing. Perhaps the most important part of the book is the part not yet written, namely, the exercises and problems which are set for the reader to do. Many of these exercises have a logical content, and in part on this account we hope that the book may also be looked upon as a "logical primer," or rather "pre-logic," which can help teach what people ought to know—but seldom do!—before they study the more rigorous and formidable sorts of formal logic. The authors are indebted to many friends and colleagues for help in writing this book. We express our gratitude to all of them, especially to Ralph William Moore, Elizabeth Opal Stone, Baker Brownell, Paul Hunsinger, and Charles D. Tenney; also Waldemer Read, William Kent, Herbert Hackett, and Marjorie Jarrett. All made helpful criticisms and suggestions. The latter four read the entire, or nearly the entire, manuscript.

R.T.H.

J.L.J.

CONTENTS

LANGUAGE

AND INFORMAL LOGIC

INTRODUCTION:

TOWARD A LOGIC FOR BETTER

COMMUNICATION

Can Communication Be Improved? • Studies of Language and
Thought • Developing a Sound Philosophy of Communication

CAN COMMUNICATION BE IMPROVED?

Once upon a time there were three brothers who lived by
themselves in a house in the woods. They were honest, hard-
working fellows, but in spite of their conscientiousness and
honesty, they were poor and sometimes hungry. But uncom-
plainingly they went their way, confident that one fine day
their fortunes would take a turn for the better. And sure
enough, a kind and powerful troll of the nearby burn, taking
cognizance of the deservingness of the three boys, made them
a visit, and announced that he happened to have left in his
hoard one old, unused wish, which he was prepared to be-
stow on one of the brothers. But which one? There was nothing to choose among them in the way of virtue, so the troll
decided to stage a small contest. "Tell me in advance the
wish you will make if you get the chance," said he, "and the
prize will go to him whose wish best expresses his need." So
the brothers retired to think, and after a time, they announced that they had made their several decisions. The
oldest brother, who spoke first, said that if the wish were his

for the making, he would wish for a million thalers, for though he was not a miser, he thought he would be able to spend the money to very good advantage so as to gratify any number of subordinate wishes. The middle brother then took his turn to say that his wish would be for good health over a long life. The youngest boy, though impressed with the projects of his brothers, took heart and boldly spoke out: "Oh troll, if the wish is to be mine I will use it to ask for the gift of *perfect communication*. For if I am able on all occasions to express myself, to make others understand exactly what I want them to know, speaking to their hearts as well as to their heads; and if I in turn can always understand what others speak and write, detecting their intent and their latent as well as their manifest meanings, then I shall have something more valuable to myself, to my brothers, and to mankind as a whole than health or wealth or any other gift I can conceive."

Now you may be astonished to learn that the troll awarded the wish to the eldest brother; and he did it on the grounds that whereas the youngest was already highly articulate, and the middle brother was the picture of health, the eldest brother was unquestionably poverty-ridden. To this day there are disputes among the trolls as to the wisdom of the decision. But the troll who made the award was really vindicated, for the wealthy brother provided the best physicians and gymnasts for the middle brother and sent the youngster to school to study linguistics, rhetoric, and logic, while he himself lived to a ripe old age, gouty and inarticulate, playing idiot's delight and eating cashews.

Prejudiced perhaps by pity for his youth and honesty, we feel some sympathy with the wish of the youngest brother. The need which he expressed is as poignant and as universally human as the needs of health and wealth. Man has been defined as the featherless biped, as the animal that cooks his food, as the rational animal; and it was William Hazlitt who said: "Man is the only animal that laughs and weeps, for he is the only animal that is struck by the difference between what things are and what they ought to be." But for the purposes of this book, a book about communication among men, man will best be thought of and defined as "the symbolizing animal."

To the definition of man as *animal symbolicum*, objections occur. Man is not the only creature that communicates. Dogs communicate their wants by barking and yelping and whining and scratching and jumping and running. Surely this is symbolizing and communicating activity. It is now known, largely through the important work of Karl von Frisch [1] that bees have fairly accurate ways of passing information, by means of dances. Having discovered a food site, foraging bees return to the hive and perform a dance, which by its tempo and its orientation, clearly indicates the distance and the direction of the site. This too is symbolizing activity. Therefore, man is not the only symbolizing animal; he has no monopoly upon symbols, their production and their interpretation. However, no one will dispute that alongside the almost infinite complexity of human symbolizing, the symbolic activity of other creatures is simple and slight.

The life of every human being is in very large measure a prolonged attempt to communicate with somebody, with his fellows, with beasts, with higher powers, with himself. Everybody knows how deep can be the frustration stemming from blocked communication. From bawling infancy, when we are enraged that our wants should go unrecognized and unassuaged, to reminiscent dotage, when we may bitterly reflect on never having been really "understood"—from one end of life to the other—we have occasion to deplore our weakheaded, insensitive, and inattentive associates who so often miss our point. We rebuke language for its poverty: "There aren't words for what I feel," "Words can't express it." We sometimes even regret our own inability to say what we mean.

[1] See his *Bees, Their Vision, Chemical Senses, and Language* (Ithaca, New York: Cornell University Press, 1950).

If we have trouble in making ourselves understood by others, we are no less impressed with the inadequacy of their attempts to get across to us. "What in the world is he talking about?" we complain, not really expecting an answer. "Do you understand what he's saying?" one coed whispers to another; and the answer may be, "Does *he?* Does the teacher?" But the teacher in his turn collects "howlers" from student papers (" 'Delete' means the very best type of English—almost perfect"; " 'Syntax' means too many forbidden words."); and the teacher tries to think how his lecture could have gone so far wrong. A politician announces that a satisfactory compromise has been reached with his opponent, and he is astonished when the newspaper headlines say, "Surrender. . . ." Another politician gets a reputation for being a fascist when a comment of his about Hitler gets quoted out of context, the qualifications omitted, the contrary evaluations left out. A romance is wrecked when something said in a playful tone does not communicate its playfulness.

So impressive are the failures in communication that we may be led to sigh, "It's hopeless." Perhaps we decide that communication always and necessarily bogs down in the slough of subjectivism; that is, each of us is a unique person, whose feelings and ideas and attitudes differ from those of everyone else. Ideas are inherently private, and hence incommunicable. "Who knows," Jeff says to his roommate, "whether what I see when I see yellow is the same as what you see? Maybe your yellow is my blue and since I can't get inside your head nor you mine, there's no way in all the world to find out. And so, maybe, with everything else. We use words like 'anger' and 'pain' and 'salty' and 'funny' when we talk to each other, but how can we tell whether we ever mean the same thing by them? How do I know right now whether you are taking my words to mean what *I* mean by them? And it won't help to use some other words, to put my meaning some other way, for whichever way I choose, there's always the possibility that the words mean something different to you."

And so saying, Jeff walks out into the night, feeling very inscrutable and very lonely.

Yet, though the argument is fascinating, there is good reason for feeling less gloomy than that. We can become aware of the dangers of motor travel without selling our car in a panic. People do continue to drive and to reach their destinations unscathed. And all of us do communicate with a wide variety of persons. We ask questions and get answers, sometimes satisfactory ones. We give directions and our hearers act, sometimes quite as directed. We express theories and get contradicted or agreed with; in either case we must have been, at least in large part, understood. We express our feelings and desires, and our associates in return make gestures and say words that indicate we have pretty well got across to them. If there are times when we fail to understand and to be understood, there are also times when we rather conspicuously succeed in communicating.

There are three basic methods of increasing our success in communication.

1. Perhaps the most important single preparation lies in clarifying the thoughts that we intend to express. Training in Logic and classes in the arts of writing or speaking will never take the place of "knowing our business." Speakers who impress us as giving a confused account usually do not really know what they are talking about. When we find it distressingly difficult to explain something, honesty will often prompt us to confess that we do not ourselves clearly understand it.

2. After knowing well what we wish to talk about, the obvious way to improve our communication is by careful practice in speaking and writing. We must cultivate good habits of expression and instill in ourselves through repeated use the various language skills. To listen acutely and to read acutely, moreover, are of the essence: "Try to be one of the people on whom nothing is lost!"

3. Still a third way of augmenting our powers of communication is by paying attention to the structure of situa-

tions where communication takes place. A basic thesis of this book is that we can improve our communication by learning something about the logic that is present in communicative processes. What are words, symbols, signs? What is the nature of human speech, and what uses does language commonly serve? And how can we make our ideas and their expression clear and effective?

STUDIES OF LANGUAGE AND THOUGHT

Several great disciplines have arisen in intimate connection with our second and third ways of improving communication and in response to widespread human need. Some of these arts and sciences that concern themselves with language and thought are new, and some are ancient.

1. *Rhetoric.* About the most ancient of all is rhetoric, with its normative approach to language. The professional rhetorician is concerned with the standards, or norms, of skillful and effective speech and writing. His is an interest in diction, style and manner. The ancient sophist's boast was that he could teach the young man persuasiveness and grace in speaking. In its lowest terms, this comes to "how to win an argument," with the emphasis upon devices and tricks. But the art of rhetoric has had many high-minded devotees who rightly insist no person is educated until he can express himself clearly, forcibly, and with a certain elegance when the occasion requires.

Aristotle (384-322 B.C.) defined rhetoric as the "faculty of discovering in the particular case what are the available means of persuasion." He defended the art in this way:

The art of Rhetoric has its value. It is valuable, first, because truth and justice are by nature more powerful than their opposites; so that, when decisions are not made as they should be, the speakers with the right on their side have only themselves to thank for the outcome. Their neglect of the art needs correction. Secondly, even if our speaker had the most accurate scientific information, still there are persons whom he could not readily persuade with scientific arguments. True instruction, by the method of logic, is here impossible; the speaker must frame his proofs and arguments with the help of common knowledge and accepted opinions.... Thirdly, in Rhetoric, as in Dialectic, we should be able to argue on either side of a question; not with a view to putting both sides into practice—we must not advocate evil—but in order that no aspect of the case may escape us, and that if our opponent makes unfair use of the arguments, we may be able in turn to refute them.... Lastly, if it is a disgrace to a man when he cannot defend himself in a bodily way, it would be odd not to think him disgraced when he cannot defend himself with reason. Reason is more distinctive of man than is bodily effort. If it is urged that an abuse of the rhetorical faculty can work great mischief, the same charge can be brought against all good things (save virtue itself), and especially against the most useful things such as strength, health, wealth, and military skill. Rightly employed, they work the greatest blessings; and wrongly employed, they work the utmost harm.[2]

Aristotle's work established what rhetoric was to be for succeeding centuries. Here is a partial list of the topics covered in his treatise:

The nature and kinds of rhetoric
Lines of arguments
Fallacies
Refutations
Delivery
Clearness and propriety
Metaphor and simile
Prejudice
Praise and blame
Causes of human action
Laws, witnesses, contracts, oaths
Character and emotion
Happiness and its constituents

[2] *The Rhetoric of Aristotle* ... trans. by Lane Cooper (New York: Appleton-Century-Crofts, Inc., 1932), 1.1.

It will be noticed that rhetoric touches upon ethics, psychology, law, sociology and the more formal types of logic. In order to know how to persuade, one must know about what is good, what makes men act in certain ways, the formalization of rules, frequent ways of mistakenly arguing, and many other matters.

When Aristotle spoke of rational persuasion, he was by no means forgetful of the emotional side of man. But he recognized what is today sometimes forgotten, that the choice need not be *between* rationality and emotionality; and in any case that the ideal is not to become just a rational machine, but to become that completer type of man whose feelings and intelligence are integrated.

Aristotle and most of the famous rhetoricians since his time have tried to lay down rules and suggestions for speaking and writing more clearly, more adequately, more convincingly. Being primarily an art and a practical science, rhetoric does not admit of as much hardness and fastness as does the general science of linguistics, but it was Aristotle too who told us that it is no small part of wisdom to require of a study only as much definiteness and scientific exactness as its subject admits of. Rhetoric, like many other important disciplines that cannot be classified as exact sciences, has much of importance to communicate.

2. *Linguistics.* The linguist, in distinction from the rhetorician, increasingly thinks of himself as a scientist, minutely recording his observations of languages as they are actually employed, and generalizing from these data. He is but little concerned with "better" and "worse" language usage, insisting that his is an objective, descriptive task that has nothing to do with norms and standards.

The story of the development of any language, English for example—its borrowings from other languages, its coining of new words as the need arises, the loss of certain inflections, the disappearance of concepts such as the familiar second

person, "thou," the alterations in meanings, changes in pronunciation and so on—is complex and fascinating.

The *general* linguist is interested in the principles of the
structure, origin, and development of language. The *special*
linguist concerns himself with the structure, origin, and development of some particular language. And the *comparative
philologist* for the most part has examined groups of languages of kindred origin.

The modern general linguist has more and more concen-
trated on the spoken languages of non-literate and semi-
literate groups in order to broaden the base for generalizations about language. He has found that if you want to know
what is universally true of language, you really must take all
kinds into account: the languages of American Indians, Afri-
cans, Australians, Polynesians, and Eskimos. The modern
linguist also has largely dispelled the older and unduly com-
placent belief that there is a clear-cut distinction between the
civilized languages, like Greek, Hebrew, Latin, German, English, French, and Spanish, and the primitive languages. The
latter were once supposed to consist mainly of mere grunts
and groans, and manual gestures sufficient to indicate the
most rudimentary needs, wants, and responses. But Edward
Sapir has written: "The gift of speech and a well ordered
language are characteristic of every known group of human
beings. No tribe has ever been found which is without language. . . . Language is an essentially perfect means of expression and communication among every known people." [3] And
Susanne Langer has made the same point graphically: "People
who have not invented textiles, who live under roofs of
pleated branches, need no privacy and . . . roast their enemies
for dinner, will yet converse over their bestial feasts in a
tongue as grammatical as Greek, and as fluent as French!" [4]

[3] Edward Sapir, "Language," *Encyclopaedia of the Social Sciences* (New
York: Macmillan, 1948). Used by permission of the publishers.
[4] Susanne K. Langer, *Philosophy in a New Key* (Cambridge, Mass.: Harvard
University Press, 1942), p. 103.

3. *Logic*. When we say that language is fluent we mean to say much more than just that it is spoken fast. We mean that it conveys meanings, that it is able to narrate something or explain something smoothly, correctly, effectively. And so in the discussion of language we soon arrive at questions about meaning and logic. The individual user of language who is an effective communicator of ideas will be one whose sentences and paragraphs are packed with meaning that is rich and clear, and whose discourse is ordered and reasoned.

If rhetoric stresses correct and effective usage of language, and linguistics aims to satisfy curiosity about the nature of language, so another great discipline, *logic,* is directed toward the principles of clear, consistent, and true thinking. Logic is the study and practice of soundness in thinking, of validity in reasoning; and also, of course, of unsoundness and invalidity. Or logic may be viewed as *the* science of order, *i.e.,* whether of thought or of real or possible things.

The authors will carefully restrict themselves in this book to the least formalized branch of logic, the logic of meaning. However, a brief defense of logic in general and a still briefer exhibition of its branches are in order.

Life may be partially characterized as a series of problems. Are we not forced into the often rather unpleasant task of thinking precisely by our need to solve problems? Where did I leave my brief case? Now let me think.... Is the T-formation weak on end-runs? I'll have to think about that. That sociologist argues that jealous blondes make untidy housekeepers. Now, let me see; why should that be?... Is the increase of the Federal government's budget a symptom of a tendency toward dictatorship? If God is truly all-powerful, is He responsible for war and disease? Since there seems always to be some cause for each of man's actions, in what sense does he possess free will? Thinking aims at an answer, at a belief which will facilitate our progress toward some goal, at "easiness" rather than "uneasiness." And is not *good* thinking exactly that which enables us to reach such ends? Crooked thinking muddles, frustrates our desire for a way out of a difficulty. The study of logic has as one of its important ends the clarification of our ideas, and clear ideas help us in the way we want to go. So much for our own thinking. We also want and need to communicate to others and to understand them. One good test of the adequacy and clarity of our own thoughts comes in an attempt to communicate. And we generally cannot put over our ideas if our presentation is not coherent and consistent. Again, we will be often fooled and duped if we are not trained in recognizing the difference between logical and illogical argument.

Some have thought that logic is unnecessary, since no one is so foolish as not to recognize some errors, and since some who have studied logic are hypercritical. Now it is true that not even logic can help little Epaminondas to follow his mother's instructions; logic is not a substitute for adaptability, intelligence, and common sense. But it is a scalpel that can serve an intelligent man to cut through sophistry. Logic can help us avoid error, as hygiene, while it cannot invariably protect us from disease, may render us less susceptible to it.

The ancient Greeks, as we have noticed, were fond of calling man "the rational animal." But some have always, rather foolishly, taken this differentia for the complete definition, as if it said that man is rational and nothing but rational. In our own time so much has been said about man's unconscious motivations, about his ability to rationalize (sometimes defined as giving *good* reasons rather than *real* reasons), and about his emotional drives, that we are almost tempted to characterize man as "the irrational animal." Still, it is hard to see what meaning can be assigned to "irrationality" unless "rationality" is meaningful. The psychoanalysts, for all their emphasis upon unconscious behavior, have as their therapeutic end the removal of psychoses and neuroses by enabling men to understand themselves, and thus to think clearly and to act reasonably. If there is a distinction between behavior that is economical, expeditious, and well-directed, and that which is confused, mixed up, and unproductive of desired ends, there is a distinction between rational and irrational behavior. Logic is studied as an aid to the former way of behaving. Consider the following little dialogue from the *Discourses* of Epictetus, a Stoic philosopher who lived early in the Christian era.

When one of his audience said, "Convince me that logic is useful," he said,

"Would you have me demonstrate it?"

"Yes."

"Well then, must I not use a demonstrative argument?"

And, when the other agreed, he said, "How then shall you know if I impose upon you?" And when the man had no answer, he said, "You see how you yourself admit that logic is necessary, if without it you are not even able to learn this much—whether it is necessary or not."

For logic is the knowledge of correct thinking processes. It discovers the norms, tells what are the marks of right thinking. Others, such as the psychologist, describe how men *do* think. The logician describes how men *ought* to conduct their thinking.

Logic is commonly but not inevitably divided into three parts: deductive logic, inductive logic, and the logic of meaning. (a) *Deductive logic,* or the theory of valid argument. A student reads in his arithmetic book: "Paul bought lemons and sugar for 25¢ and made lemonade which he sold for 40¢. What was his profit?" The student raises his hand to object that Paul hadn't had 25¢ in the first place. The derision of his classmates may be expressed as follows: It is to be assumed that Paul had this money; there are other assumptions; the assumptions are not themselves in question; we proceed *as if* they were true—their real truth being irrelevant; what we are asked to do is to deduce or infer the answer which follows from what is given.

The deductive logician is not interested in *what* people think about; he is concerned to find out how they may best think about it; he is interested in patterns of thought and other logical structures. You may correctly conclude that all cows are cunning from the assumptions that all cows are inspired by the devil and that all beings inspired by the devil are cunning. To make the inference is not necessarily to be taken in by the probably false premises. It is just to say, "If the premises *were* true, then this would be true too." If we hear someone say, "Michigan has the best football team in the country, and Labizowicz is Michigan's left tackle, so he is the best left tackle in the country," the logician will agree with us that something is rotten in Denmark, but he will want further to know *what* is wrong in principle, so that he will identify and name the same error every time.

These arguments with two premises and a conclusion are of a long-famous type called the *syllogism.* An invalid syllogism is one in which the conclusion does not follow with necessity from the premises. It may be true—Labizowicz may be All-American—but not for the reasons given. The interest of the deductive logician is, however, an abstract interest: he deals with actual arguments only as instances of types, or forms, of argument, and these types are his real subject matter. Hence he has a great tendency to use symbols: All S is M; All M is P; therefore, All S is P—whatever classes you may conceive S and M and P to be, whether shrimps, crustaceans, and prawns; or Communists, Totalitarians, and Enemies.

(b) The logician concerns himself with another kind of thinking in *inductive logic,* or the theory of true generalization. Here he is concerned with true answers, and not just with valid reasoning from given premises. Take a series of problems:

1. How do epileptics respond to insulin shock?
2. What family relations predominate in Polynesian cultures?
3. When did the English House of Commons assume the full power of appropriation of money?

4. What effect does the introduction of carp into a fresh water lake have upon the trout population?

How might you proceed to try to answer such questions? Well, you'd consider answers possibly provided by encyclopaedia and other reference works. You'd think of consulting historical manuscripts. You'd contemplate the possibility of direct observation, of statistical recording, and so on. But you probably *would not* suppose that the answers can be arrived at merely by deduction, as they can be in a formal science like mathematics. Most problems of physiology, psychology, political science, chemistry, physics, and other empirical sciences cannot be solved apart from generalization based on observation. For instance, from observing that in a very large number of cases children receiving an injection of a certain antitoxin did not contract polio, whereas of those children receiving a neutral injection, a certain percentage did contract the disease, a generalized conclusion is drawn about the effectiveness of the serum.

As to the method to employ in any given scientific problem, the best person to consult is an advanced student of the appropriate special science. The student of logic does not, as such, pretend to know about ways of counting fish or gathering ethnological data; these are not his problems. Questions which particularly interest him are: How may "scientific method" be adequately defined? What assumptions are involved in "sampling" techniques? Is it possible to achieve certainty in one's descriptions of the world? What is the role of hypothesis, or hunch, in problem-solving? That is, he is concerned to arrive at norms for good thinking in those situations where observation of actual states of affairs is necessary.

(c) A third major division of logic is made by marking off problems having to do with the linguistic tools and other means available to the thinker to express meanings and to ensure their adequacy and clarity. The *logic of meaning* studies topics like vagueness and ambiguity, kinds of words, the connotation and denotation of names, analysis, and definition. If there is no universally agreed upon title for this third division, "logic of meaning" *is* accurately descriptive. Sometimes "semantics" names the same field, and sometimes it does not.

DEVELOPING A SOUND PHILOSOPHY OF COMMUNICATION

This book draws upon linguistics, rhetoric, and the logic of meaning, but also upon the social sciences. Since its principal aim is the practical one of promoting better communication, the book is broad and informal, moving freely from field to field. The book and its logic are informal in the sense of staying close to the concrete realities of the languages of men. Logic—even the third kind—is always under pressure to dress up, to "go formal," to become neatly rigorous, elegant, abstract, and artificial. Just as the mathematician is impatient with quantifications like "several" or "a great many," so the formal logician finds ordinary language too indefinite for his purposes and takes refuge in specially constructed symbolisms. Everyone is grateful for the formal sciences with their fine discriminations, their absolute definiteness, their clean precision. But if there are times when we want our logic to be mathematically elegant, and there are such times, still there are other times when such perfectionism defeats our purpose, times when we want and need to deal with our language in all its thickness. Logic is informal when it stays close to ordinary language and syntax, when it investigates the regular and usual processes of communication, when it analyzes strategies of persuasion and ways of characterizing and defining.

This broad, informal, and elementary book starts—after this introduction—with a discussion of signs, for words are but one kind of sign, even though, for our purposes, they are the most important kind. Then emphasis will be placed upon the nature of language, upon words and names, their kinds, functions and combinations. The concern with meaning involves not only successes in meaning but also such failures as are brought to mind by the words "ambiguity," "vagueness," and "nonsense." Defining is then seen to prevent and to cure, when well used, many such failures. The principal uses of language are delineated and classified, a separate chapter being given to the problem of using language figuratively, metaphorically, analogically. The book concludes with brief discussions of persuasion, propaganda, and the individual and social advantages of improved communication.

Just as a tender and juicy steak may both delight our palates and nourish our bodies, so the most valuable of our studies are both pleasing and useful. The study of signs, language, and logic is, at its best, interesting; and any interesting study is its own excuse for being. But with the student's persistent coöperation, the study may be, in addition, useful and important.

EXERCISES

I. Distinguish between "descriptive" and "normative."

II. Distinguish by examples between "reason" and "rationalize."

III. Today the words "logic" and "logical" occur with some frequency in everyday speech. Examine the following expressions to see if in each case you can supply some reasonably close synonym *for* "logic" or "logical" and if you can tell what the speaker probably is trying to convey by his use of these words. (Naturally, *context* is important in such matters.)

1. He is the logical candidate.
2. What you say seems entirely logical to me.
3. In the logic of business, his action is quite understandable.
4. Artillery is the logic of kings.
5. The speech was logical enough, but I can't agree with his point of view.
6. The logical ending for this song is on D♯.
7. That's army logic for you.

8. "Grammar is the logic of speech, even as logic is the grammar of reason." (Trench.)

Can you think of any other usages of "logic" and "logical"?

IV. When it is said above of the deductive logician, "His is an abstract interest," what does "abstract" mean? What different meanings may it have?

V. Look up: "semantics," "semiosis," "rhetoric," "significs" (*Encyclopaedia Britannica*), "philology."

VI. Describe some situation you know at first hand in which a communication failure has resulted in serious misfortune.

VII. Balzac wrote: "Our biped soul will always accept as true what flatters his passions, caresses his hatred and serves his amours." ("The Wife's Appeal" in *Droll Stories*.) Taken seriously, how just is this observation?

NOTE: In this and the chapters to follow, there will be words, expressions, sentences and even longer bits of discourse which you will not completely understand. It is important that each reader do what he can to remove these difficulties. Three activities in particular ought to be engaged in:

1. Use a dictionary. (Get acquainted with several unabridged dictionaries.)
2. Re-read and ponder difficult passages.
3. Question yourself about the structure, scope, and content of the chapter.

SOURCES AND ADVANCED READING

1. Morris R. Cohen and Ernest Nagel, *An Introduction to Logic and Scientific Method*. New York: Harcourt, Brace and Company, 1934. Ch. I.
2. Hugh R. Walpole, *Semantics, The Nature of Words and Their Meanings*. New York: W. W. Norton and Company, Inc., 1941. Ch. I.
3. Charles Morris, *Signs, Language and Behavior*. New York: Prentice-Hall, Inc., 1946. Ch. I and Ch. II.
4. C. K. Ogden and I. A. Richards, *The Meaning of Meaning*. New York: Harcourt, Brace and Company, 7th ed., 1945. Ch. I.
5. *Language ... Man ... Society,* ed. by Harold E. Briggs. New York: Rinehart and Company, Inc., 1949.

→ II ←

SIGNS

What Are Signs? • Elements in Sign Situations • Iconic Signs and
Non-Iconic Signs • Symbols and Natural Signs • Kinds of Symbols
• Signals

WHAT ARE SIGNS?

Two lanterns hanging from Old North Church were a *sign*
to Paul Revere. A heavy layer of dark clouds *signifies* dirty
weather to the skipper of a ship. "Forward, march!" is the
signal to take off, left foot first.

Signs are sometimes difficult to interpret, requiring the
offices of an expert. "There are signs on this bell-rope," says
Sherlock Holmes to Dr. Watson, "which indicate the presence of a venomous snake." Red cheeks may be a sign of
fever and a cold or a symptom of allergy, or they may indicate momentary embarrassment or excitement, or be the mark
of an established habit of living outdoors. A sudden drop in
the Exchange may signify nothing more than a raid by the
bears; it may reflect the end of a remote military action, an
increase in interest rates, an approaching holiday; or it may
be the sign of imminent depression.

It is useful to see that words are part, but not all, of signs.
Such recognition will help us to take a practical attitude toward language. Words operate instrumentally as substitutes
for other kinds of signs; they are continuous in nature with
other kinds of signs. And verbal communication entails all

the pitfalls of sign interpretation. As Lady Victoria Welby said, "Language is only the extreme form of expression."

Many signs are read by animals. Thirsty cattle know that low thick foliage means water. A grown dog knows without putting its paw into the fire that it is hot. When a herd of deer flees from a sound, when a flock of sparrows rises from the meadow, when wild geese fly in formation following a leader and in uniform intervals, a sign or series of signs is being read and responded to. The present movements of each goose determine where it will be the next moment; and all the wing flappings of the whole "V" formation are so coördinated that the formation will persist.

Despite Longfellow's lines,

> Learned of every bird its language,
> Learned their names and all their secrets,
> Talked with them whene'er he met them. . . .

Hiawatha learned only pre-lingual sign behavior from the animals. Some of the more social animals, however, even some species far down the ladder of the animal hierarchy, respond sensitively and complexly to signs. The dances of bees have been mentioned, dances that indicate the location of a food site. Lorenz relates the following episode about an animal's intelligence:

My bitch, Stasie . . . having once eaten something which disagreed with her, wanted to go out during the night. I was at the time over-worked, and slept very soundly, so that she did not succeed in waking me and indicating her requirements, by her usual signs; to her whining and nosing I had evidently only responded by bury-ing myself still deeper in my pillows. This desperate situation finally induced her to forget her normal obedience and to do a thing which was strictly forbidden her; she jumped on my bed and then proceeded literally to dig me out of the blankets and roll me on the floor.[1]

---

[1] Conrad A. Lorenz, *King Solomon's Ring: New Light on Animal Ways* (New York: Thomas Y. Crowell Company, 1952), p. 83.

However, although a dog may prick up its ears when you say "Dinner," it cannot discuss the pros and cons of tomorrow's menu. And social birds, like geese and jackdaws, if reared singly, make their usual signals "as soon as the corresponding mood overtakes them. Under these circumstances the automatic and even mechanical character of these signals becomes strikingly apparent and reveals them as entirely different from human words." [2]

Yet even if automatic signals and responses are not always useful to the individual, they presumably have survival value for the species. Men and animals alike depend on signs to inform them what is going to happen, and what to do and what not to do. However difficult they may be to interpret, we do succeed in learning from visual and olfactory signs what things we may touch or eat; and otherwise we should not succeed in living at all.

What are the distinguishing marks of signs?

(a) Signs are everywhere: they are characterized as signs by their relations and functions. Anything at all that is noticeable may in some circumstances or other be interpreted as a sign.

(b) If it is a sign, it serves as an intermediary. A sign always signifies, is a sign of, something beyond itself. A sign may be something seen (like a yawn, a shrug of the shoulders, a mercury column, or a printed word), something heard (like thunder, a thumped melon, a siren, a dinner gong, or a spoken word), something felt (like an earth tremor, a fluttering pulse, a sample of tweed, a loose automobile clutch, a word in braille), something smelled (like smoke from the kitchen, an uncut cantaloupe, an unrefrigerated trout), or something tasted (like a sip of onion soup). To whatever sense it may appeal, in so far as anything is a sign, it is not an end in itself, but an indication of, a directive to or away from, a means of knowing or experiencing, some further thing.

[2] *Ibid.*, p. 77.

(c) Signs always communicate *through* one of our senses, but they may appeal *to* our appetite, our heart, or our head. The patriot's flag appeals to his loyalty and love of country. And some mathematical symbols appeal directly to the intellect; logical and mathematical symbols stand for relational and quantitative forms. Marks printed on paper can stand for arguments of any amount of intellectual complexity, and if you know how to read the marks, they may lead you to great knowledge and power.

(d) Our notion of a sign is pragmatic; it is of something that has reference to the future and to our future welfare. Wherever a sign is read, we suppose some creature or intelligence who is competent to read it, or perchance to misread it. We suppose that the creature can be affected by what the sign portends, and that it can respond to it, or avoid it, or attack it. Inanimate things with no future will find no signs. The disposition to read signs is the mark of life and meaning, and the degree of this disposition marks the intensity, complexity, or the elevation of life. Sensitivity to the future means, of course, sensitivity to pleasure and pain, to value and disvalue. Signs can tell you where to go; but if you are not going anywhere in particular, you are not likely to bother to read the signs. The man who doesn't care where he is going doesn't have to listen to the train caller.

Whether consciously or not, sign behavior is value-oriented. In large measure, interests determine which signs get seen. While the layman sees nothing much around the pond, the trapper is finding and identifying footprints. The skier sees the slope, the turns, and the quality of the snow, while his engineering friend is investigating the intricacies of the ski-lift.

Signs frequently imply space, as well as time and values. Animals have distance-receptors: antennae, eyes, ears, or nose. They are able, therefore, to respond adaptively to things that are more or less distant. An organism with distance-receptors may react appropriately to the sign as sign, *i.e.*, appropriately to the *things* that the sign stands for, and properly ignore the stimulus-object itself. Thus signs are the stuff of foresight; they illuminate the future for us and guide us into the field. However, sometimes our interest in signs is aesthetic; we may admire the billboard for its design rather than for its directions.

ELEMENTS IN SIGN SITUATIONS

1. Every sign situation includes an interpreter—a hearer or viewer. The interpreter is the party to a sign situation who grasps or tries to grasp the meaning of the sign. He is the receiver of meaning.

2. Then there must be the body of the sign itself—the mark, or gesture, or buzzer, or vocable which conveys meaning. This is sometimes called the sign vehicle.

3. Often there is also a producer. Whoever makes a sign for purposes of communication is a producer. If all three of these elements are present, meaning can be conveyed from the producer by means of the vehicle to the interpreter.

Accurate interpretation, like production, may require great energy and insight. Meanings signified can be easily lost or distorted. Gauges break down, clocks and bells get out of time, electrical communication systems develop short circuits. Too much faith in a seemingly 'obvious' reading of signs is an almost universal human failing. The questions are always worth posing: Is the signifying system in good order? Am I seeing and reading all the relevant signs? Is my interpretation thorough and correct?

That peculiar cloud—is it weather or is it smoke? That bugle call—is it "colors," and am I supposed to stop and salute? That yawn—is it mimetic and a sign of physical tiredness or is it a deliberate indication of boredom? And there are linguistic signs that have to be taken seriously. Your employer says, "You are certainly doing a fine job, but I do not know just what the future holds. I think that you might be wise to shop around, since that is the only way you can really know what is being paid for your kind of work." So at home that night there are doubts about what the "boss" meant. "Is he getting ready to fire me? Did he just mean what he said, 'That I ought to know what I am worth?' " This kind of interpretive analysis is part psychological, part crystal-ball gazing; but it is motivated too by the desire to be fully aware of the whole context, of the relation of this particular conversation to previous ones, of the timing, pace, tone, and so on.

Of what value are these interpretations? To interpret is to bring something from our past experience to bear in understanding a new experience. The habit of circumspect interpretation will help us reckon what kind of event to look for next. Just seeing signs is not enough. We must determine which ones are worth our attention. We must judge what is probably forecast by complex configurations. And as producers of communication, we must be kind and have insight into the problems of our hearers, as always "giving our neighbors' proceedings a charitable interpretation." The teacher will puzzle over how to put a point across to his class. The foreigner will wonder how to describe his way of life in the old country.

In interpreting, and in discussing the theory of signs, different emphases are possible. One may concentrate: (1) on the problem of the relations between the sign vehicle and the meaning (semantics proper); (2) on the relations of signs to each other: what are the principles of the combination of signs? what is the nature of the subject-predicate form? what are the parts of speech? (syntactics)· or, (3) on the relations between sign producers and interpreters: the student wonders how best to write impressively in his examination; the salesman or lover or lawyer adjusts his language according to the criterion of "persuasiveness" (pragmatics).

ICONIC AND NON-ICONIC SIGNS

One of two useful divisions of signs (sign vehicles) that we wish to make is that between iconic and non-iconic signs. An iconic sign is imitative. It is some kind of copy of that to which it refers, and it operates by virtue of the properties which it shares with the thing it stands for. Photographs of fugitives displayed in post offices are iconic signs; so are road maps, illustrations of merchandise in advertisements, the butcher's sample slice of cheese, and the perfume seller's damp dab on your wrist. There are also a few words which sound like what they mean, and they form a special word class, called "onomatopoeic." A good example is the word "ping-pong," but consider also "spatter," "screech," and "choo-choo." Such expressions often make communication effective by themselves being a sample of what is meant.

Since things may be alike in more or fewer respects, continuity between iconic and non-iconic signs is possible. A waving of the hand toward the body as a summons to another person would seem partly imitative of the action desired. But there is danger in assuming that any such bodily gestures are so purely iconic as to be universally understandable without convention. If young maidens in Nepal coyly indicated their willingness to be wed by thumbing their noses, we could not well claim any "un-naturalness" in the gesture. The employment of a gold ring in our culture to show that one is married is a matter of convention: virtually no one knows why, long ago, the gold ring became the sign of marriage. "Bow-wow" is iconic; but it is also in part conventional; the French and German equivalents, "Gnaf, gnaf," and "Wau-Wau," are more poignantly onomatopoeic. The English language is derived from many sources, and it is more highly conventionalized than most languages. In German many birds are named directly for their calls; in English, only the cuckoo and a few others. The strong tendency to conventionalize has the result that even onomatopoeic bird names take on a form related to usual English words, as, for example, in "Bob-White" and "Whip-poor-will."

Often an iconic character suffices to make you think of a certain object, but circumstances or custom and convention are needed to tell you *in what respect* to think about it. The picture of an arrow is a case in point. The (iconic) picture would just cause you to think of a real arrow except for the conventional use of arrow images to indicate direction. The arrow image by convention says, "Don't look at me, look where I point." A further relevant example is the school girl or boy painted on a sign. The iconic sign vehicle just brings to mind a school-age child. But when you stand it in the middle of the street, then it means, according to established convention, "School Crossing! Slow! Drive carefully and watch out for children in the street!"

People generally utilize, for reasons of communication, such signs as they have learned are appropriate to their purposes. The seeming fitness, or appropriateness, of a certain sign to that to which it refers is rarely inherent and rarely onomatopoeic. More often than we ordinarily realize, the "peculiar fitness" rests merely on our *being accustomed* to having the sign refer to the certain thing. Most signs used by men are neither natural nor causal nor imitative. But if we say, for example, that the name "Clem" or "Uriah" fits So-and-so to a tee, we do not refer to resemblance of the name itself to the person in sound, spelling, or any other respect, but we mean to evoke psychological associations. "Clem" was once frequent among the names of midwestern farmers; "Uriah" stands for hypocrite because of Dickens' character of that name.

SYMBOLS AND NATURAL SIGNS

Not all signs are deliberately produced; many are "natural," which is to say, they are items discovered and interpreted as signs without anyone having intended to make them signify.

Man purposefully communicates to man, but nature can also communicate. We often interpret a sign, as in the case of an inflamed skin indicating sunburn, without anyone's having deliberately produced the sign for purposes of communication.

Obviously, however, many of the signs with which human beings have to do are deliberately produced by somebody in order to put across a meaning. Since the division between natural and produced signs depends on whether or not the sign is *intended,* it is not easy, sometimes, to say whether a given sign is natural or produced. The distinction is the subject of much dispute. Are storms and floods communications from God to man? Do higher animals express themselves with deliberate intention to communicate meaning? And so on.

That noises and gestures made by human beings are deliberately communicative is not always a safe assumption. Yawning, crying, shaking may be unintentional. On the other hand, they may be intentional. If you see a child fall and begin to cry, generally you will take for granted that his crying is the unintended result of his pain. However, you should not let yourself be too amazed to see the child look around, and finding no sympathizers, suddenly stop.

Some natural signs are causes of signified effects; others are effects of signified causes. Both are commonly spoken of as causal signs, since that which serves as a sign is causally connected with whatever is signified. Smoke is caused by fire, and smoke signifies fire. Rain clouds induce you to eat your picnic lunch in the shelter instead of in the open. Smoke is an effect of the cause which it signifies; clouds are a cause of the effect which they signify. But when I point out to you the threatening clouds in the sky, I am not sufficiently conceited to believe that the gesture itself will cause rain to fall. Such an expression is not causal at all, any more than the word "cancer" is a cause of cancer. The book of nature is a great book, and we should do our utmost to read it with accuracy, always bearing in mind that we did not write it.

Natural signs are best read by scientists; they are sentences, so to speak, imprinted in the book of nature. To read them calls for a spectator with keen eye and cool head; it calls for stubborn patience and objectivity. An economist, for instance, is specialized in precisely and adequately interpreting certain kinds of indicators. The housewife exclaims, "My goodness, the price of coffee has risen again!" But the economist strives to relate the rise in coffee prices to other phenomena—he will try to connect it with drouth in Brazil, a shortage of carriers, an operation of brokers, or perhaps even with changes in habits of consumption.

Signs which may be produced by us intentionally are subject to wider control. They can be read, and we can move to or from them, as with natural signs. But we can also build them, gesture them, utter them, or write them. We can change them or erase them for aesthetic reasons; or we may keep them, out of respect for tradition. The deliberately produced signs and the conventional signs are characteristically human: Man is the animal that talks. Speech is the medium whereby men control and direct their mutual affairs. According to Aristotle, the naturalness of the political state is proved by man's faculty of talking.[3] To learn to create and handle signs, to make them serve our purposes, is an art of the greatest practical and human importance.

To read natural signs well is to know nature; to master the production of signs is to be expressive, persuasive, intelligible. Produced signs are commonly called "symbols," and their production is spoken of as "symbolization."

KINDS OF SYMBOLS

Symbols may be divided conveniently into linguistic symbols, signals, and other symbols. We shall discuss linguistic symbols at some length in the next chapter, and signals in this one. We merely mention "other symbols" in passing because

[3] *Politics*, 1253a.

they do belong to the same genus. Some of these are religious, like the symbol of the dove for the Holy Ghost or perhaps the olive branch for peace. Some of them are aesthetic or at least convey by tradition some feeling that has grown common. Consider autumn or sunset as symbols of growing old, the lily as a symbol of purity, the orchid as a symbol of luxury. There is so large a variety of expression possible through flowers that you may even hear of a "language of flowers." Man creates musical and other symbols of the fine arts, money, bookkeeping entries, and other financial and economic symbols, timekeeping and recording symbols, and many others. But these kinds of symbols, however fascinating, we cannot here discuss.

SIGNALS

A signal is a sign which has been expressly agreed upon as the occasion of concerted action. Its precise, restricted meaning has been established by deliberate pre-arrangement. It answers, in the final analysis, some definite Yes or No question. Signals are produced symbols, but in their mechanical character and limited function, they resemble natural signs. But the body of a signal, like a bell, can have any meaning we wish to attach to it.

Signal systems typically are made up of very simple units of communication, like the dots and dashes of Morse Code. But such a simple code can be charged with the conveyance of no end of complex messages; the code may be simple, and the system complex. Twenty-six little letters, along with order and punctuation, suffice to write down the entire English language and literature. Ten digits can represent the entire series of cardinal numbers.

Signalling has a long history that goes back to tree engraving and simple smoke signalling. Navies were among the first institutions to make a specialty of signals and to develop specialized equipment. The compass and the clock ushered in the modern era. Then in the last century the necessities of railroad control called for new invention and application. Trains used steam whistles, warning hands, flags, lamps, also bell-cord communicating signals from train to cab.

As the soldier responds to signalled reveille, chow-call, and taps, so the modern civilian starts his race with a shot, marks a football down with raised finger, gets up in the morning to an alarm clock, hurries to punch a time-clock; and he leaves again when the whistle blows. He travels by Baedecker and dines according to the Blue Book or Duncan Hines. A Luxembourg Guide contains the abbreviated listing:

Cloche d'Or Route d'Esch B W O G T 6391 10 70-100 110-140 15 45-60 140-175 [4]

The key in a guidebook is post-verbal and allows simple marks to stand for long paragraphs full of information. Many other kinds of contemporary signalling are non-verbal or pre-verbal. For example, learning to drive an automobile means, for the most part, learning to respond automatically and at a speed far beyond that of deliberate action or of human speech. A good driver reacts fast and selectively to all sorts of events seen beyond the windshield. He responds to road signs, hand signals, flashing lights, and sirens. Inside he watches his oil gauge, generator gauge, and speedometer and odometer.

The checklist of a commercial airliner pilot neatly illustrates how verbal activities can supplement sub-verbal and pre-verbal mental processes. The pilot and his co-pilot carefully, and in prescribed order, check whole series of gauge readings and other signals preparatory to take-off and landing. The checklist may be written out, printed, or memorized. In any case it is verbal and "objective," so that the pilot and co-pilot can use it together again and again to control consciously their many detailed operations.

---

[4] The Hôtel Cloche d'Or, on the road to Esch, offers bathroom, running cold and hot water, central heating, garage in the hotel, and telephone in the rooms. Its Luxembourg telephone number is 6391. It has ten rooms at 70 to 100 Luxembourg or Belgian francs for one person, or the same at 110 to 140 francs for two persons. Breakfast costs 15 francs, and other meals run 45 to 60 francs. Room with board is 140 to 175 francs per person.

In this chapter, to summarize briefly, we have said that there are iconic and non-iconic signs, and natural and produced signs. We have mentioned various relations of signification. The relation of iconicity is the relation of similar properties. A meaning may be conveyed by a natural relation: a shovel stands for digging because shovels *are* used for digging; clouds stand for rain because they *are* related to rain. And third, a sign vehicle can relate by symbolization to its meaning. In this case, the symbol is intentionally produced in order to represent meaning. All words are symbols, although onomatopoeic words are also iconic.

PROBLEMS FOR DISCUSSION

A. Can you think of any subtle uses of signs by dogs or cats?
B. "In the end, all referents are material objects." Discuss.
C. Give the meaning of the following:

futurity	referent
intermediary	telically
percipient	convention
exemplified	conventional

D. Read "The Gold Bug" by Edgar Allan Poe. State as economically and clearly as possible how the parchment message was deciphered.
E. Education has been defined to be the practical side of communication, "communication" being taken in its widest sense. Discuss.
F. What are the seven main approaches, historically, toward a theory of signs, according to Ogden and Richards? See the Preface to *The Meaning of Meaning.*
G. Peirce says that a symbol is a sign that is related to its object only inasmuch as it *will be* interpreted to mean that object, e.g., thanks to a convention or habit or natural disposition of the interpreter. Is this different from our definition? Can we say that one definition is better than the other?
H. Does the classification "natural sign" suggest that all others are unnatural? Can you find a better name?

I. Compare the following distinction with the relevant one in this chapter: "By a *signal* I mean nothing more than a stimulus to which a response has been conditioned.... By a *symbol* I mean something else. A symbol evokes response only in a relation to other symbols. Thus the 'same' symbol in different contexts can elicit essentially different responses, or to put it in another way, a given symbol cannot be properly defined outside of a context." (Anatol Rapoport, "The Role of Symbols in Human Behavior." *ETC.*, Spring, 1955.)

EXERCISES

I. Classify the following signs as iconic or non-iconic, and as natural signs or symbols:
1. Falling leaves as a sign of autumn.
2. A street sign on which is painted the figure of a schoolgirl, as indication of a school crossing lane.
3. A red flag as a hurricane warning.
4. The signature on a check.
5. Red hair as a sign of quick temper.
6. The sign of the cross as a blessing.
7. A white robe as a symbol of purity.
8. The Russian hammer and sickle.
9. The director of a radio show draws his hand across his throat to indicate time to quit broadcasting.
10. "Cathedral Rock" in "Meet me at Cathedral Rock."

II. Outline the chapter.

III. Is it more useful to classify the following signs as natural or produced? Why? Under what circumstances?
1. A hard slap on the back — produced to show friendly feeling.
2. The chairman pounding his gavel in a noisy convention.
3. Parasols up — interpreted as a sign of hot sunshine.
4. A bounced check — interpreted as a sign that the check signer is fraudulent.

IV. List six onomatopoeic words that are not given in this chapter.

V. Some engine whistle signals listed in the "Standard Code of Operating Rules" are as follows: ("O" is short whistle. "–" is longer whistle.)

O Apply brakes. Stop.

OO Engineer's answer to any signal not otherwise provided for.

OOO When standing, back.

OOO When running, stop at next station.

OOOO Call for signals.

Succession of short sounds: Alarm for persons or live stock on the track.

–OO A second section is following.

–– Release brakes. Proceed.

Devise a system for one-way communication to the cab from the train using only bell-rope.

SOURCES AND ADVANCED READING

1. Norbert Wiener, *The Human Use of Human Beings.* Boston: Houghton Mifflin Co., 1950.

2. Ernst Cassirer, *An Essay on Man.* New Haven: Yale University Press, 1944. Ch. II and Ch. III.

3. Susanne K. Langer, *Philosophy in a New Key.* Cambridge: Harvard University Press, 1942. Chs. II, III and X.

4. *Collected Papers of Charles Sanders Peirce,* Vol. II, ed. by Charles Hartshorne and Paul Weiss. Cambridge: Harvard University Press, 1932. Paragraphs 230-232, and 281-282, and 292-308.

5. Charles Morris, *Signs, Language and Behavior.* New York: Prentice-Hall, Inc., 1946. Ch. I.

6. *Language, Meaning, and Maturity,* ed. by Hayakawa, S. I. New York: Harper and Brothers, 1954.

✦ III ✦

LANGUAGE

AND LINGUISTIC SYMBOLS

Signs and Language • What Is Language? • Origin of Language •
Development of Languages • Learning One's Own Language •
Language: Natural or Conventional? • Language Consciousness

SIGNS AND LANGUAGE

There are ways of gaining information through signs that
are not language signs: for instance, by weather vanes. We can
sometimes express our feelings by mediation of non-linguistic signs: for instance, by laughing. There are non-linguistic
ways of indicating that something is valuable, worthless, or
dangerous, and ways of commanding "hands off."

But human communication and expression take place
usually and characteristically through the instrumentality of
language. For the most part, we even do our thinking in terms
of words, or in terms to which, at least, words are applicable
and for which they are available. Can you even *think about
yourself* without using such terms as "I," "my," "personality,"
"interests," "attitudes," "body," *etc*? Could you even *be* what
you are, if you were dependent on non-linguistic signs only?

Perhaps we have taken language—at least, our own language—for granted and thought of signs as things to be used
only when words fail us or when our voice won't reach.
Perhaps we have thought of signs and "sign-language" as instruments of the deaf and dumb, but not as instruments of

those with normal hearing and speaking faculties. Or we may have thought of signs as things to use when we must communicate with foreigners or bargain with Indians, that is, as extraordinary tools of communication to be used only when the ordinary device of our native language, in some rare cases and special circumstances, would not work.

But we have only to ask "Why do we produce signs, or read signs?" to see that linguistic symbols are a species of the genus *signs,* rather than something altogether different. Why *do* we produce signs? Many answers are required. We have stop-lights and railroad signals to organize and control behavior. We produce signs to "enjoy ourselves"! We sometimes talk merely to brag—to enlarge our reputation or to build up our ego. We may produce signs merely to exhibit our good manners or our gratitude. It is said that the Chinese, when the food is good, eat very noisily, in order to express their appreciation of the fine cooking. Among Occidentals, silence is a sign of breeding in diners. Composers and arrangers produce symbols in order to prescribe performance. Prescription and control are certainly among the major uses of language.

The giving, recording, and interpreting of information involve the use of language, as everyone knows. He knows very little about language, however, who thinks of it as merely a dictionary of words used by men for the communication of ideas. Language can serve demands for expression of emotion and prescription of action or for the lubrication of human relationships; and it can also serve superstition and magic.

Since language is thus the everyday stuff of life in all its aspects, the use of our own tongue seems entirely natural and normal. Words are subtle, and the organization of them in sentences and paragraphs is complex; but they are used so frequently, and sometimes so effortlessly, that they seem the most natural means of communication. The use of signals and other non-linguistic signs has come to seem "special"; and it is reserved for extraordinary occasions. But words perform the same intermediary functions as other signs; they refer to further things—things beyond and other than themselves, that are of interest to interpreters. Yet they are emphatically subtle and effective, even in distinctive and original ways. Grimaces and gestures, or sticks and stones, may be more forceful than language; but they are not able to convey meanings and overtones so varied and numerous. There are many sorts of forceful expression—artillery can command and money can talk—but only words can succeed, 99 per cent of the time, in making clear and distinct *what* is being forcefully expressed. So the *comfortable* feeling in hearing and speaking words only serves to accentuate the vast extent to which we use language symbols to perform essential sign functions.

Every human being uses at least one language. All but a very small number speak, and listen to their fellows speak, at least one language. In some nations almost the entire population can read and write the language that they speak, though in other places only a small number of persons are literate. And with certain languages it is impossible to be literate for the very good reason that the languages have no written form.

We all more or less know a language; but what is a language? What is language in general? What is it to *know* a language? And there are other, closely related questions: How did languages come to be? What are they for? Are some languages better (in some sense) than others? How do they function? How do they differ?

WHAT IS LANGUAGE?

Here is a definition by a linguist: "Language is primarily a system of phonetic symbols for the expression of communicable thought and feeling." [1] This is a compact statement; it deserves close inspection. Notice these emphases:

1. *Language is primarily phonetic.* Written language

---

[1] Sapir, "Language," *Encyclopedia of the Social Sciences*. Used by permission of the publishers.

typically follows after oral language, not only in that the child almost always speaks a language for several years before he reads or writes it, but also in the process of language development itself. Written languages are developed as transcriptions of oral languages; written words are symbols of sound-symbols.

2. *Language is a system.* Language is not just sounds, not just words, not just meanings; it is an organization of sounds, of words, of meanings. Language symbols are organized into a system which facilitates the variable needs of communication. Every language has a grammar. In every language, there are some ways you may combine the language units and some ways you may not—that is, if you want to get across to your fellows and be accepted by them. The grammars of primitive languages are often exceedingly complex. Just as a trained musician of our culture is sometimes baffled when he tries to put a primitive song into our standardized system of musical notation, so a grammarian finds that many Indian languages, for example, do not exhibit the same verb tenses or the same parts of speech that English and French do.

3. *Language is symbols.* Language is not just babbling and not just marks. Language symbolizes. A symbol is something which stands for something else, and does so in an intended way.

4. *Language is for expression.* By means of language we try to externalize our observations, our feelings, our ideas, our beliefs. The word "express" means, literally, "to press out," almost as you might press out the juice of an orange. We all know what it is to feel that there is something we want to say and not know how to say it. In such cases we try to put that "it" into language, to press out what is latent in our minds.

5. *Language is for the expression of communicable thought and feeling.* Perhaps there are incommunicable, ineffable thoughts and feelings; these by definition can't be put into language. But the authors and orators who especially im-

press us are those who succeed in finding the language in which to express what had seemed inexpressible. They (and then we too, perhaps) manage to communicate what had before been private. Language is not to be thought of as for the purpose of expressing just thought or just feeling. The distinction between thought and feeling is not a very sharp one, and it can be a very misleading one if its sharpness is exaggerated; in any case, through language we manage to communicate to others ways that we feel and thoughts that we think.

In order for language to serve communication needs, there must be a speech-community; that is, a group in which a given language is understood, a group whose members act alike in at least one important way, namely, in their speaking. Sometimes this point is made by speaking of the "interpersonality of language." A child may assign names to things, where the names are secret; or for purposes of keeping a diary secret a person may invent his own shorthand. We would hesitate to call a group of signs which were known to only one person, a language; though one may, of course, insist that such a secret "language" still serves communicative purposes, in that by its means one communicates with himself.

Edward Sapir, who made the definition just analyzed, wrote elsewhere an interestingly different definition: "Language is a purely human and non-instinctive method of communicating ideas, emotions, and desires by means of a system of voluntarily produced symbols." [2] This statement contains a few points not included in the other, so let us continue our analysis:

6. *Language is purely human.* Quintilian said long ago that God had properly distinguished man from the other animals, by giving to man the faculty of speech. No other animal has a language, though, as was said above, some of them have means of communicating that may be thought of as approxi-

[2] Edward Sapir, *Language* (New York: Harcourt, Brace and Company, 1921), p. 7.

mating language. We all know ways dogs, cats, and horses have of "telling us something." It is perhaps possible to teach some apes a few simple words—though the evidence is not clear-cut. Some birds, of course, can learn to repeat word-sounds, but they only echo the sounds and do not select the words to communicate. (Edgar Allan Poe's raven, who spoke the word "Nevermore," only *happened* to speak it at appropriate places.) And if no non-human animals have a real language, all human animals do have, excepting only some idiots.

7. *Language is non-instinctive.* Human infants no doubt babble instinctively, but they have to learn to babble sense. If a child could survive alone long enough, he would almost certainly come in time to walk, but without a society in which to grow up, there seems to be no reason to believe he would certainly come to talk.

8. Another characteristic of symbols is that they are *"pluri-situational."* That is, a given symbol "means the same thing" in a variety of situations and contexts. For instance, the word "red" though it does not designate *exactly* the same quality in every usage, can be applied to a number of different objects in order to indicate ways in which they are alike or nearly alike. Thus "red shirt," "red leaf," "red eye," "red sunset"— the word "red" in these several applications refers to approximately the same color. "Plurisituationality" is relative to the given language. For example, we use "hot" in both the phrases "hot coffee" and "hot weather." In Russian, the "hot" of "hot coffee" is "zharkeez," but the "hot" of "hot weather" is "gory-acheez."

ORIGIN OF LANGUAGE

If these eight points tell us some of the important characteristics of language, we might next ask: whence language? There must have been a time when language arose, as there must have been a time when men began using fire. Both language and fire have been thought to be gifts of the gods. The Egyptians prized language enough to make it the special province of the god Thoth. A Biblical account of the origin of at least a part of language follows (King James translation, Genesis 2:19-20):

And out of the ground the Lord God formed every beast of the field, and every fowl of the air; and brought them unto Adam to see what he would call them: and whatsoever Adam called every living creature, that was the name thereof. And Adam gave names to all cattle, and to the fowl of the air, and to every beast of the field . . .

It is not said that Adam also named the non-living parts of nature nor is it said that he invented the large part of language that is in addition to names; for instance, the verbs and prepositions and conjunctions. Again, it is not clear from the account in Genesis whether Adam had any principle to guide him in his naming or whether he assigned arbitrary names, as in a sense we do when we give proper names to new babies. (However, little girls have been known to look long and carefully at a doll's face before they decide on the right or appropriate name!) There is an old story which supplements what is written in the Bible, but which is inconsistent with the Bible because it speaks of Eve participating in the naming ceremony, whereas when God allowed Adam to give the birds and beasts names he had not yet provided the helpmeet; nevertheless, the story is at least amusing:

Eve, acting as Adam's secretary, took his dictation as he assigned the names. Two large birds first flew across the garden, and Adam said, "Write 'eagles'." Two great, maned creatures came by and roared, just as if they were kings of beasts, and Adam said, "Write 'lions'." Two long-eared, braying creatures grinned and Adam ordered Eve to put down "donkeys." Then two furry creatures lumbered by, and Adam said, "Write 'bears'."

At that point Eve betrayed the quality that was to prove man's undoing. "Bears?" she asked; "how do you know that those are bears?"

Adam glared at the interruption and snorted, "Because they *look like bears!*"

Somewhat similar is the Chinese myth describing the original assigning of names, an undertaking so exactly and precisely performed that by means of the names alone one could know exactly what a thing was. Of course, this is more plausible if one has in mind pictographs, or any other iconic signs, as names.

There is in the Bible at least one other interesting teaching about language. Here are the first nine verses of the eleventh chapter of Genesis (King James translation):

And the whole earth was of one language, and of one speech. And it came to pass, as they journeyed from the east, that they found a plain in the land of Shinar; and they dwelt there. And they said one to another, Go to, let us make brick, and burn them thoroughly. And they had brick for stone, and slime had they for morter. And they said, Go to, let us build us a city, and a tower whose top may reach unto heaven; and let us make us a name, lest we be scattered abroad upon the face of the whole earth. And the Lord came down to see the city and the tower, which the children of men builded. And the Lord said, Behold, the people is one, and they have all one language; and this they begin to do; and now nothing will be restrained from them, which they have imagined to do. Go to, let us go down, and there confound their language, that they may not understand one another's speech. So the Lord scattered them abroad from thence upon the face of all the earth: and they left off to build the city. Therefore is the name of it called Babel; because the Lord did there confound the language of all the earth: and from thence did the Lord scatter them abroad upon the face of all the earth.

It is a rich passage; among other things it suggests (1) the origin of languages out of one language; (2) the godlike power the human race might have if it spoke a common language; (3) the confusion and impotency that derive from a multiplicity of tongues.

The ancient Greeks were interested in everything, and not least in language. Leonard Bloomfield wrote that their "generalizations about languages were not improved upon until the eighteenth century, when scholars ceased to view language as a direct gift of God, and put forth various theories as to its origin.[3]

The richest of Greek writings on language is Plato's dialogue "Cratylus," a work in which Socrates and two philosophical students are represented as discussing various theories of the origins of names. Socrates tries to show how words often spring from roots, but that eventually there must be some primary names; then the question is, whence these? Perhaps they are vocal imitations, onomatopoeic sounds. But the objection is made that those who imitate the sounds of sheep and other animals are not thereby naming those animals. Perhaps there is some other sense in which names or even the letters into which written names can be analyzed, are imitative of things.

That objects should be imitated in letters and syllables, and so find expression, may appear ridiculous ... but it cannot be avoided—there is no better principle to which we can look for the truth of first names [i.e., roots which cannot be further analyzed]. Deprived of this, we must have recourse to divine help, like the tragic poets, who in any perplexity have their gods waiting in the air; and must get out of our difficulty in like fashion, by saying that 'the gods gave the first names, and therefore they are right.' This will be the best contrivance, or perhaps that other notion may be even better still, of deriving them from some barbarous people, for the barbarians are older than we are; or we may say that antiquity has cast a veil over them, which is the same sort of excuse as the last; for all these are not reasons but only ingenious excuses for having no reasons concerning the truth of words.[4]

---

[3] Leonard Bloomfield, *Language* (New York: Henry Holt and Company, 1933), p. 5
[4] Plato, "Cratylus," 425-26. Jowett translation.

Socrates recognizes still another theory, that

> names are conventional, and have a meaning to those who have
> agreed about them . . . and that convention is the only principle;
> and whether you abide by our present convention, or make a new
> and opposite one, according to which you call small great and
> great small — that, they would say, makes no difference, if you are
> only agreed.[5]

Socrates finds some truth in the convention theory, but also
believes that somehow names must originally be imitative in
nature.

In the nineteenth century, Max Müller, a famous linguist
and Sanskrit scholar, summarized the three chief theories of
the origin of language by the nicknames "bow-wow theory,"
"pooh-pooh theory," and "yo-he-ho theory." According to
the first, language had its beginning in imitations of the
sounds made by animals, or of other sounds, as the game ping-
pong gets its name from the sound made by the ball hitting
the table; the second suggests that the first utterances were
cries and groans and other instinctive expressions, evoked by
pain or intense feeling; the yo-he-ho theory explains the
earliest language as originating in work chants. Plato took
notice of the first theory. Democritus seems to have been the
originator of the thesis that speech arose in emotional utterances, and he was followed by Epicurus, Lucretius, and Rous-
seau, among others. Darwin, too, made much of this theory in
his book *The Expression of the Emotions in Man and Animals*. However, there seems to be no evidence that any human
group ever had an exclusively emotional language, that is, a
language in which nothing is designated or named. Sapir has
sharply criticized at least the first two of these theories by
pointing out that the onomatopoeic and interjectional aspects
of virtually all languages are relatively unimportant. He
added that in any case, such theories are inadequate, for they
fail to meet the great problem, that of explaining the emer-

[5] *Ibid*, 433.

gence of a genuine symbolic system out of whatever combination of expressive vocal sounds may have been the forerunners of language.

Otto Jesperson, the Danish linguist, has put forth the interesting speculation that language develops from song:

The further back we go in the history of languages the greater is the number of irregularities that we find, not only in morphology, and syntax, but also in vocabulary; the same thing is not always denoted in the same way, and instead of general terms as in our languages we find words with highly specialised and concrete meanings. The bigger and longer the words, the thinner the thoughts. The first framers of speech were not taciturn beings, but lively men and women babbling or singing merrily on for the mere pleasure of producing sounds with or without meaning; as an instrument for expressing thoughts their utterances were clumsy, unwieldy and ineffectual, but they served to give vent to their emotions, and that was all they cared for. One string of syllables sung to some kind of melody may have been so characteristic of a certain individual, that it came to be repeated by others to signalise his approach, thus denoting him and becoming a proper name for him—the most concrete of all words. Another song might serve to remind the tribe of some occasion when it was first intoned and might thus become an undifferentiated expression for what happened then. When a multitude of utterances of this kind had developed, each with some sort of special meaning, they might be combined in various clumsy ways and thus give rise to something that was more like the long intricate sentence-conglomerates which we find, for instance, in Eskimo.[6]

Both Sapir with his anthropological approach and Ernst Cassirer with his philosophical approach have repeatedly insisted that the problem of language origin cannot be meaningfully separated from the psychological and epistemological questions of how man came to discriminate a variety of things and qualities in his environment. Sapir freely admits that the problem is far from solved:

[6] Otto Jesperson, "Language," *Encyclopaedia Britannica*, 14th Edition.

About all that can be said at present is that while speech as a finished organization is a distinctly human achievement, its roots probably lie in the power of the higher apes to solve specific problems by abstracting general forms or schemata from the details of given situations; that the habit of interpreting certain selected elements in a situation as signs of a desired total one gradually led in early man to a dim feeling for symbolism and that in the long run and for reasons which can hardly be guessed at the elements of experience which were most often interpreted in a symbolic sense came to be the largely useless or supplementary vocal expression that must have often attended significant action. According to this point of view language is not so much directly developed out of vocal expression as it is an actualization in terms of vocal expression of the tendency to master reality, not by direct and *ad hoc* handling of its elements but by the reduction of experience to familiar forms.[7]

Language should be thought of as more than a means of communication, more, that is, than a way of transferring feelings already felt, observations already made, ideas already minted. Names and connectives apparently arise in the very act of discriminatory perceiving, that is, the naming process may be an intimate part of our discriminating various aspects of our environment. But consider a boy, lying on his back and looking at the stars, knowing nothing of astronomy. He gazes at what looks like an infinite number of points of light forming no patterns but scattered quite at random over the sky. Then suddenly he *sees* a way in which certain stars go together—not because they must and do inevitably make that configuration, but only because this is one way of seeing—and he gives a name to his constellation, perhaps a name that establishes a connection between the group of stars and something else, "the ship" or "the turtle." The naming and the perceiving go perfectly together. Once the name is firmly attached, the name can beget the perception, imaginatively

---

[7] Sapir, "Language," *Encyclopedia of the Social Sciences.* Used with the permission of the publishers.

or actually, or the perception can call up the name. When we listen and read we go from words to things; when we speak and write, we often look at things to get the words.

The vocabulary of a person is a fairly reliable index of the extent of his interests. Every job, every amusement and sport, has its own terminology; those interested in golf know about divots and number-7 irons and hooks; devotees of the stage speak easily of upstaging, striking the set, juveniles, and so on. By and large it is very difficult to build one's vocabulary by merely learning words. All of us have forgotten hundreds of words we once knew at least for a few minutes; and in many cases we forget because we have no real interest in that aspect of the universe designated by the word. But a man taken up with a new job, concerned to make good in it, usually rather rapidly acquires and easily remembers those particular tools of the trade that are its key words.

Vocabularies of different languages vary according to the needs and special interests of their respective users. It is said that in Arabic there are some five to six thousand terms used to describe camels, whereas in many languages there are, of course, no terms for camels at all. Santayana wrote: cont next page

Looking at the moon one man may call it simply a light in the sky; another, prone to dreaming awake, may call it a virgin goddess; a more observant person, remembering that this luminary is given to waxing and waning, may call it the crescent; and a fourth, a full-fledged astronomer, may say (taking the esthetic essence before him merely for a sign) that it is an extinct and opaque spheroidal satellite of the earth, reflecting the light of the sun from a part of its surface. All these descriptions envisage the same object—otherwise no relevance, conflict, or progress could obtain among them.[8]

The Greek word for moon connotes "measuring one," whereas the Latin "luna" connotes shininess, brightness. Some people would think it a very curious characteristic of

[8] George Santayana, *Scepticism and Animal Faith* (London: Constable & Co. Ltd., 1923), pp. 176-77.

English that it does not distinguish in the word "brother-in-law" among the following kin: the brother of one's wife, the husband of one's wife's sister, and the husband of one's own sister. The word "cousin" does not specify sex. "Uncle" can mean a relative on either side of the house and either a relative by marriage or a blood relative. These failures to make distinctions that other cultures find important suggest certain differences in attitudes toward kinship groupings. It would seem that in still deeper ways languages reflect differences in outlook upon the world. Thus the linguist Benjamin Lee Whorf has written:

Hopi may be called a timeless language. . . . Among the peculiar properties of Hopi time are that it varies with each observer, does not permit of simultaneity, and has zero dimensions. . . .[9]

The background linguistic system (in other words, the grammar) of each language is not merely a reproducing instrument for voicing ideas, the program and guide for the individual's mental activity, for his analysis of impressions, for his synthesis of his mental stock in trade. . . . We dissect nature along lines laid down by our native languages. The categories and types that we isolate from the world of phenomena we do not find there because they stare every observer in the face. . . . We cut nature up, organize it into concepts, and ascribe significances as we do, largely because we are parties to an agreement to organize it in this way — an agreement that holds true throughout our speech community and is codified in the patterns of our language.[10]

In recent times there has been much discussion of the ways in which our subject-predicate type of language influences our thinking. That is, to use the familiar form "The cow is purple" is to distinguish a subject, a substance, "cow," and to attribute to it a quality, a predicate, "purple." Since our lan-

---

[9] Benjamin Lee Whorf, "Science and Linguistics," *Language, Thought, and Reality:* Selected Writings of Benjamin Lee Whorf (Cambridge, Mass.: The Technology Press, and New York: John Wiley & Sons, Inc., 1956. Copyright, the Massachusetts Institute of Technology).

[10] *Ibid.*

guage so readily fits this way of thinking, it may seem to us that it is inevitable for anyone so to think, just as, before one has heard of Hopi, one may suppose that all languages must by necessity refer directly to time. Yet in some languages, the classification of nouns and adjectives is difficult or impossible. Again it has been argued that in some societies there is no real concept of causality, and so no words to designate the causal relations. Paul Henle has tried to show that in languages constructed in certain ways it would be literally impossible to think of certain matters that seem ordinary to us. But these are very difficult problems, and still much controverted; the statement of them at least suggests an extension of our thesis that languages arise as men learn more and more complex ways of abstracting from and discriminating within the environment, and that languages closely reflect the interests of groups and individual persons.

DEVELOPMENT OF LANGUAGES

The languages of primitive peoples are both highly complex and relatively adequate for the needs of their users. But this is not, of course, to say that such languages are altogether like the languages of "civilized" races. Perhaps the chief difference is that primitive languages tend to be highly concrete rather than abstract.

Boas has written:

In primitive culture people speak only about actual experiences. They do not discuss what is virtue, good, evil, beauty; the demands of their daily life, like those of our uneducated classes, do not extend beyond the virtues shown on definite occasions by definite people, good or evil deeds of their fellow tribesmen, and the beauty of a man, a woman, or of an object. They do not talk about abstract ideas. The question is rather whether language makes impossible the expression of abstract ideas. It is instructive to see that missionaries, who in their eagerness to convert natives have been compelled to learn their languages, have had to do violence to the idioms in order to convey to the natives their more or less abstract ideas, and that they have always found it possible to do so and to be understood. Devices to develop generalized ideas are probably always present and they are used as soon as the cultural needs compel the natives to form them.[11]

Today linguists who are anthropologically sophisticated ordinarily insist that one language is not "better" than another, but only "different"; that there is no meaning to any assertion that languages progress. No doubt everyone has some inclination toward believing that his own language is better than the others, that there is something "natural" about it. About language as about many other parts of culture we tend to be ethnocentric. The anthropologist A. L. Kroeber says:

It is impossible to rate one speech trait or type as inherently or objectively superior to another on any basis like that which justifies the placing of a metal culture above a stone culture. If wealth of grammatical apparatus is a criterion of superiority Latin is a higher language than French, and Anglo-Saxon than English. But if lack of declensions and conjugations is a virtue, then Chinese surpasses English almost as much as English surpasses Latin. There is no reason for favoring one of these possible judgments rather than its opposite. *Amabo* is no better or worse than *I shall love* as a means of expressing the same idea. The one is more compact, the other more plastic. There are times when compactness is a virtue, occasions when plasticity has advantages.[12]

Dr. Johnson uttered in the preface to his famous dictionary a fine Johnsonism when he laid it down that "Tongues like governments have a natural tendency to degeneration"; but Jesperson makes out a strong case for preferring, on the whole, modern languages to the ancient, arguing that though progress has been slow and fitful, there has nevertheless been progress

11 Franz Boas (ed.), *General Anthropology* (Boston: D. C. Heath & Co., 1938), pp. 141-42.
12 A. L. Kroeber, *Anthropology* (New York: Harcourt, Brace and Company, 1923), p. 113.

toward greater clearness, regularity, ease and pliancy. No one language has arrived at perfection; an ideal language would always express the same thing by the same, and similar things by similar means; any irregularity or ambiguity would be banished; sound and sense would be in perfect harmony; any number of delicate shades of meaning could be expressed with equal ease; poetry and prose, beauty and truth, thinking and feeling would be equally provided for: the human spirit would have found a garment combining freedom and gracefulness, fitting it closely and yet allowing full play to any movement.[13]

One sort of change that seems to go on in the development of civilized language might be called the achievement of interchangeable parts. The tendency in primitive languages is toward entirely different expressions for two closely similar situations. Thus the fact that there is an edible bird in the bush might be noted by a phrase altogether different from that used to signify the presence of a green bird in the bush. As languages develop they appear more and more to permit the expression of facts by the combining of simple elements which retain a definite meaning in comparative isolation. However, such generalizations are dangerous because of the great variations even among the so-called highly developed languages. English, for instance, is a language which relies very heavily on the order of the words to communicate, say, who did what to whom (the difference between *Sam hit Jack,* and *Jack hit Sam;*) yet the difference between *who* and *whom* is an inflexional difference of a kind very common in Latin. German is a language in which there are many compound words, words whose components are other words with their independent meanings. This is rarer in English, though we have such words as "skyscraper" and "undertaker," and many hyphenated words. In Chinese little or no use is made of prefixes or suffixes; words tend to be isolated units. Where in English we make a time distinction, for instance, by adding

[13] Otto Jesperson, *Language: Its Nature, Development, and Origin* (New York: The Macmillan Company, 1949), pp. 441-42. Reprinted by permission.

"-ed" to a verb, the Chinese will add a whole word to indicate past tense. Or again, in English there are few words with gender except the pronouns of the third person,[14] whereas in French, for instance, every noun is feminine or masculine.

LEARNING ONE'S OWN LANGUAGE

In a witty passage, Bertrand Russell makes fun of the theory that the larger unit of speech precedes the simpler:

Certain philosophers who have a prejudice against analysis contend that the sentence comes first and the single word later. In this connection they always allude to the language of the Patagonians, which their opponents, of course, do not know. We are given to understand that a Patagonian can understand you if you say "I am going to fish in the lake behind the western hill," but that he cannot understand the word "fish" by itself. (This instance is imaginary, but it represents the sort of thing that is asserted.) Now it may be that Patagonians are peculiar — indeed they must be, or they would not choose to live in Patagonia. But certainly infants in civilized countries do not behave in this way, with the exception of Thomas Carlyle and Lord Macaulay. The former never spoke before the age of three, when hearing his younger brother cry, he said, "What ails wee Jock?" Lord Macaulay "learned in suffering what he taught in song," for, having spilt a cup of hot tea over himself at a party, he began his career as a talker by saying to his hostess, after a time, "Thank you, Madam, the agony is abated." These, however, are facts about biographers, not about the beginnings of speech in infancy. In all children that have been carefully observed, sentences come much later than single words.[15]

If, in a sense, the race has had to learn to speak, so does each separate child. The old phrase, "Ontogeny recapitulates Phylogeny" argues that we can learn about evolution from embryology. It has been proposed that by the same token a good way of investigating the origins of language is to study

---

[14] Others are "ewe," "actress," "aviatrix" etc.

[15] Bertrand Russell, *Philosophy* (New York: W. W. Norton and Company, Inc., 1927), pp. 51-52. (It was not Macaulay but Samuel Johnson.)

how children come to speak. Although an obvious dissimilarity weakens the analogy, namely that the child learns language from adults who already know the language, whereas early man must somehow *create* the language, there is nevertheless something relevant to be gained from the field of child psychology.

The most notable worker in the area of linguistic and rational development of children is the French psychologist, Jean Piaget. On the basis of exceedingly close observation of children at play and in school, he worked out classifications of child language. The division of such language into two large groups, "egocentric" and "socialized" is especially interesting. Piaget points out that in children (say, aged six) a very great deal of speech is, even when others are present, monologue. The child speaks about himself and for the most part to himself. Even his questions often require and ask for no answer.

It should be remembered... that throughout the time when he is learning to speak, the child is constantly the victim of a confusion between his own point of view and that of other people. For one thing, he does not know that he is imitating. For another, he talks as much to himself as to others, as much for the pleasure of prattling or of perpetuating some past state of being as for the sake of giving orders. It is therefore impossible to say that the monologue is either prior to or later than the more socialized forms of language; both spring from that undifferentiated state where cries and words accompany action, and then tend to prolong it; and both react one upon the other at the very outset of their development.[16]

Though a child may seem highly socialized, prattling to his friends and parents and teachers, actually

the child has less verbal continence simply because he does not know what it is to keep a thing to himself. Although he talks al-

[16] Jean Piaget, *The Language and Thought of the Child*, translated by Marjorie Gabain (New York: The Humanities Press, Inc., 1948), p. 17.

most incessantly to his neighbors, he rarely places himself at their point of view. He speaks to them for the most part as if he were alone, and as if he were thinking aloud.[17]

No wonder that language seems natural! We cannot recollect the day when we did not use it to express ourselves: we learn it too early in life. There are solid reasons for believing that our recollection and conscious memory are symbolic. In a sense, then, there was no *I* before the acquisition of language. The child learns language by imitation and repetition (self-imitation), and much of his early speech is entirely egocentric and non-communicative. It rests on a confusion between the I and the not-I. "At his most imitative stage, the child mimics with his whole being, identifying himself with his model." [18]

Child psychologists now believe that an indispensable period for language-learning is the first six months, when the child knows no language at all! It is a time of babbling, though of course there are simple emotional expressions that a mother is ordinarily sensitive to. But without the babbling, there could be no speech; for we learn to speak by learning to channel the sounds we are already making. The first time a baby speaks a word, perhaps when he is a year old, it is no doubt an accident, though the delighted parent will assure you that he is unusually smart. But the accident is important, for immediately the adult goes to work to re-enforce it.

The great proportion of his early words are nouns: "mama," "daddy," "chair," "house," "doggy," "baby," and simple imperatives, like "see." But by the age of two, he begins to acquire or to discriminate two or three prepositions, like *in* and *on* and then gradually, certain pronouns, *I* and *you* and *me*. Perhaps the child does not at first distinguish words from longer linguistic expressions which (for adults)

17 *Ibid.*, pp. 39-40.
18 *Ibid.*, p. 11.

consist of several words in combination. What a child is striving to do—or what nature is striving to do in and for him—is to learn to talk and to hear successfully: learning individual words is incidental to learning speech. By the time he's ready to enter kindergarten he has at his command (i.e., both recognizes and speaks) some 2000-3000 words, which vocabulary increases in size until when he is ready to enter high school, he may be able to use 8000-10,000 words. The vocabulary of the average adult has been estimated at 18,000-20,000 words; a person of bookish tastes uses perhaps 35,000 words; and C. K. Ogden, inventor of a system of Basic English which permits the expression of most things by the use of 850 carefully selected words, estimates the vocabulary of professional scientists at 60,000-80,000 words.[19]

But let us take a somewhat closer look at the child acquiring his first speech. We have noticed that though a child may cry and by his cry betray his hunger, it is the mother, not the child, who consciously makes the connection between the produced sound and the feeling — at first. Gradually, of course, the child becomes aware of a relation between certain producible sounds and alleviation of discomfort and uneasiness; herein is the ground for deliberate communication of needs and desires. Parents too have certain demands to make upon the baby, and increasingly they find it important to establish a verbal basis for communication. This is accomplished by juxtaposing certain sounds with certain other sensory stimulations, such as the sound "Mama" with the sight and touch of the mother, or the sound "Clap" with the activity of briskly joining one's palms, either done for the baby to see or accomplished with the infant's hands, so that he may experience the motor feelings. In general, the child more readily learns the meaning of words spoken by others than he learns

[19] A. F. Watts, *The Language and Mental Development of Children* (Boston: D. C. Heath and Company, 1944), Ch. II. However, such estimates vary widely. Thus for some different figures, see "Language" in *Encyclopaedia Britannica*, 14th Ed.

to produce words himself. However, rather frequently he will reproduce sounds of words before he has learned their meaning. Yet, gradually he comes to be able not only to anticipate the taste of food and the alleviation of hunger by means of the mother's word "dinner," but to say the word himself, perhaps in order to call forth the subject.

One of the big problems in learning to understand others' speech is to know what, precisely, a given word refers to. The adult sometimes encounters this same problem. Suppose a guide in an art gallery points to a painting and says, "That is an example of *pointillisme.*" Now you may direct your eyes as his finger points and be completely puzzled about whether he is designating the subject matter of the painting, the manner of its framing, the period in which it was executed, the medium used, or the stylistic technique of the painter. Consider the child's problem in learning the meaning of "red" from the parent's pointing in the direction of, say, a tomato. Three kinds of mistakes can easily occur in this sort of learning: (1) One might select the wrong property, associating, for instance, "red" with the roundness of the object; (2) one might particularize too much, so that "red" would be learned as this particular shade and no other; or (3) one might overgeneralize so that "red" means anything colored. Certainly everyone has encountered in a child simple mistakes in naming, a tendency, for example, to call all adult males "Daddy," and the refusal to admit that any but his own home is "house."

LANGUAGE: NATURAL OR CONVENTIONAL?

It is reported that when a famous classical scholar at Oxford was asked to defend the study of Greek, he replied, "Not only is Greek the immediate tongue of God, but its study leads to positions of great dignity and great emolument." No doubt men everywhere have thought and have liked to think that their own language was God's language, was the proper language of the universe, was the only right means of expression and communication, or was, at the very least, the one "natural" language. Consider Jim and Huck Finn:

. . . I told about Louis Sixteenth that got his head cut off in France long time ago; and about his little boy the dolphin, that should 'a' been king, but they took and shut him up in jail, and some say he died there.

"Po' little chap."

"But some says he got out and got away, and come to America."

"Dat's good! But he'll be pooty lonesome — dey ain' no kings here, is dey, Huck?"

"No."

"Den he cain't git no situation. What he gwyne to do?"

"Well, I don't know. Some of them gets on the police, and some of them learns people how to talk French."

"Why, Huck, doan' de French people talk de same way we does?"

"*No,* Jim; you couldn't understand a word they said — not a single word."

"Well, now, I be ding-busted! How do dat come?"

"*I* don't know; but it's so. I got some of their jabber out of a book. S'pose a man was to come to you and say Polly-voo-franzy — what would you think?"

"I wouldn' think nuffin; I'd take en bust him over de head — dat is, if he warn't white. I wouldn't 'low no nigger to call me dat."

"Shucks, it ain't calling you anything. It's only saying, do you know how to talk French?"

"Well, den, why couldn't he say it?"

"Why he *is* a-saying it. That's a Frenchman's *way* of saying it."

"Well, it's a blame ridicklous way, en I doan' want to hear no mo' 'bout it. Dey ain' no sense in it."

"Looky here, Jim; does a cat talk like we do?"

"No, a cat don't."

"Well, does a cow?"

"No, a cow don't, nuther."

"Does a cat talk like a cow, or a cow talk like a cat?"

"No, dey don't."

"It's natural and right for 'em to talk different from each other, ain't it?"

"Course."

"And ain't it natural and right for a cat and cow to talk different from us?"

"Why, mos' sholy it is."

"Well, then, why ain't it natural and right for a *Frenchman* to talk different from us? You answer me that."

"Is a cat a man, Huck?"

"No."

"Well, den, dey ain't no sense in a cat talkin' like a man. Is a cow a man? — or is a cow a cat?"

"No, she ain't either of them."

"Well, den, she ain't got no business to talk like either one er the yuther of 'em. Is a Frenchman a man?"

"Yes."

"*Well,* den! Dad blame it, why doan' he talk like a man? You answer me dat!" [20]

Today we cannot believe either that any single language is *the* natural one, nor even that language is natural in the sense of being possessed innately rather than requiring to be learned.

Nevertheless, languages *are* natural in various senses. They are natural in the sense that they are used habitually, without requiring the *focus* of our attention. They are natural in being something that we caught on to so early in life that we seem always to have had the possession. And language is natural in the sense that it does have a physiological-psycho-

---

[20] Mark Twain, *The Adventures of Huckleberry Finn.* Ch. 14.

logical basis, and in being a possession of all human groups. Languages, moreover, have their own individual structures and histories and can be observed and studied as a kind of cross between natural and cultural facts.

Paradoxically, languages are conventional, as well as natural. They are, perhaps, more often called conventional than natural. The question is, however, what is the meaning of "conventional" in this connection? Does it mean "arbitrary"?

In speaking of another kind of conventional sign, the logician Lewis Carroll wrote up the following episode in *The Hunting of the Snark*. He was writing of travelers and a crew who scorned the conventional symbols on navigation charts, and who admired the eccentricity of their Bellman navigator:

The Bellman himself they all praised to the skies—
   Such a carriage, such ease and such grace!
Such solemnity, too! One could see he was wise.
   The moment one looked in his face!

He had bought a large map representing the sea,
   Without the least vestige of land:
And the crew were much pleased when they found it to be
   A map they could all understand.

"What's the good of Mercator's North Poles and Equators,
   Tropics, Zones, and Meridian Lines?"
So the Bellman would cry: and the crew would reply
   "They are merely conventional signs!"

"Other maps are such shapes, with their islands and capes!
   But we've got our brave Captain to thank."
(So the crew would protest) "that he's bought us the best—
   A perfect and absolute blank!"

Using language, like map reading, is not conventional in what might be called "the weak sense"; it is not merely a nice custom like taking off your hat when an old lady steps onto the elevator. Obedience is forcibly demanded to the kind of conventionality that belongs to language; it is as if the elevator would stop if you did not remove your cap and stay stopped until you doffed it. In fact, if you have your arms full of packages, for instance, you may leave your hat on. It is not the same with grammatical forms and the meanings of words; you have to take your hat off to them regardless!

If you do not want to speak English, say, that is your own concern. There are many languages that no one speaks any more. If you do want to speak English, however, and if you want to be understood, then you must use certain words to mention certain kinds of objects, actions, and relations. The degree of individual liberty available in this respect is amazingly small, although, of course, there is a little. Dr. Brown's facetious storyteller had "a windmill that used to lay eggs and hatch young ones." When that produced a sort of stare, the storyteller explained, "Ah, but you are to know that when I say a windmill, I mean a goose." [21] A degree of individuality of expression is allowable; it is even desirable; but a degree of conformance to traditional symbolization is unavoidable.

If you want to be understood, you must speak the common tongue. If a man calls geese "windmills," he exhibits mere eccentricity. He exhibits individuality, however, if he knows and respects the popular language medium, but uses it freshly and interestingly. In most cases, perhaps, the difference between individuality and mere eccentricity in linguistic usage lies precisely here, namely, in whether or not expression precedes or follows on proper acquaintance with the medium.

In recognizing that language is only one division of signs, we are not placing ourselves in agreement with the Bellman navigator. We do not scorn words any more than we scorn maps, mileage charts, gasoline gauges, and the warning whistle on the pressure cooker. A primary reason for calling languages conventional is just to point up that linguistic conventions do require obedience!

Languages are cerebral, and in *some* sense, no doubt,

[21] Related by Jeremy Bentham in commenting on Blackstone's *Commentaries*. Bentham thought that many of Blackstone's words would prove geese.

thought is involved in their creation. But from the point of view of the individual, a language is like a natural fact. It is presented to him ready-made, to be learned by him. The expression, "to master a foreign language" for the most part means "to learn it," not "to boss it." Francis Bacon's famous aphorism (or paradox) applies to language: "Nature to be commanded must be obeyed." To force a language, or to be obstreperous and half-cocked with it, is not to master it, but to be thrown and turned into a laughingstock. If you want to learn German, for example, you will have to treat it like a natural fact, in the sense that you will have to obey *its* rules. You will have to pronounce German the German way, if you want to be understood by German-speaking people. And you will have to follow the German grammar. Your own creativity and originality will not take you very far until you have learned the language as it already is.

People often remark how easily little children pick up a language or two. They do have important advantages over adults, but still they perform millions of little experiments in learning to use their tongue. They listen carefully to hear how others speak. They repeat errors for years. They often stammer and stutter. Languages are very complex facts; they are what they are; and effort has to be expended in order to learn them. In any community, the child will find plenty of playroom for cerebration in learning the customs and language of those around him.

However, some of those who defend the thesis that speech is cerebral sometimes overdefend it. According to what they *say,* speech in being cerebral is something explicitly agreed upon, as if each of us had at some time determined what each word in his vocabulary would mean. The natural languages which we learn as children certainly are *learned* and absorbed by us; they are not concocted, or cut from whole cloth. The English language was there before I was!

The more nearly perfect a language is, and the more honest its users, the better will its signs serve to convey the meaning of one organism to that of another. Signs constituting a language must be signs which an individual himself can produce and signs capable of meaning the *same* thing to him as to those who interpret them. Most readers will recall the legend:

A mischievous Shepherd's Boy used to amuse himself by calling, "Wolf, Wolf!" just to see the villagers run with their clubs and pitchforks to help him. After he had called this more than once for a joke and had laughed at them each time, they grew angry. One day a wolf really did get among the sheep, and the Shepherd Boy called, "Wolf, Wolf!" in vain. The villagers went on with their work, the Wolf killed what he wanted of the sheep, and the Shepherd Boy learned that liars are not believed, even when they do tell the truth.

Here we see a partial breakdown of language through the destruction of interpersonality. As later chapters will show, individuals and institutions confuse us—whether deliberately or not—when they juggle language.

LANGUAGE CONSCIOUSNESS

In reaction to the plethora of books on how to avoid being neurotic, on how to think properly, on how to practice good mental hygiene, James Thurber once wrote a witty book called *Let Your Mind Alone*. In reaction to all of this discussion about what language is and where it came from and how it develops and so on, someone might impatiently exclaim: Let your language alone.

Although language does not consist in moans and groans and sighs, it can be, and is, used non-consciously. This is as it should be. When we are repeating old and habitual actions, we do not want to have to think out our statements about them or in connection with them. When our attention is on the things that we would communicate, we do not want to distract ourselves by reflecting on the relevant symbols. The freest use of speech, as of other things, is the use that has become habitual and unconscious.

That we should be always and totally unconscious of our language does not follow. We should not always be unconscious when we speak! Our speech will be most effective if we have it both ways. There are frequent occasions when it is convenient to be able to observe our speech, both our oral and written communication, in order to grasp it better as an instrument and as a skill.

On the other hand, the fairly widespread feeling that we should never speak other than self-consciously is unwarranted. As our automobile driving illustration in the last chapter suggested, there are important actions which we must be able to do by habit, in order to do them fast enough. Too much self-consciousness in speaking puts us on the road to stammering and stuttering, or, even worse, it may bring us to a complete halt, and reduce us to silence and inactivity. The silence of good Billy Budd was catastrophic. Language is not just a mess and we should ignore the hyper-critical advice of those semanticists who would have us so suspicious of words that we cannot relax and enjoy them. We need to use words, no matter how much we prefer the celebrated goldenness of silence. These extremists among the semanticists are like the physicist who drowned rather than swim in water, which he knew had a low relative density. Swim we must, and speak we must, but we can be observant and improve both stroke and statement.

Language is like a pair of bifocals, if we may change the figure. As long as you are home reading, or quietly walking down the street, if your glasses fit well, and if they are a habit, you are not likely to be at all aware of them. But if you join a game of basketball or go for a swim, you will want to recall that you wear glasses. Or if you go suddenly from reading to walking, you surely should recollect that you are wearing bifocals, or there is danger of misjudging your step. But, in respect to speech, let each of us be his own oculist; every one of us needs to be at least semi-professional in the field of communication. We need to use speech as an instrument, with our attention on the object which we would describe or on the emotion which we would convey, but we also need the power at will to turn our attention on speech itself. It is not the kind of instrument that works best with no attention and maintenance at all. We ought to want to know what kind of instrument it is, what various uses it has, and how the best results can be obtained from it. Moreover, our own language is like the green spectacles that Dorothy wore in Oz: were we *never* self-conscious about our language, we might forget that the emerald tint on the Emerald City belongs to our way of looking at it. But on the other hand, we do not throw our glasses away just because they are tinted.

PROBLEMS FOR DISCUSSION

A. Aldous Huxley once wrote: "For evil . . . as well as for good, words make us the human beings we actually are. Deprived of language we should be as dogs or monkeys. Possessing language, we are men and women able to persevere in crime no less than in heroic virtue, capable of intellectual achievements beyond the scope of any animal, but at the same time capable of systematic silliness and stupidity such as no dumb beast could ever dream of." (*Words and Their Meanings,* Los Angeles: The Ward Ritchie Press. Quoted in Irving J. Lee (ed.), *The Language of Wisdom and Folly,* 1949, p. 58.) Discuss Mr. Huxley's claims.

B. Compare the following definition with those of Sapir given in the text: "A language is a structured system of arbitrary vocal sounds and sequences of sounds which is used, or can be used, in interpersonal communication by an aggregation of human beings and which rather exhaustively catalogs the things, events, and processes in the human environment." (John B. Carroll, *The Study of Language,* Cambridge, Mass.: Harvard University Press, 1953, p. 10.)

C. A ten-year old girl once said, "When people thought of a language, how did they think of it if there were no words to think with? After they had thought of it, how did they get other people to understand it? If they went from door to door explaining it, people would think that they had gone crazy because they wouldn't know what the words meant. After the first language was started how were others formed? These are the questions that make me say, 'I wonder how people learned to talk.' " (Janet Baker, Letter to *Look*, Vol. 13, No. 20, Sept. 27, 1949. Quoted in Ruesch and Bateson, *Communication: The Social Matrix of Psychiatry* (New York: Norton, 1951), p. 203.) Are these questions entirely naïve? Discuss them.

D. Psammetichus, king of Egypt, desired to find out whether Egyptians or Phrygians were the more ancient race. "This king, finding it impossible to make out by dint of inquiry what men were the most ancient, contrived the following method of discovery: He took two children of the common sort, and gave them over to a herdsman to bring up at his folds, strictly charging him to let no one utter a word in their presence, but to keep them in a sequestered cottage, and from time to time introduce goats to their apartment, see that they got their fill of milk, and in all other respects look after them. His object herein was to know, after the indistinct babblings of infancy were over, what word they would first articulate. It happened as he had anticipated. The herdsman obeyed his orders for two years, and at the end of that time, on his one day opening the door of their room and going in, the children both ran up to him with outstretched arms, and distinctly said Becos. . . . Psammetichus then himself heard them say the word, upon which he proceeded to make inquiry what people there was who called anything becos, and hereupon he learnt that becos was the Phrygian name for bread. In consideration of this circumstance the Egyptians yielded their claims, and admitted the greater antiquity of the Phrygians." (Herodotus, *The Persian Wars, Book II*, tr. by George Rawlinson. Mod. Lib., pp. 116-117.)

What assumption was Psammetichus making? Are you willing to permit the assumption to be made?

E. Criticize this definition: "Language is the tool for communicating ideas."

F. If you know some foreign language, give an example of a word or an expression which has no entirely adequate translation into English. Is this because in our language we have no *need* for such an expression?

G. From your own observations would you agree with Russell that children always learn single words first?

H. What are the meanings of the following words that were used in this Chapter?

intermediary	interjectional	syntax	category
phonetic	taciturn	discriminatory	concrete (adj.)
transcription	inflection	configuration	culture
ineffable	morphology	terminology	ethnocentric
plastic			

EXERCISES

I. Illustrate the three errors listed at the end of the section "Learning One's Language" with more important instances of confusion.

II. As against the notion that language is entirely "conventional" in its origins, it would be possible to argue that after all certain sounds are very appropriate to certain meanings. For instance, why is the short "i" sound common to such words as "pretty," "twig," "kid," "slip" (of a girl), "chick"? And notice the similarity in sound among these words: "clumsy," "blunder," "bungle," "muddle," "slobber," "slovenly." Give five other instances, and explain their appropriateness.

III. Compose a fable of your own — make it different! — "explaining" the origin of language.

IV. The Latin sentence, "Pater filium amat, sed, si peccat, castigat," means "A father loves his son, but, if the latter commits some error, he corrects him." It has been said that the Latin expression, despite the lack of pronouns and articles, is a model of precision. State clearly why you agree or disagree.

V. Find five words of Anglo-Saxon origin, three of Celtic, five of Latin, five of Greek, five that are onomatopoeic, and five that are none of these. Can you distinguish between words of Norman French origin and those that were imported from France long after the Norman Conquest?

VI. Compare the definitions of language of Sapir with the following statement assigning characteristics to language by Anatol Rapoport, who works in the tradition of Count Korzybski and "General Semantics." Rapoport has listed five characteristics of symbolic-language as distinct from mechanical or conditioned-response signalling. A symbolic language is grammatical, logical, abstract, metaphysical, and psycho-logical. *Grammar* consists in the allowable forms of combining the constituents of language, and *logic* prescribes "certain relations among certain assertions." The *abstractness* of symbolic language "allows humans to acquire symbolic repertoires quite immense compared to the signal repertoires which constitute the languages of other animals. This is so because words can be associated with objects, actions, qualities, and situations without a separate conditioning in each instance." To say that language is *metaphysical* is to say that "a particular language imposes on its user a framework of perception and reasoning into which his observations of the events around him must fit." "Finally, symbolic languages are characterized by being *psycho-logical* [the word is hyphenated as in Korzybski's writings]. This is to say, a language impresses on us not only a metaphysical framework but also an affective one. It does not only a good deal of our thinking for us but also a good deal of our feeling." (Anatol Rapoport, "The Role of Symbols in Human Behavior," *ETC.* (Spring, 1955), pp. 181-182.)

SOURCES AND ADVANCED READING

1. Articles on "Language," *Encyclopaedia Britannica, Encyclopedia Americana, Encyclopaedia of the Social Sciences.*
2. Mario Pei, *The Story of Language.* Philadelphia: J. B. Lippincott Company, 1949.
3. Otto Jesperson, *Language: Its Nature, Development, and Origin.* New York: The Macmillan Company, 1949.
4. Leonard Bloomfield, *Language.* New York: Henry Holt and Company, 1933.
5. Edward Sapir, *Language.* New York: Harcourt, Brace and Company, 1921.

6. Plato, "Cratylus." Jowett translation.

7. Benjamin Lee Whorf, *Four Articles on Metalinguistics*. Washington: Foreign Service Institute, 1949.

8. John B. Carroll, *The Study of Language*. Cambridge: Harvard University Press, 1953.

9. George Lyman Kittredge and Frank Edgar Farley, *An Advanced English Grammar*. Boston: Ginn and Company, 1913, pp. 316-19, "The English Language."

10. Paul Henle, "Mysticism and Semantics," *Philosophy and Phenomenological Research,* Vol. IX (1949), pp. 416-22.

11. Sheridan Baker, "Scholarly Style, or the Lack Thereof," *Bulletin* of the American Association of University Professors, Vol. XL, No. 3 (Autumn, 1956), pp. 464-70.

·→ IV ·←

WORDS AND GRAMMAR

Kinds of Words and Word-Functions ● Propositions and Terms ●
A Word about Grammar

KINDS OF WORDS AND WORD-FUNCTIONS

A word is really a *class* of sounds or marks, as we usually
use "word," and not a member of a class and not an individual. That is why the six-year-old girl exaggerated when she
came home from school, thrilled at learning, and claimed she
could already read five words, and the five words were "Look,
look, oh, oh, oh!" She was using the word "word" the way we
use it when we count the words in a manuscript or theme.
But a word or other expression is ordinarily a *class* of sounds
or marks, and it includes a broad variety of members and
eccentrics. Consider the difference, for instance, in the sound
of "New Orleans," as pronounced now by a soprano, now by
a bass; now by a Vermonter, now by a Louisianan; now by a
Frenchman, now by a Chinese. We as hearers can tolerate
quite a good deal of difference in sound and still know what
word is being said: these sounds which we interpret as the
oral equivalent of "New Orleans," form the class which is the
word or phrase in its sound aspect. Most of the time when we
hear a certain sound, maybe it's *Nyu Orlens or Noo Orleens*
or *Nu Orlayahn,* we "bring to mind" the southern city and
prepare ourselves to regard it as the setting for some incident
or the like. But sometimes when we hear a sound rather dif-

ferent from what is indicated by any of the above spellings, we are puzzled: "What did he say?" "What was that word?" Then perhaps the light breaks: "Oh, he means New Orleans." In such a case the doubtful sound acts, at least for a moment, as the sign of the proper sound, which in its term designates the city. At other times, the sound made by the speaker, though it was intended by him to designate the city, is too different, and we simply cannot recognize it. People vary among themselves in their aural acuity in the recognition of words; some can tolerate a wide range of pronunciations while others require a close approximation to a given sound before they know what word is being used. In general, the better we know a language, it seems, the more variations we can accommodate; in the case of a foreign language upon which we have but a very shaky hold, a word must be said very nearly as we learned it or we will be baffled.

Similar considerations obtain in written language. Here is one written form of a word: *elder*. But now look at this: ELDER. Every letter is different in shape and size. Consider, further, the different type faces that might be employed in printing it. And when we think of handwriting, and of the great variations there, we begin to see that it is hard to know exactly what we mean when we speak of *the* written form of a word. Still, we know that all of us who are literate can handle a certain variety. But the fourth grade child may be able to read printing and not script, and most of us would find our difficulties greatly increased by the use of a German script type. And all of us have come across illegible handwriting, perhaps even our own.

One way of expressing this is to say that, for a person to *know* a word, he must be able to recognize a certain variety of sounds which are sufficiently similar to be called the "same": and so too with written or printed marks, with the additional complication that one may have to know two or more alphabets, like capital and lower case letters, some of which differ only in size, but many of which differ in shape as well.[1]

We have spoken of what can be learned about language from reflecting on the typical experiences of children in mastering their native speech. Let us now consider a hypothetical case involving two adults on a desert island—for our present purposes, let us say, two males. Now these men must be thought of as completely ignorant of each other's language, but friendly and eager to converse. The more aggressive and ingenious one of the two (and luckily for us, the one who speaks English) decides that he will be teacher. He soon sees that the methods of the language textbooks are no help, for they can be written only by one who knows two languages: words are defined by means of equivalences or translations. But the idea soon occurs that English words can be supplied for objects that can be pointed at, and so, a minimum vocabulary, consisting of such words as "rock," "tree," "sand," "sky," "eye," "hand," etc. is provided. By drawing pictures in the sand, the teacher further manages to get across such useful words as "cat," "house," and "automobile." Some conversation is now possible. The two friends can spend many happy hours pointing at things and pronouncing their English names. But this does not long suffice. The English-speaker, now firmly established in authority, has great difficulty in making commands understood. Upon occasion he wants to say, "Get the water," "Build a fire" or "Bring the pineapples but not the cocoanuts"; however, he finds that certain words in these sentences are especially hard to communicate. Perhaps the articles "the" and "a" are not of great importance, but what about "or" and "but not"? Any analysis will reveal these as of crucial significance in the sentences. But how do you teach them? To what can you point?

Certainly such words do not designate things or qualities

---

[1] See Bertrand Russell, *Analysis of Mind* (London: George Allen & Unwin, Ltd., 1921) Ch. X: Throughout this section we are heavily indebted to Lord Russell.

(as "red" or "round" designates a quality) or actions (like "build" or "get") or classes of things (e.g. "green apples"). Let us call them "logical-relation" words. (The careful reader will notice that we still haven't told how they might be taught. It *may be* that they can be taught behavioristically. Thus, the word "not" or any other negation may be associated with gestures of rejection, "or" with bodily indications of hesitation, etc.)

At this stage in the educational process, the teacher remembers something of his early study of grammar—enough at least to notice that those words which he has used to designate things are what he once learned to classify as substantives, i.e., nouns and pronouns. Having thought of substantives, however, he recalls certain words that are classified as nouns, but seem incapable of being defined ostensively, that is, by *showing*. For instance, there are nouns like "ripeness," "nonchalance," "chastity," "confusion," "friendship," whose meanings must be indicated in some way other than by pointing. Perhaps the *must* in the last sentence is too strong; with a great deal of luck one might point to a confused situation, pronounce "confusion," and be understood, but in such a case it would be much more likely that confusion would be spread than that "confusion" would be understood. Such words as these are commonly thought of as words whose meaning consists in certain qualities (notice the adjectives: "ripe," "nonchalant," "chaste," "confused," "friendly") which have been abstracted from concrete instances. This ripe peach, that ripe apple, those ripe pears yield the classification *ripeness*. A word of this sort is usually called *abstract*. If one wanted to convey the meaning of "ripeness"—that is, assuming one already knew the meaning himself and wanted another to understand it—one might be well advised to indicate a number of objects with only the one quality in common; like a teacher trying to show that 2 plus 2 equals 4, no matter whether the pairs are pieces of chalk, erasers, fingers, or girls. But the original *finding* of this or any other common quality in seemingly very different objects is quite another matter and a harder one.

To state precisely an adequate distinction between abstract and concrete names is by no means easy. One can think of extreme examples: "Socrates" is a concrete name and "mortality" is an abstract name; but what is "book" or "red" or "under"? Perhaps the best way to make the distinction is to say that concrete names are those which apply to singular objects or events or situations ("this shoe," "The War of Roses," "that fight") while abstract names are those which apply either to classes ("shoes," "boxing," "women") or to attributes or relations ("red," "redness," "being to the left of," "truth") considered apart from instances or real cases. Yet it is sometimes useful to be able to speak of degrees of abstractness, of the more abstract and the less abstract. This is perhaps always a matter of generality; that is, of the two abstractions "apparel" and "shoes" the former is the more abstract in being more general. In a similar way, "$x + y = y + x$" is more abstract than "$3 + 4 = 4 + 3$." But once we admit degrees of abstractness, it is hard to rule out degrees of concreteness, so that we will perhaps want sometimes to speak of going from the more to the less abstract as "becoming more concrete." This usage requires, of course, a modification in our definitions in order to make abstractness and concreteness relative to each other, so that "chair" is concrete relative to "furniture" but abstract relative to "that armchair." Will "that armchair" be abstract relative to anything? That is, is there something even more concrete? Perhaps some such awkward expression as "this brown-soft-wooly something now" names a momentary experience, and our conception of what *that armchair* is, is made up of such experiences and expectations of more of the same kind. If so, the name "that armchair" will be more abstract than the expression which names a constituent of the same conception.[2]

---

[2] This, of course, is a very big subject, one which has fascinated metaphysicians from the time of Plato, who argued that Justice and Goodness and

It is popular among some people to speak slightingly of abstractions, abstract words, abstract studies and talk. The objection is usually twofold: Abstractions are so far from the "everyday world" as to be particularly liable to error, error of a sort that is subtle, hard to put one's finger on; and, secondly, dealing with the abstract is an impractical task—not necessarily harmful but quite fruitless because of the notorious possibilities for attaining to good theory (abstract) that does not work out in practice (concrete). Both objections are sound—up to a point. Many great philosophers have insisted upon the importance of verifying theories by observation of immediate experience; and practically all scientists worthy of the name have guided their practice by this admonition. It is, on a high level of abstraction, possible to be ingenious without arriving at truth. Nevertheless, science and philosophy— kinds of learning—are not possible without abstraction. The botanist must broaden his interest beyond a particular flower: the one flower must be regarded as a specimen, as typical. He must describe the abstract daisy; thus you might say that he is principally interested in daisies, i.e., in that abstract set of qualities which are manifested by particular daisies. The philosopher cannot amount to much as a philosopher until he extends his inquiry beyond a particular instance of moral or immoral behavior into the realm of principles. The mathematician, perhaps more than any other scholar, scorns the concrete, favoring the abstract. If this latter statement seems surprising, it is probably because of a confusion between the terms "abstract" and "vague." Abstractions are often vague, but are sometimes scrupulously clear-cut, exactly determinable. In part, the second objection is already answered, but it needs to be said further that although it is frequently a

---

such Ideas have a permanent reality quite apart from the concrete objects to which they apply (this just government, that good man), to A. N. Whitehead who discusses the "fallacy of misplaced concreteness"—that is, the fallacy of supposing that the name for some object ("that arm chair") is as concrete as you can get. On the other hand, what is the most completely abstract name that can be conceived? Some philosophers have answered: "Being."

mistake to arrive at a theoretical position independently of the concrete, seldom can theory and practice be meaningfully separated. There are some "formal" studies such as pure mathematics and pure logic which are not tested by their application to concrete reality; but aside from such exceptional cases, theory *is* good or bad as it does meaningfully and helpfully apply or fail to apply to the world in which we live. It is quite misleading to say: "That plan is all right on paper but not in practice," for if it turns out to be bad in practice it thereby turns out to be bad on paper. It would be silly to say of an architect's drawing that it was very good, except that a building erected according to these specifications would be poor. And so, too, of any other sort of plan or theory. It is of course true that what *looks* good on paper may turn out to be bad in practice; but this is hardly worth uttering.

We have disparaged the importance of the articles, "a," "an," and "the," but we shall now demonstrate their importance under certain circumstances:

First islander: "Did you say to bring a pan?"

Second islander: "No, I said to bring *the* pan."

Just what sense is to be made out of this correction? "A pan" is equivalent in meaning to "anything which answers to the description of 'pan'." Thus if I ask you to hand me *a* pan, I presumably mean any pan, not just some particular one; not the pan with the chipped enamel or the frying pan with the hump in the middle, but just any member of the class of pans. But if I speak of *the* pan, I may be understood as meaning one and only one pan. It may be the only one in sight; it may be the only one I own; it may be the one we have just been discussing; it may be that you can see me getting ready to French-fry potatoes, and I assume you know that there is a particular pan I use for this operation. In any case, I thus indicate an individual, not just a member of a class.

In the case of the indefinite article "a," (such words as "any," "each," and "one" are also called "indefinite determiners") it may just happen that there is in fact only one such thing as is designated by the substantive employed; but unless I have reason for assuming this singularity, I have no right to use the definte determiner "the." Suppose a fussy girl asks her roommate to get her a date with a fellow exactly six feet tall, weighing precisely 186 pounds, 22 years old, unmarried, a college graduate, a butcher by trade, and a Seventh-Day Adventist by religion. (This rather long phrase can be construed the same as a simple name, such as "a date": just suppose all the words joined together with hyphens.) There may be no one like this or there may be just one in all the world. Nevertheless, unless the petitioner happens to know that there is just one (which, by the way, would be an astounding piece of knowledge), she still must say, "*a* fellow . . ." For if there happened to be two and the less desirable one (according to some new criteria) were selected, there could be no reasonable ground for complaint.

But if the date-wanting girl had gone to just a little more trouble, she might have been able to specify her choice by name, that is by proper name: "Get me a date with Fred Nelson." Those objects get proper names which are for some reason memorably distinctive. In so far as he is a boy, Fred is just one member of a numerous class; in so far as he is Fred Nelson, he is unique. (Of course, there may turn out to be other Fred Nelsons, that is, other users of this name, and this may force us further to specify, as "The Fred Nelson who comes from Illinois," but it remains the case that in anyone's usage "Fred Nelson" is intended to designate one unique individual.) From what has been said it can be inferred that proper names form a sub-class of singular names. "This blade of grass" designates, if we want to be technical, something absolutely unique also; if there were any need to remember it particularly, we might even call it "Oscar." The title "general name" is traditionally given to class-names, like "automobiles," "pencil," "army," "universities." (Notice that a class name may be grammatically either singular or plural.)

There are some other traditional classifications of words to which we now turn. Thinking of words as a means of expression and communication, we may note a distinction between those words which, singly or in combination, have a *naming* function and those which do not name but only connect with other words in order to facilitate the forming of a proposition. The first kind are called categorematic words, or, as we will say, *names*. Examples are: "tree," "government," "John Adams," "dreams," "sobriety," "the Trinity," "the highest mountain peak on earth," "unicorns." Syncategorematic words, those which have a syntactical function only, have as instances: "of," "by," "only," "the," "is," and "and."

Collective names are those which refer to collections that somehow can be treated as a unit: "The 81st Congress," "regiment," "Phi Beta Kappa," "the football team," "the New York Public Library." *Distributive* names refer to one member of a collection, which a collective name can never do. "Juryman," "football player," "a member of Phi Beta Kappa," are examples of distributive names.

A name is called *relative* when it designates a quality or object closely associated with another quality or object. "Parent" is never applicable unless there be offspring. "Cold" is familiarly defined as the absence of heat. "Up" is meaningless without a notion of down. A sale requires a buyer. Alice, asked by the Mad Hatter whether she would have more tea, objected that since she hadn't had any, she couldn't have *more*. The Hatter rebuked her by saying that she could always have more; it was *less* she couldn't have. Non-relative names, those that are not necessarily paired with others, are called absolute. Examples are "man" (consider Adam before Eve), "water," "God." However, this distinction is not very precise; because of the very ubiquity of relationships, it is not always possible to determine whether a certain relationship is inevitable.

A final traditional classification of names, and again one that is of a limited use, distinguishes *positive, negative,* and *privative* names. A name is positive when it designates the presence of a given quality, negative when it designates the absence of the quality, privative when it suggests the absence of a quality which would normally be expected to be present. "Red" and "not-red," "mortal" and "immortal," "coöperative" and "uncoöperative," are positive-negative pairs. "Blind," "destitute," and "fatherless child" may be instances of privative names. Sometimes the negative word is much better known than the positive. For instance, we may be stumped by "maculate" until we remember "immaculate."

PROPOSITIONS AND TERMS

Not all words are names, as we have seen, but only those which designate persons, places, things, events, situations, groups, or other entities. Not all sentences are propositions, but only those which assert something that can be believed or denied, something which is either true or false. "My car is black" is a proposition and so is "All cars are black," and it is not the less a proposition for being patently false. "Rain fell in Shanghai January 1, 1939" is a proposition even though one may utter the sentence without the slightest idea of whether it is true. "There are complex organisms on Mars" is a proposition in spite of its truth being presently unascertainable. "Slow down!", "Here's mud in your eye!" "Oh to be in England" are, on the other hand, all expressions to which it would be wholly inappropriate to answer, "Yes, that's right" or "I doubt it"; for they are not propositions.

It is usual to list three types of non-propositional sentences: questions, commands, and exclamations. In a general way this will do, but there are some subtleties that make for qualification. It is not a proposition to say "Is it raining?" but the question may be contained *in* a proposition; for instance, "He said, 'Is it raining?'" is a proposition—that is, it is true or false that he did say that. The same holds true with commands and exclamations; it may be worth remarking further that the exclamation of wishes is particularly tricky. Thus, if "Oh for an apple" is non-propositional, to say "I wish I had an apple" is possibly to draw the comment, "Oh, you don't wish that at all"—a comment that clearly denies a proposition. But from this point it is a short step to noticing that whenever a question, command or exclamation is uttered, it is plausible to say of the questioner, "He wants to know if . . ."; to say of the commander, "He wants me to do . . ."; to say of the exclaimer, "He feels . . ." In short, we—the hearers or readers—frequently utter propositions as interpretations of the questions, commands, and exclamations that we receive.

Again, so-called "non-propositional utterances" may *implicitly* contain propositions. Suppose someone says, "Close the window." I might reply, "Oh, you're wrong—the window isn't open." Or to someone who expressed a wish for a pleasant voice, the reassurance might come: "But you *do* have a pleasant voice," a denial of the implicit proposition that he didn't have. Somewhat similar is the familiar case of the rhetorical question: "How much longer can we tolerate this outrage?" But in such a case we say that it is not a question at all, but an assertion that is disguised as a question. The main point for practice in all this is that one often needs to search behind the form of the utterance to see whether there be a proposition lurking about the premises. And sometimes when a person hears his question (for example, "Do you believe in communism?") evoke an indignant denial, he may retort, "But I only asked a question"; and perhaps he did.

Propositions are typically analyzable into terms and relations. A responsible tradition in logic holds that every proposition has three principal parts, a subject term, a predicate term, and a copula. It may be doubted whether every proposition can, without serious distortion, be fitted into this scheme, but a very great many can, and so the pattern deserves close scrutiny.

Each of the terms is a name for an individual or a class, and the copula relates the subject to the predicate by inclusion or exclusion, partial or entire.[3] Thus in the proposition "All tyrants hate civil liberties," the class of tyrants (subject term) is asserted to be entirely included within the class of haters of civil liberties (predicate term). "Some musicians dislike Berlioz" asserts a partial inclusion (by convention, "some" is taken to mean "at least one") of the class of musicians (subject term) within the class of "dislikers of Berlioz" (predicate term). It will readily be seen that the proposition "Some musicians do not dislike Berlioz" may be read as a partial exclusion of the same subject class from the same predicate class. Finally, "No carrots contain calcium" asserts an entire exclusion of the subject class (carrots) from the predicate class (things which contain calcium).

This same analysis is usable when the terms are negative rather than positive. Every time a class is formed (e.g. books), another class is implicitly formed, namely the class of all things outside of the formed class (non-books); and the term "non-books" is just as usable in a proposition as the term "books": "All magazines are non-books."

Terms may be said to contradict each other (or the one to be the contradictory of the other) when the two classes they designate entirely and necessarily exclude each other. Another way of saying the same thing is: Of any term "S" and its contradictory "non-S" it may be said: "All S is excluded from non-S."

Sometimes mistakes are made when it is assumed that two terms which are strikingly different from each other are therefore contradictories: for instance, "bored" and "interested" or "wise" and "foolish." And when Socrates asked of his wise teacher: "But who, then, Diotima, are the lovers of wisdom, if they are neither the wise nor the foolish?" he was told, "They are those who are in a mean between the two . . ."

---

[3] Modern logicians sometimes distinguish four uses of *is*: *class inclusion* as in "All Mamelukes are soldiers"; *predication* as in "Ellen is a peasant"; *identity* as in "She is my wife"; and *existence* as in "It is raining."

Strictly speaking, every pair of contradictories taken together includes everything there is. Thus, the class "living kings" has only a few members, but its contradictory includes not only dead kings but cabbages and curlews and everything else that is other than a living king. However, practically, there is almost always an implicit restriction intended. One who has occasion to speak of non-union men (the contradictory of "union men") is doubtless confining himself to *workers* who do not belong to a union. Such an implicit restriction may be spoken of as a "universe of discourse." The context of the discussion specifies the universe of discourse. If one is talking of dahlias and non-dahlias, the universe of discourse is very likely the universe of flowers, and if of language and non-language, the universe of signs is probably implied. Such terms may be called "contraries." Contraries are of such nature that, though both of them together cannot be used as a predicate for a single subject, neither one of them alone has to be. One cannot (in the same way at the same time) be both bored and interested but he may be neither.

A WORD ABOUT GRAMMAR

As some grammarians of our own time have themselves best shown, a surprisingly large amount of what has been taught in the schools about English grammar is not gospel but apocrypha. Every language (except, of course, artificial languages or newly constructed languages, like modern written Chinese) comes into existence and continues for a long time without grammarians. But, as every reader of this book knows, language, quite as much as bees and weather and economics, is a proper object of investigation. After Greek became a highly developed language, there came into existence the study of its form. Sanscrit received a definitive treatment several centuries before our era by Panini, in a work described by linguists as one of the marvels of all ages—some have gone so far as to say that no other language has received such a nearly perfect treatment. English finally came to be blessed by its grammarians, too, many of whom flourished in the eighteenth century, before which time there prevailed what now seems to us a shocking looseness in writing. Thus, Shakespeare can be discovered in "grammatical errors"; what's more, the Bard seems to have been variable in spelling his own name. The eighteenth century grammarians set out to rectify this confusion, and they proceeded (as now appears) not just to describe the language, but to *prescribe* its usage. That is, their procedure was normative; and, indeed, every child who goes through school is conscious of some "rights" and "wrongs" of speaking and writing, and knows—at least hazily—some of the rules for *proper* language usage.

How many errors can you find in the following sentence?

Irregardless of what you say, it don't make sence to separate mens' classes — lockers — and etc. off by themselfs.

But why should one call them *errors*? Is it then an error to say "None were there"? Grammarians of a hundred years ago certainly thought so. How can these things change? Is it a mistake to split an infinitive? To say, "It is me"? If we encounter a difference of opinion about these usages, who is to decide? The authorities? But who are they, and how did they become authorities? Many contemporary linguists appear to believe that propriety of usage, so far as grammar is concerned, is, to a considerable extent, a sociological matter. Thus, a description of the way people write and talk reveals certain separable groups differing in their societal status not because of the way they use language particularly, but because of their occupations, their ownership, their family traditions, and the like. Frequently, there is pressure on persons in groups of lesser status to pattern their language after the most respected. A man will, under certain circumstances, make a genuine and often successful effort to stop using double negatives when he realizes that his preacher and his banker and his doctor avoid such expressions, whereas, though

he may be taught in school, year after year, that it is incorrect
to say, "It looks like it's going to rain," he remains unchanged
in his non-schoolroom usage because he feels no pressure (from
the groups having prestige) about that particular speech form.
For the construction just cited violates a rule that exists because of a prescription of a grammarian and not because it
reflects actual usage. It may seem that the expression "Aren't
I?" is illogical; that is, that if we are going to say "I am not"
we must also say "Am I not?" But consistency has less to do
with the matter than most of us are willing to believe. If
"Aren't I?" sounds all right to our ears, if it is the usage we
hear on all sides and not just the usage of an unapproved
group, we too, in all likelihood will employ that way of speaking.

The division of words into parts of speech is pretty inexact.
It may be of some help to the student of language to learn to
classify words in this way, but two important objections can
be made against the accepted classification into the eight
parts of speech: (1) The traditional definitions of these categories seriously violate the logical requirements for sound
classification. The point can be made in this way: if someone
averred that there are only three kinds of fraternity men—
the handsome, the stupid, and the athletic—you would suspect that the speaker was trying to make a joke rather than
offering an observation. Obviously there are three different
criteria here employed: physical appearance, intelligence, and
physical prowess. Now, in the same way, it is said that every
word is a noun, a pronoun, an adjective, an adverb, a verb, a
preposition, a conjunction, or an interjection; but a noun is
defined as "the name of a person, place, or thing" whereas an
adjective is defined as "a modifier of a noun." An examination of these two definitions will reveal that when you classify
a word as a noun, you must take into account its meaning,
that is, the sort of object it designates; but when you find a
word to be an adjective, you may ignore its meaning in order
to pay particular attention to its function in a sentence or at

least in a phrase. Other inconsistencies of this sort may readily be discovered. But there is another objection to this grammatical standby: (2) It is a serious error to suppose that the English language is typical in this multiplicity of parts of speech; in some languages only three parts are to be distinguished, in others just two. As Leonard Bloomfield put it: "It is a mistake to suppose that our part-of-speech system represents universal features of human expressions. If such classes as objects, actions, and qualities exist apart from our language, as realities either of physics or of human psychology, then, of course, they exist all over the world, but it would still be true that many languages lack corresponding parts of speech." [4] Provided with this salt of scepticism, one may still find the hoary theory about parts of speech useful.

It is now rather widely held by experts in language study that a very great many grammar rules are matters of good manners: to say, "I come to see you yesterday" is like eating peas with one's knife. To continue this analogy, it might be possible to find in Emily Post's book some rule of etiquette that in fact does not correspond with the ways refined and elegant persons behave. In such an instance, it isn't [5] likely that many persons will be affected in their own behavior by the injunction. Everyone has been taught that the future tense of the verb *to be* is conjugated: I shall, you will, he will, we shall, you will, they will; but the number of persons who consistently speak this way is very small. A recent authoritative study has shown that this distinction between "shall" and "will" is not now and never has been consistently made by the "better people" either in England or the United States.

However, grammar is not just a matter of the way people do in fact speak. The usage of our own group or of the group we especially admire is a strong determinant in our speech

---

[4] Leonard Bloomfield, *op. cit.*, p. 198.

[5] In this book such contractions as "isn't" are used. Some persons regard this as colloquial practice and thus of insufficient dignity for the printed page. However, even purists regretfully recognize that the trend is in the direction of informality.

patterns, but it is possible to be deliberately different, at least to a degree. It may be very, very hard for a girl not to follow the fashion in the hem length of her skirt, but it is at least *possible* to be eccentric. The study of grammar may be helpful in making us not just conformists, but better handlers of our language and more effective communicators. Even if it should become almost unanimous practice to use pronouns with vague reference, this still would not warrant the practice, and the grammarian can help us see why we should and how we can avoid the fault.

Perhaps it is fair to distinguish three different kinds of criticism which the grammarian makes:

1. "I can't hardly manage it." (Not conventional in high-status classes. Say "I can hardly manage it," or "I can't manage it.")
2. "In the very heart of the woods, an aged crone often reviled by the children of the nearby farms, lived." (Awkward, inelegant.)
3. "Being in somewhat poor health, her mother rather humored the child." (Unclear.)

PROBLEMS FOR DISCUSSION

A. It has been said that everyone has four vocabularies, one each for speaking, reading, writing, and hearing. Explain in your own case certain concrete discrepancies among your different vocabularies. Are these justifiable? If to any extent they are not, how may they be overcome? In this text have you passed over any words which you understood only vaguely or not at all?

B. Some linguists have asserted that it is easier for a Chinese child to learn Chinese between the ages of two and four than for an American or German to learn Chinese between the ages of thirty-eight and forty. Does this seem to you true? Why?

C. How may mistaking an abstract name for a concrete name lead to confused thinking? How may this kind of error be guarded against?

D. Can you think of any good reasons why in general a high score on a vocabulary test is an unusually reliable indication of superior intelligence?

E. Discuss Spinoza's saying: "To say definitely what a thing is, is at the same time to say what it is not."

F. Discuss the following:

Misnaming is not a trivial or laughing matter. If I misname I shall mislead others, and I shall also misunderstand information given by others to me. "Of course I knew all about his condition perfectly, but I never realized that was *diabetes.* I thought it was cancer, and all the books agree that's incurable: if I'd only known it was diabetes, I should have thought of insulin at once." Knowing *what a thing is* is, to an important extent, knowing what the name for it, and the right name for it, is. (J. L. Austin, "Other Minds" in *Essays on Logic and Language,* Second Series; A. G. N. Flew, editor. New York: Philosophical Library, 1953.)

G. Bertrand Russell, after discussing the interesting etymology of "apricot," drily comments: "All this makes the fruit taste much sweeter." ("In Praise of Idleness.") Can etymology be justified by any results?

H. William James says: "Names are arbitrary, but once understood they must be kept to. We mustn't now call Abel 'Cain' or Cain 'Abel.' If we do, we ungear ourselves from the whole book of Genesis, and from all its connections with the universe of speech and fact down to the present time." Does he exaggerate?

I. If you heard an Arizona sheepherder say about the desert, "There ain't a nubbin of nothin' growin' nowhere," would you disapprove of his speech? Why?

EXERCISES

I. Classify the following as singular or general, proper or common, collective or distributive, concrete or abstract, relative or absolute, positive, negative, or privative. Normally, a name will, of course, be classified in *several* ways.

1. clocks
2. *Hamlet*
3. this razor
4. the world's longest river
5. drunkenness
6. the human race
7. infinite
8. inflammable
9. blameless
10. short
11. a statue
12. fascism
13. sibling
14. enemy
15. desirability
16. Canada
17. group
18. the present emperor of Mexico
19. Zeus
20. a Nero
21. bronchitis
22. rationality

II. Write a short paper suggesting how the study of a foreign language can make one conscious of certain peculiarities in his mother tongue. Give specific examples.

III. Construct the vocabulary of an artificial language sufficient for writing several sentences. Translate the sentences into English. Can you determine in what ways you were influenced by your knowledge of English or some other language?

IV. Show how the description of a given word as a class of sounds substantially applies to a given written word. Give an example of a sentence that might be confusing because of the possibility of mistaking a word for its homonym. How do we ordinarily avoid confusion in the use of homonyms?

V. "Bang," "hiss," "gurgle," "splash," "whisper," and "crackle," are onomatopoeic words. Name five more. Are some of them borderline cases?

VI. These lines from Tennyson's "Princess" are often cited as a poetic use of onomatopoeia:

> The moan of doves in immemorial elms,
> And murmuring of innumerable bees.

What does the poet gain here by choosing words that imitate sounds?

VII. State the contradictory of each of the following terms and specify the probable universe of discourse implied: "animal," "dramatic poetry," "cannibals," "those with an I.Q. under 75," "philosophy," "green things."

VIII. Find at least one plausible implicit proposition in each of these non-propositions:

1. Put that down.
2. Are you coming or not?
3. Take me with you.
4. How do you know he passed?
5. Ouch!
6. I wonder who's kissing her now.
7. Fight, team, fight!
8. Oh, if only this would last forever.

SOURCES AND ADVANCED READING

1. Bertrand Russell, *The Analysis of Mind.* London: George Allen & Unwin, Ltd., 1921. Ch. X.
2. Mario Pei, *The Story of Language,* Philadelphia: J. B. Lippincott Company, 1949. Part II, Chs. II, III, IV, and V.
3. C. C. Fries, *American English Grammar.* New York, London: D. Appleton-Century Company, 1940.
4. A. M. Frye and A. W. Levi, *Rational Belief.* New York: Harcourt, Brace and Company, 1941. Ch. III.
5. W. Stanley Jevons, *The Elements of Logic.* New York: Sheldon and Company, 1883. Ch. I.
6. G. L. Kittredge and F. E. Farley, *An Advanced English Grammar.* Pp. xv-xvii.

MEANING

AND FAILURES OF MEANING

Meaning and Meaninglessness • Ambiguity • Vagueness • Some Meanings of Meaning

---

MEANING AND MEANINGLESSNESS

"Do, as a concession to my poor wits, Lord Darlington, just explain to me what you really mean."

"I think I had better not, Duchess. Nowadays to be intelligible is to be found out."

Lady Windermere's Fan

In order for words to function in communication, they must *mean* something; and they must not mean too much or too little. But some words are to some of us on some occasions meaningless, ambiguous, vague, or incorrect. When a word is unknown to us, when we don't know what it signifies, when we don't know what its user is trying to say by means of it, that word is for us *meaningless*. When the word means more than one thing and there are not clear indications of which meaning is intended, the word is *ambiguous*. When a word means something but means it in a misty, uncertain way so that it fails to mark off some aspect of the universe, then the word is *vague*. These failures of words are always relative to a given context of communication: what is meaningless to one person may be meaningful to another; a word ambiguous in print may have its meaning clarified by being pronounced in a certain tone of voice; an expression that in isolation seems vague may in its larger linguistic setting be sufficiently precise. Another obvious way in which words may fail us—or perhaps it would be better to say, in which we fail words—is in *incorrect* meanings. Everyone has had the experience of finding out that some word he had used for years and years, he had used all that time incorrectly. It might, for instance, be possible to stumble through a decade of life thinking that "inadvertently" was a synonym for "inexcusably," so that every time one came across the word or heard it spoken, he made this misinterpretation; probably, in the vast majority of cases, the mistake would be relatively harmless.

Even the person with the bulging vocabulary may be made humble by leafing through the pages of an unabridged dictionary; no single person, not even the chief editor of the greatest dictionary knows nearly all the words of a specific language. And whether our working vocabulary be 10,000 words or 50,000, we have had, of course, to learn the meaning of each one of those words. How have we learned? In many ways. By connecting words with accompanying gestures and actions, as when a person says, "I'm leaving" and leaves; or says "This pencil . . ." and picks up a pencil; or says "No!" and slaps. And we ask questions: "What does that mean?" "I don't understand that expression; what does it mean?" "What's a synonym for this word?" "Can you give me an example?" Still another way of learning words is by looking them up in dictionaries and glossaries.

The expression "learning a word" is misleading. It seems to suggest that we either know a word or do not. But there are many words we have learned and forgotten. Suppose someone reading a book were to look up and ask you, "What does the word *otiose* mean?" You've run across the word before and have *some* idea of its meaning. Perhaps you recall, for instance, that it is an adjective used to describe an argument or a speech, but you can't quite specify its meaning. Perhaps a glance at the context in which it occurs in the book will bring

more of its meaning to mind. Sometimes we will remember
that a certain word means either such-and-such or the opposite of that; does *enervate* mean to make energetic or to drain
of energy? Avid readers "know" a lot of words they have never
heard pronounced and never have occasion themselves to say.
Then again, I may know a word such as "burglar" without
knowing it well enough to distinguish its meaning from that
of "robber" or "thief." Or I may be acquainted with "fell" as
the past tense of "to fall" without knowing its use as an adjective or as a noun.[1] Sometimes we will smile at a foreigner who
says something like "That rose stinks," not because he doesn't
know the meaning of "stinks" at all but because he doesn't
sufficiently know its meaning; he knows it means "smells"
but doesn't know it means "smells bad."

Can we properly say that we know the meaning of a word
when we know what the word *refers to?* This has some plausibility. I know the meaning of "Abraham Lincoln" if I know
that it is the name of the sixteenth president of the United
States. I know what "chalk" means if I can, when I am asked,
select a piece of chalk from among different objects. I don't
know the meaning of "troglodyte" if I know not at all the
sort of thing named by that word. In such a case the word is
meaningless to me, though it will become meaningful as I
find out, say from a dictionary, what it names. Or perhaps the
word is not only meaningless to me, but meaningless to everybody—just a nonsense word—and doesn't refer to anything.
But what about a word like "justice"? Does it have *meaning?*
Certainly we use the word and recognize that it is appropriate
and proper to speak of "The justice of a court's decision" and
inappropriate and improper to say "Justice was a thin wire,
forty feet long."[2] But to what does "justice'" refer? If the

---

[1] This is not altogether accurate. The noun "fell" as used in Gerard Manley
Hopkins' line, "I wake and feel the fell of dark, not day," is a *different word*
from "fell" as in "Jack fell down and broke his crown." They are two words
that are spelled alike.

[2] It is somewhat dangerous categorically to deny sense to such an expression; perhaps one can imagine a context in which it would be appropriate.

object of a referring must be a physical thing, then "justice" would not have meaning. Some writers have adopted this position, saying quite flatly that every meaningful word must refer to some palpable object. Yet we do not, presumably, want to say that "justice," however vague the term may be, is meaningless in the way that "ogluteen" is meaningless. Or again are not prepositions, like "of" and "to" and "in" words with meaning? There surely are "right" and "wrong" uses of such words. They help us say things, express ourselves, communicate our ideas and feelings. Yet prepositions do not seem to refer to objects. It might even be doubted that adjectives, like "green" and "small" and "meaningless" *refer* in the way that names refer.

Of course it may very well be the case that while certain words like "green" and "in" and "the" do not themselves individually refer, phrases of which they are a part, like "the green bird in the tree" do refer. And this is no doubt the case; what is referred to is not just bird and tree but a total situation, complete with a quality and a spatial relation. Even the articles play a part, as was noticed in the previous chapter, there being a difference in designation between "a tree" and "the tree."

There remain, still, certain words which seem to have a meaning (in some sense very hard to specify) but which do not, at least not in the same way we have already noted, make reference, even if they are put into a larger context. Let us take as examples, now, not the kind of word we used above when we inquired about "justice" but a word like "ouch" or a word like "help." A person who calls "Help!" is most certainly understood by users of the English language to be meaning something quite different from a person who says, "Go away!" or "Bother!" But is the difference a difference in reference? Possibly so, in the sense that you might be inclined as an observer to look for a different situation for the cause of the yell for help than for what would cause a mild exclamation like "Bother!", but this is not quite the same as saying that the word "Help" means a certain distressing situation by referring to it. The referential meaning of "Help!" is sideshow; the main tent meaning seems to be of an altogether different kind.

These initial considerations about *meaning* and *lack of meaning* will be discussed before an approach is made to the problem of *what it means to "mean."*

AMBIGUITY

A verbal expression may be said to be ambiguous when its use gives rise to uncertainty as to which of two or more possible meanings to assign to it. Words given in isolation are very apt to be ambiguous. Take an ordinary word like "chair" for instance. It may designate not only a certain kind of article of furniture but also the dignity attached to the office of presiding over a meeting. Doubtless the latter meaning is an extension of the former, but it is nonetheless quite a distinct and legitimate meaning. And in practically any context it would be clear which of these meanings was intended. There is even a feeble joke about someone at a meeting being asked to "take the chair," whereupon he walks off with the furniture in which the presiding officer was supposed to sit. This and many other better jokes derive whatever humor they possess from an ambiguity. "Man" is often cited as a highly ambiguous term. The following pairs of contrasting terms suggest some of the scope of the ambiguity: man and boy, man and woman, man and wife, man and beast, man and master; add such expressions as "man the lifeboat" and "Take him all in all, he was a man" and it will be admitted that there is considerable variety of meaning. Nevertheless, it is just as apparent that there is little or no ambiguity in many of these instances, however much there might be in the isolated term.

Occasionally all of us will make mistakes of interpretation because of taking a given vocalized sound to be another word than that intended. Thus, in conversation, we might mistake "rain" for "reign," "beer" for "bier," "dye" for "die." Spelling clarifies these mistakes (for most of us), but would not help if we understood "lie" in a certain instance to mean prevaricate where it was intended to designate a recumbent posture. Then again, some words which pronunciation distinguishes are spelled alike: for instance, "tear." Reader, which way did you pronounce it or think of it, just now? (A psychologist might take your interpretation as an index to your tendency toward lugubriousness.) But again, mere location in a context is usually sufficient. If we encounter the phrase "tear a page" we will not be likely to think of a page being bespattered with drops from an eye.

However, we are not always so fortunate. Sometimes the context of an expression not only does not remove an ambiguity but seems positively to intensify it. Here is an instance cited by the logician Jevons:

"A thoroughly benevolent man cannot possibly refuse to relieve the poor, and since a person who cannot possibly act otherwise than he does can claim no merit for his actions, it follows that a thoroughly benevolent man can claim no merit for his actions." According to this kind of argument a man would have less merit in proportion as he was more virtuous, so as to feel greater and greater difficulty in acting wrongly. That the conclusion is fallacious every one must feel certain; but the cause of the fallacy can only be detected by observing that the words *cannot possibly* have a double meaning, in the first case referring to the influence of moral motives or good character, and in the second to circumstances entirely beyond a person's control; as, for instance, the compulsion of the laws, the want of money, the absence of personal liberty.[3]

One of the key words in formal logic is "or." Yet it is frequently ambiguous. If I say, "Either go or don't go," the two alternatives are mutually exclusive and the "or" is not ambiguous. If I say, "Will you have sugar or lemon in your tea?"

[3] W. S. Jevons, *Elements of Logic* (New York: Sheldon and Company, 1883), pp. 30-31.

and you reply, "Both, please," I may not admire your taste but I will admit that you properly understood me to mean that taking both was an alternative. But suppose a scholar to write, "Either the manuscript is a forgery or it is over five hundred years old"; does he intend by that "or" to say that at least one of these conditions obtains and possibly both, or to say that if one is the case, the other is automatically ruled out? We cannot tell. The expression "and/or" is sometimes used in legal documents, presumably to suggest that the stated alternatives are not to be construed as excluding one another.

William James told a story that has become famous as an illustration of how arguments are sometimes merely verbal, in the sense that they hinge upon an ambiguity. Let the ambiguity be detected and the argument disappears. In such cases, it is literally the case that it *all* depends on what you mean by the word. Here is the story:

Some years ago, being with a camping party in the mountains, I returned from a solitary ramble to find everyone engaged in a ferocious metaphysical dispute. The corpus of the dispute was a squirrel — a live squirrel supposed to be clinging to one side of a tree trunk; while over against the tree's opposite side a human being was imagined to stand. This human witness tries to get sight of the squirrel by moving rapidly around the tree, but no matter how fast he goes, the squirrel moves as fast in the opposite direction, and always keeps the tree between himself and the man, so that never a glimpse of him is caught. The resultant metaphysical problem now is this: Does the man go round the squirrel or not? He goes round the tree, sure enough, and the squirrel is on the tree; but does he go round the squirrel? In the unlimited leisure of the wilderness discussion had been worn threadbare. Everyone had taken sides and was obstinate; and the numbers on both sides were even. Each side, when I appeared, therefore appealed to me to make it a majority. Mindful of the scholastic adage that whenever you meet a contradiction you must make a distinction, I immediately sought and found one, as follows: "Which party is right," I said, "depends on what you practically mean by 'going round' the squirrel. If you mean passing from the north of him to the east, then to the south, then to the west, and then to the north of him again, obviously the man does go round him, for he occupies these successive positions. But if on the contrary you mean being first in front of him, then on his left, and finally in front again, it is quite obvious that the man fails to go round him for by compensating movements the squirrel makes, he keeps his belly turned towards the man all the time, and his back turned away. Make the distinction, and there is no occasion for any further dispute. You are both right and both wrong, according as you conceive the verb 'to go round' in one practical fashion or the other."

Although one or two of the hotter disputants called my speech a shuffling evasion, saying they wanted no quibbling or scholastic hair-splitting, but meant just plain honest English "round," the majority seemed to think that the distinction had assuaged the dispute.[4]

Sometimes a word or a phrase will be employed so that it quite deliberately has multiple meanings. A simple example is afforded by a pun, for instance, Wordsworth's saying, "If I had a mind to, I could write like Shakespeare." Then too, very frequently a poet plays upon and exploits the richness of meaning within a word. Thus Andrew Marvell begins his poem "The Garden," "How vainly men themselves amaze," and in the very second word we detect a double meaning: (1) in vanity (2) futilely. Is this a fault in the poem? Clearly not, for Marvell wants to say both these things; it is a great advantage that one word will so effectively compress both meanings.

As we have defined "ambiguity," the intentional use of multiple meanings is not an instance. Ambiguity is a *fault*, something which blocks clarity of communication, something which needs to be removed.

A special kind of ambiguity, often given the title "amphiboly," is that in which a confusion as to which meaning is

<hr/>

[4] William James, *Pragmatism* (New York: Longmans, Green and Company, 1931), pp. 43-45. Permission to reprint granted by Paul R. Reynolds & Son, 599 Fifth Avenue, New York, N. Y.

intended arises from the very construction of the clause or sentence itself instead of from the words. The classical illustrations are the pronouncements of the ancient oracles. "Cyrus this day a mighty nation will destroy" is a prediction that has a fair chance of panning out because of the several possibilities of interpreting it: (1) a mighty nation will this day destroy Cyrus, (2) Cyrus this day will destroy a mighty nation, which might be (a) his enemy's or (b) his own. Our hesitation between (1) and (2) illustrates amphiboly, whereas the confusion between (a) and (b) is an example of the other type of ambiguity, which, if it needs a name, may be called *equivocation*. Inexpert writers are often amphibolous in their constructions, especially through the use of carelessly placed modifiers and through unclear reference. The following sentences illustrate: "When properly pickled, no man can resist good, ripe cucumbers." "If the water seems to upset the baby, boil it." (Of course we would not expect the latter to be really confusing in our particular culture.)

The meanings which concepts have differ for (1) different epochs (2) different contemporaneous cultures (3) different individuals. It is no small part of our constant job of trying to understand what other persons mean, to recognize these differences.

(1). Here are a few translations culled from a Shakespeare glossary:

Shakespeare	Modern Equivalents
ecstasy	madness
jealousy	suspicion
conceit	thought
indifferently	fairly well
thrift	profit
idle	insane
presently	immediately

To know what Shakespeare's *Hamlet* means, it is most helpful to know the meanings which he assigned to his words. He meant by "presently" something different from what we commonly mean, and it is his meaning and not ours that is important to our reading.

When a Plato translation says "art" we often need to know, for accuracy of reading, that the Greeks had no concept of art quite like ours. "Democracy" meant to Alexander Hamilton something sufficiently different from what we commonly mean today, that we are likely to go wrong in interpreting his thought if we do not exercise due caution.

(2). It was George Bernard Shaw who said that "England and America are two countries separated by the same language." Tourists sometimes run into snags when they assume that a given word has the same meaning in two different countries or that a translation of a foreign word is a precise translation. In English we speak to a second person as "you" whether he is a stranger or an intimate, but there are whole chapters in the novels of Thomas Mann, for example, which center around the delicacy of shifting from the impersonal second person pronoun to the form reserved for use with close friends, children, and certain inferiors. It is especially hard that the British and Americans should use the "same" word with different meanings. No doubt most of the examples which come to mind are slight, yet they are symptomatic of the difficulties of understanding. An American in England might ask for a biscuit and be served a cracker, engage an apartment only to find himself put in a single room, find that a billion is written with three more digits than he is used to.

(3). Far more subtle, yet perhaps far more important, is the difficulty of understanding what another person means just because he is another person. Every one of us learns a language and a language belongs not to one person only but to an entire language community. Yet no person's language is quite like another's. Every single word that each of us has learned, every phrase, every manner of speaking, has been learned under unique circumstances. Every word that each of us has in his vocabulary has its own career in our own psyches. Chances are that when Mr. A says, "wicked" or "virtuous" or "selfish" or "loving," he means, because of the unique configuration of his own experiences, something a little bit different from what his hearer would mean in using these expressions. So it becomes the hearer's job to use all the clues at his disposal to interpret the speaker's special meanings.

VAGUENESS

A well-known advertisement reads approximately as follows: "When ordering Scotch, don't be vague; say 'McKutcheon, McKutcheon, McKutcheon, and Smith, please.'" The brand name is less vague than just the class name in the sense of vagueness that is opposed to specificity. Thus "Scotch" is less vague than whiskey, which is less vague than "liquor" which is less vague than "beverage" and so on. But more often "vagueness" refers to a certain indefiniteness of class membership. Take the word "old" in the question "Is he an old man?" One is inclined to answer the question by another question: "How old is old?" Presumably 80 is old, but is 60? How about 65? And so on. In such a usage, "old" is vague. An applicant for a stenographic job might answer the employer's query, "Are you a fast typist?" with the single word, "Yes," and it would serve the employer right for not having asked a sharp enough question.

The degree of vagueness that is admissable varies with the communicative situation. We may instruct the barber to "take a little off the top" without having to specify the exact number of hairs. On the other hand our hostess at tea may reprove the answer "Lots" by asking "How *many* lumps?"

Value terms tend to be vague, notoriously so. Sometimes it is not necessary to be any more precise than to say, "Dick is a good student"; but at other times "good" must be pinned down. As good as an "A" grade? In the upper five per cent of his class? Better than Lawrence?

Recently, the United States Supreme Court handed down

a unanimous ruling on a case involving the constitutionality of the State of New York's censoring as "immoral" the French film "La Ronde" and the State of Ohio's censoring the movie "M" as "inciting to crime." In a previous case they had ruled on New York's censorship of "The Miracle" as "sacrilegious." In all these instances, the court found the grounds for censorship "vague and indefinite." That is, the laws of the states involved did not provide any standards for determining when a film is sacrilegious, or for telling whether it incited to crime.

The courts, naturally, are constantly having to clarify the vagueness of laws. Practically every phrase in the Constitution of the United States has been found to be vague in some case or other. What is "due process of law"? Is *this* an instance? Is *that*? In recent years there has been much talk about the clause: "Congress shall make no law respecting an establishment of religion or prohibiting the free exercise thereof. . . ." Does this bear upon a bill to provide federal funds for busses for students attending a parochial school? Does it give clear guidance to the Federal Communications Commission in deciding upon the claim of an avowed atheist to be granted radio time to answer the broadcast of a sermon? Constitutional law, of course, *has* to be highly vague, or it would not be of sufficient generality to provide a principle to guide lawmakers and judges, and it would not be sufficiently flexible to cover different times and different conditions.

We quite naturally think of scientific language as the very model of precision. And so it is, but the history of science may be read as in part a succession of clarifications of the imprecisions and vaguenesses of previous theories and laws. Isaac Newton, for instance, whom his successors criticized for the vagueness of his key term "force," was himself highly critical of the "occult qualities" about which his predecessors talked. Newton wrote:

Such Occult qualities put a stop to the improvement of natural philosophy, and therefore of late years have been rejected. To tell us that every species of things is endowed with an occult specific quality, by which it acts and produces manifest effects, is to tell us nothing: but to derive two or three general principles of motion from phaenomena, and afterwards to tell us how the properties and actions of all corporeal things follow from those manifest principles, would be a very great step in philosophy, though the causes of those principles were not yet discovered.[5]

SOME MEANINGS OF MEANING

In discussing ambiguity and vagueness we have indirectly been discussing meaning, but it is time now to return to a direct concern with this central concept.

"Meaning" is ambiguous. That is the least debatable proposition that can be made about this tricky word. In his authoritative book *Signs, Language and Behavior,* Charles Morris, a leader in the field of semiotic, dismisses the word "meaning" as not having "the precision necessary for scientific analysis." [6] Nevertheless, for our elementary purposes, the word may be retained, though of course it must be analyzed to sort out some of its most important significations. Here are eight sentences:

1. You mean a lot to me.
2. "Little" means "small." Or: "Pferd" means "horse."
3. Do you mean him or her?
4. "Pedantic" means affectedly learned.
5. What do you mean to do?
6. I mean what I say.
7. Do you mean that you like him?
8. When I say "One," that means to get ready.

Ignoring entirely such alien uses (different words) as "the meanest flower that blows," "a mean, nasty man," and "arithmetical mean," let us briefly examine the function of the word "mean" in each of these eight cases.

[5] Newton, *Optics,* IV.

[6] Charles Morris, *Signs, Language and Behavior* (New York: Prentice-Hall, Inc., 1946), p. 19.

1. "You mean a lot to me." "Mean" here is a value term. It signifies the placing of value by the speaker on the one addressed. Is there any symbolizing function played in this instance by "mean"? Perhaps there is, in the sense that the person spoken to is said by the speaker to "stand for" an important value.

2. " 'Little' means 'small'." This can be thought of in two ways: (a) that the first word symbolizes the second; (b) that both words symbolize the same thing or designate the same property. Translation from one language to another is the same matter.

3. "Do you mean *him* or *her?*" This question presumably arises from a need to clarify an ambiguity of reference. Something was said that might have had as its object either "him" or "her." To mean "him," for example, is to say something *about* "him." "He" was meant as that being to whom certain actions or qualities were ascribed.

4. " 'Pedantic' means affectedly learned." The term "pedantic" is to be understood as marking off a certain complex of qualities. It names these qualities.

5. "What do you mean to do?" "Mean" in this instance is interchangeable with "intend."

6. "I mean what I say." This is an intensifying statement. The speaker ascribes to himself a sincerity, a seriousness of assertion. He tries to guard against an interpretation of his words as "just words," as not having been expressive of a real feeling or belief or intent.

7. "Do you mean that you like him?" Here the question is about whether some verbal expression or other form of behavior may properly be interpreted as indicating a feeling of liking, directed in such and such a way.

8. "When I say 'One,' that means to get ready." This is an announcement of a signal.

From these examples (and of course more might be given) we can learn to notice certain differences regarding: (a) who or what does the meaning; (b) what is the object of the meaning;

and (c) what relationship between subject and object or what action of the subject is indicated by the expression "means."

(a) Sometimes a person does the meaning, directly: you mean, I mean, he means (#'s 1, 3, 5, 6, and 7); sometimes a *word*, like "little" or "pedantic," is said to mean (#'s 2, 4, and 8). But of course where there's a word, there's a speaker or writer behind the word, who means, somehow, through his expression; though a person may mean without the use of words, as possibly is the case in #'s 5 and 7.

(b) A word may be meant (#2) or qualities may be meant (#4) or a person or other object may be meant (#3). An action may be meant (#'s 5 and 8), an evaluative expression may be meant (#7), or an assertion may be meant (#6). Perhaps a value or an ascription of worth can be meant (#1). The sense in which these various kinds of objects *are* objects varies, of course, with the nature of the action of meaning in each case.

(c) The relationship of pointing to, pointing out, singling out, or referring to, is commonly expressed by "means." (#'s 3 and 4). "Is substitutable for" or "is the same as" may be the relationship exhibited by #2 and perhaps #7. "Mean" sometimes bespeaks an intention or a certain attitude of seriousness (#'s 5 and 6). Sometimes, though probably rarely, "mean" is directly expressive of a value (#1). And sometimes it indicates a signal (#8).

Bertrand Russell makes a fundamental distinction between the meaning of the *indicative* and the meaning of the *imperative*:

In the indicative, a word A means a feature B of the environment if (1) when B is emphatically present to attention, A is uttered or there is an impulse to utter A, and (2) when A is heard it arouses what may be called the "idea" of B, which shows itself either in looking for B or in behavior such as would be caused by the presence of B.[7]

---

[7] Bertrand Russell, *Human Knowledge: Its Scope and Limits* (New York: Simon and Schuster, 1948), p. 71.

An imperative, on the other hand, expresses (a word that Russell distinguishes from "means") a wish on the part of him who utters the command and "means" the external effect which it commands.

Russell's suggestions are interesting but not altogether satisfying. In the first place, it can be doubted whether in the indicative, the "idea" aroused by the word A does necessarily show itself in looking for B or in other behavior such as would be evoked by the sensible presence of B. Pavlov's famous experiments which showed that if dogs are given their food at the same time as a bell is rung, then, after a while, the sound of the bell itself will make the dogs' mouths water—these experiments are often cited as an example of behavior in the presence of a symbol such as would be caused by the presence of the thing itself. But the behavior of most of us in the presence of the word "desk" as in somebody's saying to us, "I guess I must have left the paper home on my desk," does not ordinarily start us looking around for the desk and certainly doesn't start us acting in any overt way as we might in the presence of a desk, such as putting our feet up or making a motion like opening a drawer. Still, we want to recognize that the word "desk" does in a sense substitute for the piece of furniture itself, in that the word takes the place of a gesture in the presence of the object, whereby we might indicate "that thing over there." By means of the word "desk" our behavior is oriented toward the desk without the desk itself acting as a stimulus.

As to imperatives, it sounds a little odd, perhaps, to say that a command "means" the external effect which is ordered. Do we really want to say that "Close the window!" means the window closed? If someone hearing the command were to ask a companion, "What does that mean?" a proper reply would be, "It means that he wants the window shut." This suggests that rather than saying that the command first expresses a wish and then means an effect, that it really means a wish-for-a-shut-window.[8] In this case too the words act as a substitute stimulus for the listener or reader; what is substituted for is non-verbal wishing behavior. In another sense the command means the effort of the one commanded.

Charles Morris, who uses the word "signifies" instead of "means," helps us understand the function of signifying by distinguishing four *modes*. Two of them correspond, roughly, with what Russell called the "indicative" and the "imperative." Morris' names are: the *designative* mode and the *prescriptive* mode. Another mode is the *appraisive*, and a fourth, the *formative*, about which we will say only that it has to do with what in Chapter IV were called the syncategorematic expressions, words which help order discourse.

A homely dialogue will help us understand these ways of meaning. Suppose that a tourist is quizzing a service station operator:

T. Where's a good place to eat around here?

O. "The Greasy Spoon" is about the best place in this town.

T. Where is it?

O. Across the street and down two blocks. Tell the manager I sent you.

The two questions may be taken as prescriptive: they are demands for information, they prescribe a verbal response. The first answer is clearly appraisive: "The Greasy Spoon" is given a clean bill of health. The restaurant is located for the tourist, and this is a designative matter. And the parting shot is prescriptive in suggesting an action.

This brief analysis indicates that meaning or signifying is in its broadest sense a matter of the various functionings of signs or more particularly of language. A given use of language has meaning when it is a relatively successful *means*

---

[8] The imaginative reader will conceive of other possible interpretations of this command: perhaps the commander is primarily interested in showing his power over us, or perhaps he is practicing a part in a play. In our examples, we will always be offering possible and plausible interpretations, but not inevitable ones.

for the end of communication. A person means; he means through his words, so words subordinately mean; his words have meaning for somebody, the person communicated to; and they mean something: they mean in the sense of designating or indicating, or they mean in the sense of appraising or evaluating or expressing desire or preference, or they mean in the sense of recommending or suggesting or demanding a certain action. Correspondingly, language can fail in these same ways—or, if one prefers a more precise statement—persons can fail in their use of language in these same ways. I may want to tell you about something and not be able to; I may give you a mistaken notion of what I like; and I may misdirect you unintentionally or intentionally, in which case what I say and what I "mean" may be very different.

Normally for a bit of discourse to have meaning, it is required (1) that the words fit together in an acceptable pattern; (2) that we know *what* is being talked about; (3) that we understand what the producer is driving at, what relevance his language has.

(1) "Yesterday another Arthur cannibalism" doesn't make sense, unless of course the words are assigned new meanings, as in a code. The expression is basically ungrammatical; it is not a proper way of speaking. (2) "Enantiopathy is now discredited" is to most readers an only partly meaningful expression. The grammar looks right and one probably knows what it is to be discredited and suspects that the subject of the sentence is something capable of being discredited, like a practice or a belief, rather than something to which discrediting is totally alien, like paper or the sun. But until one knows what that long word means, the meaning of the whole sentence is dim. (3) An expression has meaning when by means of it, the producer and one or more receivers are enlighteningly related. We read in *Othello,* "I understand a fury in your words, but not the words." We often understand the fury or the threat or the tenderness or the invitation in words in

virtual independence of the other kinds of meanings the words may have. And, conversely, we sometimes understand the words, in a literal sense, without knowing what their speaker is driving at.

A single expression may mean in different ways (as distinct from having different meanings, as with an ambiguity) for different receivers. Suppose three persons, A, B, and C to hear the following sentence spoken by D: "I wonder where she's at." A, being a stylist and rather finicky, says, "That's a very awkward expression." B, having been prompted by the sentence to think of the woman too, says, "Yes, where could she be? Maybe on a date." C, being more of a psychologist, says, "Now, why did he say that? He seems unduly worried."

Ruesch makes a similar point:

A verbal statement perceived by an observer can be interpreted in different ways. For example, a compulsive or legalistic mind might confine itself to purely syntactical or semantic interpretations, omitting all pragmatic considerations. In contrast, the psychologically oriented person will listen to the same statement in an attempt to detect the implied values of the speaker. A politically minded person with common sense will in turn interpret the statement as an expression of the feeling of the population at large and without particular consideration of the individual who makes the statement. Thus the legalistic mind acts primarily as an observer, the psychologically minded person as a participant, and the politically minded person, while he may pretend to participate, is in reality manipulating, campaigning, and observing the effects of his actions.[9]

A return will be made to this subject in a later chapter where the variety of language usage is discussed, but we must now look at a further distinction within the designative mode of meaning.

[9] J. Ruesch and G. Bateson, *Communication: The Social Matrix of Psychiatry* (New York: W. W. Norton and Company, Inc., 1951), pp. 76-77. Note that the types of interpretation here discriminated do not exactly correspond with those above.

The distinction is the traditional one between connotation and denotation. (1) The word "eraser" means or refers to any member of the class of erasers; (2) The word "eraser" means an instrument for obliterating marks. (1) is denotation. (2) is connotation. A word *denotes* an object or a set of objects. "Jane" denotes that girl. "Thief" denotes any and all of the *persons* who steal. A word *connotes* a complex of properties or qualities. "Vertebrate" connotes animal-with-a-backbone. As W. E. Johnson puts it: "While extension [denotation] stands for a set of substantives, intension [connotation] stands for a set of adjectives.[10] Some words connote without actually denoting. It is possible to describe a unicorn without there being any; that is, "unicorn" connotes a set of properties but has no denotation.

It is sometimes said that a proper name like "Dwight Eisenhower" denotes without having a connotation, but it seems that in such a description as "thirty-fourth President of the United States" one is giving a connotation.

Now the connotative phrase "bone china tea cups" enables us, theoretically, to construct a class of all the objects in the world which answer to that description and this will be the denotation of that phrase. But it will no doubt be the case that the objects which find themselves classified thus together will have some other properties in common besides those which served as the basis of the classification; for instance they may all be white, even though their being white was not taken into consideration in lumping them together. The entire set of properties which is possessed in common by the whole denotation of a term has been called the *comprehension* of that term.

A question may be raised about whether a term denotes only the *actual* things delimited by its connotation or all the possible, thinkable things as well. The question may be answered by stipulating that the latter will be meant unless the

10 W. E. Johnson, *Logic, Part I* (London: Cambridge University Press, 1921), p. 100,

expression "actually denotes" is employed.[11] Thus "Don Quixote" (the name of the character, not the name of the book) denotes but does not actually denote. "Round square" has no denotation. It will have occurred to many readers that oftentimes the word "denotation" is used to mean the same as what here is meant by "connotation," and that the latter word is used to indicate the emotional toning of an expression. Thus, on this usage, "communist" denotes subscription to an economic doctrine of the common ownership of property, but connotes a disagreeable, dangerous, frightening fellow. This kind of emotional suggestiveness is doubtless an important aspect of language and will be dealt with later. In this book it will *not* be called "connotation."

Thinkers have known for many centuries that it is not only possible but usual for men to get so rapt with their *words* as to be neglectful of *things,* to become trapped in merely verbal arguments, to become so used to certain words as to assume that these words have referents in the non-verbal realm. "Witch" is a real word; it even has a meaning in the sense that we know what the attributes of such a creature are or would be; still, we believe that there are no actual witches. "Witch" has no actual denotation. Or again some persons are extraordinarily glib with such words as "ideal," "beauty," "justice," "rightness," and "freedom"; yet their verbal facility may seem fatuous and otiose; one suspects them of mere word juggling.

Such complaints are well grounded and indicative of need for corrective action. But the reform cannot be simple without being simple-minded. Periodically there have been wars waged on words. "Let's confine ourselves to tangible matters. Away with abstractions. Stick to the facts; let the facts *speak for themselves.* Down with Words! Vive Things!" For the

---

[11] For a different handling of this classification, see C. I. Lewis, *An Analysis of Knowledge and Valuation* (La Salle, Illinois: The Open Court Publishing Company, 1946), Ch. III.

present, Jonathan Swift's satire in *Gulliver's Travels* is a sufficient answer to the anti-word fanatics.

We next went to the school of languages, where three professors sat in consultation upon improving that of their own country.

The first project was to shorten discourse by cutting polysyllables into one, and leaving out verbs and participles, because in reality all things imaginable are but nouns.

The other project was a scheme for entirely abolishing all words whatsoever; and this was urged as a great advantage in point of health as well as brevity. For it is plain that every word we speak is in some degree a diminution of our lungs by corrosion, and consequently contributes to the shortening of our lives. An expedient was therefore offered, that since words are only names for things, it would be more convenient for all men to carry about them such things as were necessary to express the particular business they are to discourse on. And this invention would certainly have taken place, to the great ease as well as health of the subject, if the women, in conjunction with the vulgar and illiterate, had not threatened to raise a rebellion, unless they might be allowed the liberty to speak with their tongues, after the manner of their ancestors; such constant irreconcilable enemies to science are the common people. However, many of the most learned and wise adhere to the new scheme of expressing themselves by things, which hath only this inconvenience attending it, that if a man's business be very great, and of various kinds, he must be obliged in proportion to carry a greater bundle of things upon his back, unless he can afford one or two strong servants to attend him. I have often beheld two of those sages almost sinking under the weight of their packs, like pedlars among us; who, when they met in the streets, would lay down their loads, open their sacks, and hold conversation for an hour together; then put up their implements, help each other to resume their burdens, and take their leave.

But for short conversations a man may carry implements in his pockets and under his arms, enough to supply him, and in his house he cannot be at a loss. Therefore the room where company meet who practice this art, is full of all things ready at hand, requisite to furnish matter for this kind of artificial converse.

Another great advantage proposed by this invention was that it would serve as an universal language to be understood in all civilized nations, whose goods and utensils are generally of the same kind, or nearly resembling, so that their uses might easily be comprehended. And thus ambassadors would be qualified to treat with foreign princes or ministers of state, to whose tongues they were utter strangers. (Part III, Ch. V.)

PROBLEMS FOR DISCUSSION

A. In one year it was reported that Philadelphia had only one-fifth as many thefts as Washington, D. C. and that Miami had three hundred times as many robberies, proportionate to the population, as Lowell. Is it possible that recognition of the ambiguity of certain words would make these statistics less impressive? Explain.

B. Early in the nineteenth century a ship and its cargo, bound from the United States for Ireland, were insured. In the policy was the provision that if the vessel and its cargo were insured in England, the U.S. policy would be cancelled. The vessel was lost. A suit arose because the vessel but not its cargo was insured in England. Explain the ambiguity that is the heart of the trouble.

C. It is sometimes asserted that a sentence is meaningless if there cannot be specified some way in which it could be discovered to be either true or false. On this criterion, which of the following sentences are meaningless? For those you call *meaningful,* describe how the statement might be verified.

  1. There are man-made canals on Mars.
  2. Right this minute, it is raining in Shanghai.
  3. God exists.
  4. Swiss cheese is better than Roquefort.
  5. When you die, you stay dead.
  6. Every human being has an invisible, immaterial soul.
  7. No one has ever seen or could possibly ever see an electron; still electrons exist.
  8. Count Korzybski was the founder of "General Semantics."
  9. Forward march!

EXERCISES

I. Look up the etymology of "ambiguous," "equivocal," "dictionary," "vague," and "designate."

II. Devise an argument in which some key word is used ambiguously. Make it as subtle as possible.

III. Find in a newspaper or magazine an instance of a sentence in which there is real doubt as to which of two or more possible meanings is intended.

IV. In three or four sentences give a simple explanation of Swift's satire, quoted in the chapter.

V. A person who says, "But that's not what I meant!" may sometimes be understood to be saying, "Though I perhaps meant that then, I no longer want to mean that now." Explain.

VI. Re-write each of the following sentences without using the word "means," but so as to retain the meaning of the sentence as you understand it:
   1. He means me.
   2. When I say "Jump!" I mean *Jump*!
   3. He means to say that he does not believe the proposition.
   4. "Rubber" means "something which rubs."
   5. What does the expression "fresh vegetable clerk" mean?
   6. "Cougher" and "coffer" sound rather alike but do not mean at all the same thing.
   7. My dog means everything to me.
   8. I mean to go as soon as I get ready.
   9. Do you mean the one with red hair?
   10. What does "holophrastic" mean?

VII. Correct the ambiguity: "There has been much discussion of values, but very little of value."

VIII. Find in three advertisements a deliberately *vague* use of words.

SOURCES AND ADVANCED READING

1. E. M. Adams, *The Fundamentals of General Logic*. New York: Longmans, Green and Company, 1954. Ch. III.
2. C. K. Ogden and I. A. Richards, *The Meaning of Meaning*. New York: Harcourt, Brace and Company, 7th ed., 1945. Ch. IX.
3. John Neville Keynes, *Studies and Exercises in Formal Logic*. New York: The Macmillan Company, 4th ed., 1906. Part I, Ch. II.
4. Charles Morris, *Signs, Language and Behavior*. New York: Prentice-Hall, Inc., 1946. Chs. III and IV.
5. Frederick A. Philbrick, *Understanding English, an Introduction to Semantics*. New York: The Macmillan Company, 1942.
6. Max Black, *Critical Thinking*. New York: Prentice-Hall, Inc., 2nd edition, 1952. Ch. 10.

❖ VI ❖

DEFINITION

Are Words the Master or the Mastered? • Meanings of Definition • Ways of Defining • Characterization and Empirical Propositions • Deductive Propositions • Definition and Ambiguity • Not All Arguments Are Verbal

---

ARE WORDS THE MASTER OR THE MASTERED?

Multae terricolis linguae, coelestibus una.
—*Bible* (King James translation), title page.

Everything that can be thought at all can be thought clearly. Everything that can be said can be said clearly.

—WITTGENSTEIN

Did you ever hear a third party break into an altercation to say with some vehemence:

This is the silliest argument I ever heard. You guys talk and talk and neither one of you knows what the other is talking about. You say "communism," "free enterprise," "democracy," "totalitarianism"—and so on. What do these words mean? Anything? What, then? Define your terms.

"Define your terms!" It is a chilling challenge. Not only the big words, "Honor," "Justice," "Truth," "Democracy," and such, but even words like "chair" or "book" or "pencil" are hard to define, except very roughly. Still, how can we know what we are talking about if we don't know what our words mean?

When we don't know the meaning of a word, or when we suspect we may have connected the wrong meaning with the right word, or when for us a word is ambiguous or vague, we feel the need for a definition. We may ask, "What does this *word* mean?" Or we may ask, "What do *you* mean by this word?" In the former case, the supposition is that the word has some standard, regular, normal, correct meaning. In the latter case there seems to be implicit the recognition that a word's meaning may vary with its user.

"There's glory for you!"

"I don't know what you mean by 'glory,' " Alice said.

Humpty Dumpty smiled contemptuously. "Of course you don't — till I tell you. I meant 'there's a nice knockdown argument for you.' "

"But 'glory' doesn't mean 'a nice knockdown argument,' " Alice objected.

"When I use a word," Humpty said in rather a scornful tone, "it means just what I choose it to mean — neither more nor less."

"The question is," said Alice, "whether you *can* make words mean so many different things."

"The question is," said Humpty Dumpty, "which is to be master — that's all." [1]

Is it the word that means or is it Humpty-Dumpty who means—by means of the word? Or suppose I am writing a speech and trying to communicate the idea that my opponent's remarks contain, though not explicitly, his belief in the inherent superiority of white-skinned people to Negroes. I write, "Mr. Y. strongly . . . that Negroes are inherently inferior to whites." I don't know quite what word to use. Should I say "infers" or "implies" or some other word? Perhaps I ask a friend, one who knows a great deal about language, what word to use and he tells me that "implies" would be correct and "infers" incorrect. But how does he know that a word

[1] Lewis Carroll, *Through The Looking Glass*. Ch. VI.

is incorrect? What does it *mean* for a word to be incorrect? Why can't I use any word I want to? Am I the master or the mastered?

MEANINGS OF "DEFINITION"

John Stuart Mill wrote: "The simplest and most correct notion of a Definition is a proposition declaratory of the meaning of a word. . . ." If we may take Mill's sentence to be itself a definition, we find him assigning "correctness" to a certain indicated meaning. If one runs the risk of incorrectness, then it is not true that he can mean by a word anything he chooses to mean. But in their monumental work *Principia Mathematica*, Bertrand Russell and Alfred North Whitehead say that "A definition is, strictly speaking, no part of the subject in which it occurs. For a definition is concerned wholly with the symbols, not with what they symbolize. Moreover, it is not true or false, being the expression of a volition, not of a proposition." Whom are we to believe? But in the quotation above, we unfairly cut Mr. Mill off in mid-sentence (a device often used by advertisers and political commentators quite deliberately); let us hear him out:

The simplest and most correct notion of a Definition is, a proposition declaratory of the meaning of a word; namely, either the meaning which it bears in common acceptation, or that which the speaker or writer, for the particular purposes of his discourse, intends to annex to it.[2]

This shows the ambiguity of "definition" in such a question as "Is a definition either true or false?" The answer would seem to be: a definition is either true *or* false if it claims to declare the meaning a word bears in common acceptation, but is neither true *nor* false if it only declares the meaning a particular user attaches to a word for purposes of his own discourse. Let us call these two *kinds* of definition

[2] John Stuart Mill, *A System of Logic* (London and New York: Longmans, Green and Company, 1948), Book I, Ch. VIII.

and name them, respectively, Reportorial Definition and Stipulative Definition.

Reportorial Definition. Suppose two persons to be arguing about the correct pronunciation of "decadent." They finally agree to settle their dispute by consulting a dictionary. But why is the dictionary an authority on such a matter? Presumably because the dictionary reports how most persons or how most of a selected list of persons pronounce the word. This is what the Merriam-Webster unabridged dictionary says about determination of pronunciation:

The standard of English pronunciation . . . so far as a standard may be said to exist, is the usage that now prevails among the educated and cultured people to whom the language is vernacular. . . .[3]

But if two dictionaries disagree about the pronunciation of a word, say "decadent," and they both claim to report the prevailing usage at a given time of "the educated and cultured people to whom the language is vernacular," then at least one of the dictionaries must be wrong.

Precisely the same thing is true of reportorial definitions. If one is asked, "What does the word 'sacerdotal' mean?" he would probably understand the question to ask about the established meaning-usage of the term among educated and cultured people, though this particular word probably has little currency among uneducated and uncultured people. If the reply came: "Oh, that means impudent," this definition would be inaccurate whether or not it was believed. The fact of the matter is simply that hardly anyone who uses the word "sacerdotal" means by it impudent, and therefore the claim that such is the common usage is an erroneous claim.

Sometimes, of course, there isn't any single, clearcut prevailing usage, but two or more common meanings, and in

---

[3] The entire section, "A Guide to Pronunciation" in the Second Edition is fascinating.

that case, a correct reportorial definition would report the plural usage.

A definition may be reportorial in being based not on general usage or on usage among the élite, but on some particular usage, as that of some writer (e.g., "In Plato, the word usually translated 'Idea' means the universal and permanent forms") or of some class or group (e.g., "To the Communists 'revisionist' means one who has tried to reinterpret the basic theories of Marx") or of the inhabitants of a geographical region (e.g., "In England, 'corn' stands for all grains").

Stipulative (or Humpty Dumpty type) *Definition.* Sometimes a speaker or writer will announce: "When I use the word 'x' I will use it to mean so-and-so." He has defined "x" in such a way that if someone says, "Oh, but that's not what the dictionary says" or "That's not what I take the word to mean," the reply is, "That's very interesting, but what *I* mean by 'x' is so-and-so." He is stipulating the meaning, making no claims about common usage or dictionary authority or truth. This kind of definition is, as Russell and Whitehead put it, "the expression of a volition, not of a proposition."

"I *will* use the word to mean such-and-such" is a prediction and as such is either true or false. Certainly it has happened more than once that a speaker has begun by announcing his intention of using some key word in one way and then, consciously or unconsciously, has shifted the meaning of the word in the course of his remarks. In this case his prediction was untrue, but in so far as one is predicting his own verbal behavior he is doing something different from stipulating.

Now sometimes the way a stipulative definition comes about is through the assigning of a name, perhaps a new name, one coined for the purpose, to an object or a class of objects or an activity, etc. Thus suppose an anthropologist wants to attach a name to all the relatives on the mother's side of the family, and proposes to call this class of relatives, "matives." In assigning this concocted name, he is of course defining it. There is no question about its truth or falsity, for the word is new, it has no usage as yet except his own, and it is not likely that anyone will challenge his right to mean by his own word whatever he chooses to mean by it. Of course, someone might object that there was already a suitable name for this purpose, or that no name was needed because the classification was unimportant, or that from the definition it was not clear whether one's mother's uncle by marriage was a matative, or that the name was hard to pronounce, and so on. But these are not matters of truth or falsity.

However, the word which is defined by stipulation need not be a new word. One *can* define "glory" as "a nice knock-down argument," but the trouble with such a stipulation is that it's very hard to remember that *that* is what "glory" now means. Every time you hear it, you have to make a little translation and that's a bother.

Mixed Stipulative and Reportorial Definition. The commonest and most important use of the device of stipulation is when a choice is made between several possible ways in which an expression might be interpreted or when a vague term is assigned a more precise meaning than it normally has, but still a meaning similar to its usual one. Thus, a writer may be about to put down the word "necessary" when he recalls that there is a certain difference between the kind of necessity which is mathematical and that which is non-mathematical: (1) "If one interior angle of a triangle equals more than 90 degrees it is necessary that the sum of the other two be less than 90 degrees." (2) "If you are going to vote, it is necessary to register." The writer may then wish to specify that it is the second type of necessity which he has in mind. This will be a stipulation in the sense that he will be expressing his intention to use the word in a certain way, but the way in which he chooses to use the word is *one* of the accepted ways. Or again, someone may find it important to define very precisely the word "sedition" in order to know how a law employing this term is to be enforced, and he may decide that no one is guilty of sedition unless he specifically advocates the overthrow of established government by force. This is making the word have a rather more specific meaning than is usual and yet a meaning that is entirely consistent with the usual more vague signification. Thus it is stipulative to the extent that the claim could not be made that the word does in fact have only this precise meaning, yet the claim can be made that in general the definition conforms to what dictionaries report.

WAYS OF DEFINING

So far we have considered defining as it relates to the intention of the word-user and to established usage. But if, as John Locke put it, definition is "nothing but making another understand by words that idea the term defined stands for," [4] we need now to ask *how* one goes about this "making another understand." Once again distinctions must be drawn, for there is no single way, not even any single *right* way.

Defining by Giving an Example. If you had just selected a golf club from the bag and walked onto the green when a novice asked, "Say, what is a putter?" you would prove yourself a very tiresome person indeed by going into a long verbal description instead of gesturing and saying, "One of these." Sometimes we may feel impatient with a definition that starts out, " 'Misdemeanor' means like when..." but there are times when we feel almost totally helpless to define in any other way than by pointing, by making some imitative gesture, or by referring to an instance of the class in question. Children like to ask adults "What's an accordion?" or "What's a spiral staircase?" and then laugh at the descriptive gesture that almost invariably comes by way of answer.

Defining by exemplifying embraces two distinguishable species: (1) verbally citing an instance, an example; (2) pointing to or showing an instance or a sample. The latter is frequently called *ostensive* definition. Simple sensory qualities like *salty* or *red* or *rough* particularly need ostensive defining;

---

[4] John Locke, *Essay on Human Understanding*, Book III, Ch. 3, Sec. 10.

words seem particularly futile to describe, for instance, an odor. What does sassafras smell like? Is there any good answer except producing a bit of the bark for a good whiff?

In many cases we perfectly well get the point of the exemplification and feel ourselves well answered, but not always. The trouble may lie in telling what precisely about the example is characteristic of the whole class. The following account by a missionary among primitives is instructive:

I remember on one occasion wanting the word for Table. There were five or six boys standing round, and, tapping the table with my forefinger, I asked, "What is this?" One boy said it was a *dodela,* another that it was an *etanda,* a third stated that it was *bokoli,* a fourth that it was *elamba,* and the fifth said it was *meza.* These various words we wrote in our notebook, and congratulated ourselves that we were working among a people who possessed so rich a language that they had five words for one article.

But these language-learners were doomed to disillusionment, for they came to discover that

one lad had thought we wanted the word for tapping; another understood we were seeking the word for the material of which the table was made; another had an idea that we required the word for hardness; another thought we wished for a name for that which covered the table; and the last, not being able, perhaps, to think of anything else, gave us the word *meza,* table — the very word we were seeking.[5]

Of course the missionary here was doing what might be thought of as the opposite of defining by exemplification, in that he was passing from meaning to word rather than the other way around, but the difficulty is the same either way; for if our query about a word's meaning is answered by pointing toward an object, we may mistake *what exactly* is being pointed at. We say, "What is a quarto volume?" and in answer we are directed to look at a certain book. But what makes the

5 J. H. Weeks, *Among Congo Cannibals* (Philadelphia: J. B. Lippincott Co., 1913).

book a quarto: its length and breadth? its thickness? the material in which it is covered? its color? the subject matter?

Defining by Giving a Synonym or an Antonym. If we are asked what "tome" means, we are likely to respond: "book." "Tome" means—that is, it means the same as—"book." The two words can be used interchangeably; they are synonyms. "Versus" means the same as "against." "Monsieur" means the same as "mister." These are definitions of a sort, and are very often satisfactory. If we are reading and encounter the sentence, "He was devoted to the gay science"; we may be puzzled enough to ask, "What's 'gay science'?" If we are answered, simply, "Poetry," chances are we will be satisfied. A known word is substituted for an unknown expression.

But such defining is by no means always satisfactory for the reason that synonyms are only more or less rough substitutes and there are times when we will "accept no substitutes." Children often have to be offered especially rough synonyms because of the need for simplicity. When the child is told that "melancholy" is the same as "sad" or that "planet" means the same as "star," he is being helped, probably, but also being somewhat misled, and future experience, it is hoped, will gradually correct the error.

A variant of this way of defining consists in specifying an *antonym*. "Quick" means the opposite of "slow." "What is 'sweet'? Well, it's the exact opposite of 'sour.'" "Infinite" means the same as "not-finite." The shortcoming of this sometimes useful kind of definition springs from the ambiguity of "opposite." Aristotle usefully distinguished two kinds of opposite, the contradictory and the contrary. The contradictory class is that class which includes everything excluded by a given class. For instance, the contradictory opposite of "red" is "not-red"; everything that falls outside the class of red falls inside the class of not-reds. A contrary class, on the other hand, is any class which shares no members with the given class, but which in conjunction with that class does not necessarily include everything there is. For example, "red" and "green" are contraries, in that anything that is red (all over) is (at the same time and in the same way) necessarily not-green; still there are many things that are neither red nor green. "Infinite" and "finite" are contradictory opposites; "sweet" and "sour" are contrary opposites. But if it is said merely that "war" is the opposite of "peace" or "Democrat" is the opposite of "Republican" or that "fair" is the opposite of "dark," what are we to understand in each case by the word "opposite"?

Defining by Giving the Connotation. Probably the commonest meaning of "definition" is "to determine the essential qualities of." (Merriam-Webster) "Essence" may be defined as that whereby a thing is what it is, or that without which a thing would be a different kind of thing from what it is. There are some qualities which something must possess in order to be a chair; those qualities constitute the essence of chair or "chairness." Or, to state it another way: you want to decide what it takes to be beautiful. What are the "marks" of everything that is beautiful? What do all beautiful things have in common and which of those qualities are absolutely necessary to beauty? We define "beautiful" when we "determine the essential qualities" that the word "beautiful" stands for.

There is an old and much debated distinction between "verbal definition" and "real definition." The first has to do with words, the latter with things. But in few cases is this distinction a sharp one. In purely stipulative definition the concern may be *wholly* with words, and possibly in many cases of synonymous definition. But in connotative definition one is concerned with both words and things. Notice that Webster's phrase says "*determine* the essential qualities" which perhaps puts the emphasis upon an investigative, inquiring process by which we seek to find out what there is about, say, biscuits that makes them biscuits. But this determination will be reported in words. And, indeed, the determination seems to be no different if we describe our task as deciding what the word "biscuit" refers to, or deciding when it applies and when not.

One of the oldest descriptions of the process of definition is that of Plato's which is known as "dichotomous division." This calls for giving the essence of something through displaying its two principal parts. This is best illustrated by the so-called "Tree of Porphyry." [6] Substance is defined as that which includes the corporeal and incorporeal; animal consists in rational and irrational things; and man is not dichotomized but is exemplified:

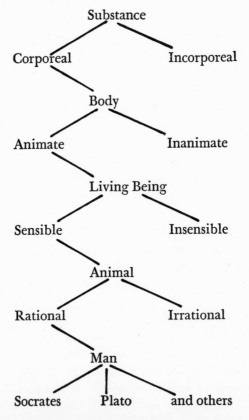

---

[6] Porphyry was a neo-Platonic logician of the third century A.D. What is here given is a popular adaptation of Porphyry's model.

It will probably not be amiss here to say a word about "false dichotomies." If someone should tell us that there are only two kinds of person, Americans and un-Americans, we would do well to be on our guard. For this might lead to such a line of argument as the following: "Englishmen are of course not Americans and are therefore un-American. But every American must be opposed (else he will himself be really un-American) to anybody guilty of such feelings. Consequently it is our patriotic duty to oppose and try to put down Englishmen." From this it is fairly easy to see that the word "un-American" as it tends to be used, is not equivalent to such a virtually neutral word as "non-American." Every person may be said to be either American or non-American, but many persons who are non-American are not un-American in the sense of being anti-American.

Aristotle, the greatest logician of antiquity, decided that definition (at least one kind of definition) proceeds best the other way around; that is, by first specifying the larger class to which that-to-be-defined belongs. We have begun our definition of "sofa" when we notice that a sofa belongs to the class of furniture. But of course "sofa" and "furniture" are not synonyms. All sofas are furniture, but not all furniture is sofas. We need to know further that which distinguishes the sofa from other members of the class, furniture. Having put *sofa* into the genus *furniture*, we need the differentia, that which differentiates. So we say something like this: A sofa is that kind of furniture which is designed to seat more than one person, is upholstered, and has arms and a back. Is that a good definition? Formally, at least, it fits the specifications. It tells us the kind of thing a sofa is, and it gives us the marks which distinguish it from other sorts of furniture.

This defining by specifying genus and differentia (the Latin phrase is still often used in texts: *per genus et differentiam*) is today often followed in spirit if not in letter. Here is a dictionary definition: "Stridulate" means "to make a shrill, creaking noise." The genus "noise" and the differentia, "shrill, creaking," can easily be detected.

Nevertheless, the need for defining is by no means always met by this ancient device. Aristotle was above all a biologist in his interests, and of course classifications by species and genus are especially useful and plausible when one is dealing with plants and animals. But today we are a little wary of the assumption that everything in the universe has its "natural" place in an elaborate hierarchy of classes, and most of the concepts that really bother us into a defining activity do not seem to call out for placement in a genus. Think of a word like "freedom," for instance. It is used constantly, but everyone except the most semantically naïve person recognizes the word to be highly ambiguous and terribly vague in most of its usages. There are times when all of us want to use the word and some of those times we would like, if possible, to use it a little more carefully than we usually do. So we try to define it, at least in the sense of talking about it a little. We try, to use an expression that is very much in vogue, to *analyze the concept*. What does this mean?

In order to explore the nature of analysis, we start with the so-called "analytic proposition." An analytic proposition may be defined (among other ways) as that type of proposition in which the predicate is truly ascribed to the subject for the very good reason that the meaning of the subject term includes what the predicate means. The simplest case is that in which there is just literal repetition: "A rose is a rose." "Virtue is virtue." [7]

[7] However, notice that such an expression as "Business is business" may be construed to mean something like this: In the commercial world (the subject, roughly) the profit interests precede the interests of friendship and even of some rules of 'fair play.' So the predicate here only *apparently* repeats the subject, but does not do so in actuality. Sigwart makes the same point as follows: "In the proposition, *Children are children,* the subject-term means only the age characteristic of childhood; the predicate-term, the other characteristics which are connected with it. By the proposition, *War is war,* we mean to say that when once a state of warfare has arisen, we need not be surprised that all the consequences usually connected with it appear also. Thus the predicate adds new determinations to the meaning in which the subject was

But this is hardly a case of analysis at all, if we think of analysis as consisting of "taking apart." A clearer instance is afforded by: "Queen Elizabeth is a queen"; or "A dray horse is a horse." There is perhaps little excuse for uttering such sentences—certainly they would seldom be helpful, except for writers desperate for an example—but that they are true, and true because the subject contains what is manifestly already part of the subject. The case is not quite so simple when we get to: "A triangle is a three-sided plane figure." Suppose someone asks, "Yes, but suppose you find one with four sides, what then?" The answer readily comes, of course: "Oh, but you can't do that. A triangle has *got* to have only three sides. If it has more or less it isn't a triangle. Having three sides is part of what it means to *be* a triangle." We are, therefore, spreading out in the predicate the meanings packed together in the subject. The situation is not altered if we complicate the instance in this way: "A cubical parabola is a plane cubic curve which meets the line at infinity in three coincident points and having a point of inflection as center and a cusp at infinity." All that comes after "is" in the sentence merely reveals what is already there in the subject, if only you have the eyes to see.

This explanation of the "analytic proposition" suggests what it is to analyze: that is, to make explicit what was implicit, to open up and show the contents of an expression. What is analyzed may not be just a single word or a simple phrase, but may be a whole proposition, or a law, or indeed a whole book. Thus there are whole libraries of volumes which analyze the Bible, making no claim, of course, to add to it, but only to help get out of it what is there.

Analytic activity is sometimes impatiently explained away as "just reading a lot of meanings into something." Of course one may "read meanings into" an idea; that is, add to its meanings, ascribing some thoughts of one's own to what was

---

first taken." *Logic*, I. p. 86. Quoted in J. N. Keynes, *Studies and Exercises in Formal Logic* (New York: The Macmillan Company, 4th ed., 1906), p. 52n.

intended by the user of the expression in question. But analyzing proper is "reading out of" rather than "reading into," and because one himself had not recognized what is revealed to be the complexity of a given idea is no sign that that idea was not really so complex.

Many essays and whole books are attempts to define-by-analyzing some difficult concept like *art* or *freedom* or *philosophy* or *democracy*.

W. E. Johnson tells of a related type of definition useful in mathematics. Let us assume that our job is to define "factor." If we can presuppose that the expression "a x b = c" is understood, then we define "factor" by saying that in such a proposition *a* is a factor of *c*.[8]

Defining by specifying an operation. If the teacher asks what it means for a number to be *even* and little Johnny replies, "Oh that's when you divide by two and if it works, the number is even," the answer might be reproved by the teacher as crudely expressed, but an advanced mathematical physicist like P. W. Bridgman might well applaud. Johnny has given an *operational* definition of *evenness*—that is, he has shown a way of operating that constitutes the very meaning of the term in doubt. Bridgman's famous description of *operational definition* is:

In general, we mean by any concept nothing more than a set of operations; *the concept is synonymous with the corresponding set of operations.*[9]

His clearest example is the concept of length.

We evidently know what we mean by length if we can tell what the length of any and every object is, and for the physicist nothing more is required. To find the length of an object, we have to perform certain physical operations. The concept of length is there-

[8] W. E. Johnson, *Logic* (London: Cambridge University Press, 1921), Part I, p. 108.
[9] P. W. Bridgman, *The Logic of Modern Physics* (New York: The Macmillan Company, 1927), p. 5. Quoted by permission of the publishers.

fore fixed when the operations by which length is measured are fixed: that is, the concept of length involves as much as and nothing more than the set of operations by which length is determined.[10]

Incomplete Definitions.

The only adequate definition of a name is . . . one which declares the facts, and the whole of the facts, which the name involves in its signification. But with most persons the object of a definition does not embrace so much; they look for nothing more, in a definition, than a guide to the correct use of the term — a protection against applying it in a manner inconsistent with custom and convention.[11]

Mill goes ahead to remark that the most famous definition of all, "Man is a rational animal," is a good illustration of an incomplete definition. Though rationality and animality are essential qualities of every man, it is entirely possible to imagine a rational animal we would not consent to call a man: one of Jonathan Swift's super-intelligent horses, a Houyhnhnm, for instance. Thus the definiens (i.e., the defining expression) in this case gives us a part only of the essence of *man*. To put it still another way, in order to be a man it is necessary to be both rational and animal, but being animal and rational does not suffice to make one a man. A full definition states the conditions *necessary and sufficient* for the definiendum (i.e., the term to be defined) to be a name applicable to a given entity.

Oftentimes we will be stumped by a demand for a definition, but that does not necessarily mean that we "don't know what we're talking about." How many of us could give, offhand, a definition of "capitalism" that would satisfy an economist? Yet all the while we may have a practical notion of when an economy is capitalistic and when it is not. We might

---

[10] *Ibid., loc. cit.*

[11] J. S. Mill, *A System of Logic* (London and New York: Longmans, Green and Company, 1948), Book I, Ch. VIII. No definition could give "the whole of the facts." Mill is suggesting the ideal limiting case.

say, "*One* thing that is essential to capitalism is the profit system. Perhaps the presence of a profit system isn't enough to make an economy capitalistic, but at least if there is no provision for making profits, it isn't capitalistic." Here there is a defining activity being carried on, right enough, even if what emerges is not a complete definition.

Sometimes a useful concept can best be defined by the specification of characteristics which *tend* to be present. Thus it may be helpful to say of "pencil" that it designates a writing instrument usually employing graphite, etc., even though the use of a red wax core would not disqualify the object. An eminent theoretical biologist has pointed out a difficulty in defining a species:

There is no single criterion of species. Morphological differences; failure to interbreed; infertility of offspring; ecological, geographical, or genetical distinctness — all these must be taken into account, but none of them singly is decisive. . . . A combination of criteria is needed, together with some sort of flair. With the aid of these, it is remarkable how the variety of organic life falls apart into biologically discontinuous groups.[12]

CHARACTERIZATION AND EMPIRICAL PROPOSITIONS

A complete, connotative definition, as we have seen, is one which expresses the whole *essence* of what is being defined. An *essential* quality is one without which a thing would not be the kind of thing it is. Having just four interior angles, each a right angle, is part of the essence of a *square*. Now man is said to be the only mammal which mates the year around. Are we here giving part of the essence of man? No, for it is not enough that this be true of all men and true only of men; it must—in order to be essential—also be *necessarily* true of all men. If there could be turned up a being who in all other

---

[12] J. S. Huxley, *The New Systematics* (New York: Oxford University Press, 1940), p. 11. Quoted in "Definition and Specification of Meaning" by Abraham Kaplan, *Journal of Philosophy*, Vol. XLIII (May 23, 1945), p. 282.

respects was human but whose mating instincts operated only on the ides of March, we would not deny this being admission to the class of men; and if it turned out that what we have hitherto called "yaks" mate in all seasons, we would not be seriously tempted to move over to make room for these new "men." This and many other characteristics of men have been traditionally called "accidents" or "accidental qualities." Not all accidental qualities belong universally to a class. Thus, some but not all dogs are brown. The brownness of any given brown dog is not the quality that makes him a dog. We will speak of the process of attributing accidental qualities to objects as "characterization"; it is description, or describing. Sentences which attribute accidental qualities to a subject are "synthetic," as opposed to "analytic." That is, the predicate is a positive addition to the subject and something which cannot be known by an examination of what it means to be the sort of being the subject names.

What reasons can be offered for a characterization? I know some dogs are brown because I have seen brown dogs. I know this knife is sharp because I feel it to be sharp. I know that this book will drop if I let it go because I have observed many such objects fall. I know that there is a place called Wales, because I have had eye-witness accounts from persons I trust. I know about how far away the moon is because I have learned this from scientists whose observational techniques I have confidence in. In short, the reasons are empirical. If someone were to tell me that all the philosophical books in the library are catalogued between the numbers 100 and 300, I would doubt the accuracy of this statement, but I would immediately think of some observations I could make in order to check the assertion. Or if a question arose as to whether the averted face of the moon is mountainous (Bertrand Russell's irresistible example), I would know what sort of observations might conceivably be made to settle the matter, even though I know we are presently actually helpless to make such observations.

In short, to characterize is to make an empirical assertion. It is to say that a certain relation exists or that such and such an object has such and such qualities, not because these qualities belong to that object *essentially* but only because they happen to belong to it.

It is not by any means always clear whether a given sentence is intended by its user to be analytical or to be synthetic, a sentence in which something is characterized. Many misunderstandings arise because of this lack of clarity; many arguments would fade into nothingness if only it were realized that what looks like an empirical statement is just a disguised tautology. For instance, two persons might debate endlessly about whether all ruminants are cloven-footed when all the while one disputant was unwilling to *call* anything a ruminant unless it was cloven-footed. Or for that person whose definition of "God" includes the quality of omnipotence the question about whether it is possible that there should be a supreme being with limited power is not really a question at all.

It is to be noted also that what constitutes the essence of any class will vary with the person thinking about the class.

DEDUCTIVE PROPOSITIONS

Some propositions are known to be true not because what is predicated of a subject already belongs to the subject by definition and not because there is empirical evidence to show that the subject really does in fact have such characteristics. An example of this new type of proposition is: The interior angles of a triangle equal, in sum, 180 degrees. Normally we would not discover that such and such a figure *is* a triangle by determining (among other things) that such was the sum of its angles. And we certainly would not consider it relevant to go around measuring the angles of a large sample of triangles and increasing the probability of the proposition with each new one which came to exactly 180 degrees. No, but we can prove the proposition by employing certain accepted rules of deduction on certain initially stated definitions and showing that from these definitions this proposition *follows*.

Deductive propositions are more closely related to analytic propositions than to empirical propositions, for they are certain rather than just probable.

DEFINITION AND AMBIGUITY

Definitions are good or bad as they are helpful or unhelpful. A good definition is one that clarifies, that gets rid of *merely verbal* disagreements and misunderstandings.

The logician James MacKaye has given an especially helpful series of steps for dealing with an ambiguity around which an argument turns.[13] First, single out the issue or the question at stake. Next isolate the word or expression that is thought to be ambiguous. Give that definition of the ambiguous expression which *fails* to resolve the dispute, the one which is apparently employed by the disputants. Substitute a finer definition, or more properly a pair of definitions, one for each of the meanings discovered in the expression. Then, finally, restate the question and answer it according to the corrected definitions. Let us observe how this works out in practice, by following out these steps in William James's story.

1. Question: Does the man go around the squirrel?
2. Ambiguous word: Around
3. Inadequate definition: "Around" means "on every side."
4. Corrected definitions: (a) "Around" means "first to the right side, then to the back, then to the left side, and finally front again."

[13] James MacKaye, *The Logic of Language* (Hanover, New Hampshire: Dartmouth College Publications, 1939), Ch. V.

     (b) "Around" means "first to the
      north, then to the east, then
      to the south, and finally back
      to the west, the presumed
      point of departure."

5. Question again: Does the man go around the squirrel?

     (1) If the question is understood to
      use "around" in sense (a), the an-
      swer is NO.

     (2) If the question is understood to
      use "around" in sense (b), the an-
      swer is YES.

Perhaps it should be said further, at this point, that should someone now say, "But which is the *correct* meaning of 'around'?" the best answer is that both meanings are rather commonly employed, that one is not necessarily better than another, but that sometimes it is important to know *which* meaning you want to use and to be careful to make it understood that it is that meaning which you have in mind. It's rather like routing traffic: it doesn't matter whether the cars drive on the right as in the United States or on the left as in England, but it is important that in any given place, one of these directions be decided upon and made clear to all concerned.

Now let us apply this machinery for dealing with an ambiguity to a somewhat more complicated case. John Stuart Mill in his *System of Logic* deals with the classical paradox attributed to Zeno of Elea.

The ambiguity of the word Infinite is the real fallacy in the amusing logical puzzle of Achilles and the Tortoise, a puzzle which has been too hard for the ingenuity or patience of many philosophers. . . . The fallacy, as Hobbes hinted, lies in the tacit assumption that whatever is infinitely divisible is infinite; but the following solution (to the invention of which I have no claim) is more precise and satisfactory.

The argument is, let Achilles run ten times as fast as the tortoise, yet if the tortoise has the start, Achilles will never overtake him. For suppose them to be at first separated by an interval of a thousand feet: when Achilles has run these thousand feet, the tortoise will have got on a hundred; when Achilles has run those hundred, the tortoise will have run ten, and so on forever; therefore Achilles may run forever without overtaking the tortoise.

Now the "forever" in the conclusion means, for any length of time that can be supposed; but in the premises, "ever" does not mean any *length* of time; it means any *number of subdivisions* of time. It means that we may divide a thousand feet by ten, and that quotient again by ten, and so on as often as we please; and there never needs be an end to the subdivisions of the distance, nor consequently to those of the time in which it is performed. But an unlimited number of subdivisions may be made of that which is itself limited. The argument proves no other infinity of duration than may be embraced within five minutes. As long as the five minutes are not expired, what remains of them may be divided by ten, and again by ten, as often as we like, which is perfectly compatible with their being only five minutes altogether. It proves, in short, that to pass through this finite space requires a time which is infinitely divisible, but not an infinite time — the confounding of which distinction Hobbes had already seen to be the gist of the matter.[14]

MacKaye then reduced this to his schematism as follows:

1. Question: Can Achilles ever overtake the tortoise?
2. Ambiguous word: "Ever."
3. Inadequate definition: "Ever" means "at any time, in any case, under any circumstances."
4. Corrected definitions: (a) "Ever" means "in any duration of time."
   (b) "Ever" means "in any number of subdivisions of time."
5. Question again: Can Achilles ever overtake the tortoise?
   (1) If the question is understood to use

[14] J. S. Mill, *op. cit.*, p. 535.

"ever" in sense (a), the answer is
YES.

(2) If the question is understood to use
"ever" in sense (b), the answer is
NO.[15]

NOT ALL ARGUMENTS ARE VERBAL

There are some questions which are merely verbal, merely matters of definition. Sometimes it will happen that, as in the classic story, we will say, "Ah but now I see that what he calls 'God' I call 'the Devil'." And that will be all there is to it. But to get hold of the idea that disputes are often verbal is to take hold of a very vicious tiger by the tail: it is hard to let go and yet we may want to and need to very much indeed. The person who forms the habit of saying about disputes he encounters: "Oh but it's all a matter of words" will often dismiss disputes which are most certainly *not* just matters of words. Many of the disputes which are partly matters of words are not altogether matters of words. It will be worth our time to consider an example.

A sophisticated sophomore comes upon an argument about immortality and pronounces his malediction upon the entire conversation as follows: "There's no point to this argument. It's all a matter of words. Some people define 'immortality' in one way, as for instance, the permanent continuation of individual consciousness; others define it quite differently, for example so that any work of ours, any contribution to the world, in continuing after our own death, makes us immortal. Define it as you like, but don't argue about it." This may possibly be the end of the conversation, but should it be? May there not be some non-verbal questions left over after definition has done its work? It may be the case that when "immortality" has been defined, let us say, in something like the first way suggested by the interrupter, the dispute will continue

15 Adapted from James MacKaye, *op. cit.*, p. 138.

as to whether immortality, *so defined,* is a real hope for a man. Definition will have clarified the discussion but not terminated it.

It is quite possible to be oversold on definition and other types of linguistic clarification. They are not panaceas. After all the verbal puzzles have been cleared up — as if they ever could be! — there will be enough aching problems of other kinds left over to keep the aspirin-makers in business.

PROBLEMS FOR DISCUSSION

A. In the following dialogue (continued from the one quoted early in the chapter) distinguish between those definitions which strike you as purely arbitrary and stipulative and those which can be explained in some way. What sorts of explanations and justifications are offered?

"You seem very clever at explaining words, sir," said Alice. "Would you kindly tell me the meaning of the poem called 'Jabberwocky'?"

"Let's hear it," said Humpty Dumpty. "I can explain all the poems that ever were invented—and a good many that haven't been invented just yet."

This sounded very hopeful, so Alice repeated the first verse:

> " 'Twas brillig, and the slithy toves
>   Did gyre and gimble in the wabe:
> All mimsy were the borogoves,
>   And the mome raths outgrabe."

"That's enough to begin with," Humpty Dumpty interrupted; "there are plenty of hard words there. *'Brillig'* means four o'clock in the afternoon—the time when you begin *broiling* things for dinner."

"That'll do very well," said Alice. "And *'slithy'?*"

"Well, *'slithy'* means 'lithe and slimy.' 'Lithe' is the same as 'active.' You see, it's like a portmanteau—there are two meanings packed up in one word."

"I see it now," Alice remarked thoughtfully. "And what are *'toves'*?"

"Well, *'toves'* are something like badgers—they're something like lizards—and they're something like corkscrews."

"They must be very curious-looking creatures."

"They are that," said Humpty Dumpty, "also they make their nests under sundials—also they live on cheese."

"And what's to *'gyre'* and to *'gimble'*?"

"To *'gyre'* is to go round and round like a gyroscope. To *'gimble'* is to make holes like a gimlet."

"And *'the wabe'* is the grass-plot round a sundial, I suppose?" said Alice, surprised at her own ingenuity.

"Of course it is. It's called 'wabe,' you know, because it goes a long way before it, and a long way behind it."

"And a long way beyond it on each side," Alice added.

"Exactly so. Well, then, *'mimsy'* is flimsy and miserable (there's another portmanteau for you). And a *'borogove'* is a thin, shabby-looking bird with its feathers sticking out all round—something like a live mop."

"And then *'mome raths'*?" said Alice. "I'm afraid I'm giving you a great deal of trouble."

"Well, a *'rath'* is a sort of green pig: but *'mome'* I'm not certain about. I think it's short for 'from home'—meaning that they'd lost their way, you know."

"And what does *'outgrabe'* mean?"

"Well, *'outgribing'* is something between bellowing and whistling, with a kind of sneeze in the middle; however, you'll hear it done, maybe—down in the wood yonder—and when you've once heard it you'll be *quite* content. Who's been repeating all that hard stuff to you?"

"I read it in a book," said Alice.

B. "If . . . two persons contend whether Augustus deserved to be called a 'great man,' then, if it appeared that the one included, under the term 'great,' disinterested *patriotism,* and *on that ground* excluded Augustus from the class, as wanting in that quality; and that the other also gave him no credit for that quality, but understood no more by the term 'great,' than high intellectual qualities, energy of character, and brilliant actions, it would follow that the parties did not differ in opinion, except as to the use of a term, and that the Question was Verbal. If, again, it appeared that the one *did* give Augustus credit for such patriotism, as the other denied him, both of them including that idea in the term 'great,' then the Question would be Real." (Richard Whately, *Elements of Logic*. Boston: James Munroe Company, 1859, p. 212.)

Invent one other plausible argument in which the question is only verbal. How might it happen that even after a Verbal Question had been by definition turned into a Real Question, there might still be disagreement?

C. Find in the chapter three definitions not given specifically as examples of definitions. Tell what kind you take each to be.

D. There is an old logical maxim to the effect that a view of the thing itself is the best definition. What qualifications should be put on this assertion?

E. Discuss the differences between the two following descriptions of man. Is one more *correct* than the other? Is one more adequate than the other?

What a piece of work is man! How noble in reason! How infinite in faculty! in form and moving how express and admirable! in action how like an angel! in apprehension how like a god! the beauty of the world! the paragon of animals! (Shakespeare, *Hamlet*)

Scientist L. A. Borradaile: Man is metazoan, triploblastic, chordate, vertebrate, pentadactyle, mammalian, eutherian, primate . . .

(Theodore H. Savory, *The Language of Science*. London: André Deutsch, 1953, p. 19.)

F. Here is a list of traditional "rules for defining." Explain each. Criticize any that seem weak.

   1. A definition should state the essential qualities of what is defined, usually giving genus and differentia.

   2. The definition should not be circular, repeating in the defining term what is in the term to be defined.

3. The defining term should be substitutable for the term to be defined; that is to say, the definitions must be neither too broad nor too narrow.

4. If possible the definition should be affirmative rather than negative.

5. The definition should not be couched in obscure, figurative, or ambiguous language.

6. The definition should describe, not praise or condemn, what is to be defined.

G. Above all what is to be remembered in using definitions is that a definition is good or bad, effective or ineffective, adequate or inadequate, depending on its explanatory value in a given situation. A definition that would be suitable for adults would hardly enlighten children; physicists might not be satisfied with a definition of "atom" that sufficed for laymen; and so forth. Thus a successful communicator will clarify his discourse by defining words that might otherwise be misunderstood, and defining them in such a way that the intended meaning is as clear and distinct as possible.

Tell what is wrong with the following definitions, specifying, when possible, a rule that is broken. When a definition might be suitable under certain restricted circumstances, specify the circumstances.

1. A net is "anything made with interstitial vacuities." (Samuel Johnson's Dictionary)

2. Edam cheese is a nasty-tasting milk product.

3. Religion is man's noblest achievement.

4 A spinster is a disgruntled unmarried woman.

5. Democracy is a form of government employing a bicameral legislature.

6. Poetry is rhymed speech.

7. Religion is the opiate of the people.

8. Socialism is an alien philosophy of state.

9. Literary classicism is a return to the high standards of antiquity.

10. Money is the root of all evil.

11. Intuition is the strange instinct that tells a woman she is right.

12. Conscience is a small still voice.

13. A flirt is a woman who winks at you.

14. Oxygen is the element which makes combustion.

15. An historical novel is fiction about history.

16. Champagne is the drink that bubbles.

17. Gambling is a way of making money without sweating.

18. The heliocentric theory is the theory that the earth goes around the sun.

19. A university is where high school graduates learn still more.

20. Speed is velocity.

21. Adolescence is the springtime in human life.

22. A register is what heat comes out of.

23. A dress is a woman's outergarment.

24. An address is where somebody lives.

25. Evil is the absence of good.

26. A verb is the part of speech describing action.

27. White onions are between French onions and Bermuda onions.

28. A syllogism is a logical argument.

29. A point is a position without magnitude.

30. Rhetoric is the art of using words in such a way as to produce a desired impression.

31. "Man is the ungrateful biped." (Dostoevsky)

H. It is sometimes argued that defining is an activity like that of deciding to number the freezing point 32 degrees on a scale. How good is the analogy? Is a Centigrade scale just as arbitrary as the Fahrenheit?

I. Professor Zechariah Chaffee writes of a couple whose divorce decree carried the provision that in case the wife remarried the dividends from certain bonds allowed her in the financial settlement would cease and go to the children. But the woman remarried her former husband. Now should the payments go to the children? The question arises: what did the husband *intend* by the word "remarry"? But probably he hadn't even thought of this possibility. Is it fair to ask what he would have intended if he had thought of it?

J. What is meant when a legal decision is called wrong or unsound? Chaffee suggests six possible meanings: "(1) The decision offends our sense of justice. (2) It does not fit into the logical symmetry of earlier cases. (3) It is likely to produce undesirable social consequences. (4) It is likely to be over-ruled or disregarded in later cases. (5) It has already been overruled or disregarded by courts. (6) Our client lost." (From "The Disorderly Conduct of Words," *Columbia Law Review*, Vol. 41, March, 1941. Quoted in *Language . . . Man . . . Society*, Harold E. Briggs, ed. New York: Rinehart and Company, Inc., 1949, p. 192.) Discuss.

K. "A story, probably fictitious but certainly in character, is told of two patriotic Americans who met on the streets of an un-named town. 'What's this I hear about you,' demanded one, 'that you say you do not believe in the Monroe Doctrine?' The reply was instant and indignant: 'It's a lie. I never said I did not believe in the Monroe Doctrine. I do believe in it. It is the palladium of our liberties. I would die for the Mon-roe Doctrine. All I said was that I do not know what it means.' " (Thomas A. Bailey, *The Man in the Street*. New York: The Macmillan Company, 1948.)

Name one other doctrine in which people are likely to believe without really knowing the meaning of what they profess belief in.

EXERCISES

I. Long after the lights in most of the dormitory rooms are out, the roommates in B-310 are most earnestly arguing about the true nature of religion. One maintains that an atheistic religion is possible—a religion that includes in its set of beliefs a specific denial of the existence of a God. The other claims that this is absolutely impossible, that part of the *meaning* of "religion" is a belief in a supreme supernatural power. The argument includes the following maneuvers:

1. There is an appeal to the dictionary to see how the word "religion" is there defined.
2. There is an appeal to several authorities on the subject, to see how they define the term.
3. Numerous examples of religions are brought up in order to examine the place they give to God-worship.

4. One of the arguers insists that he may define the word to mean anything he wants it to mean.

5. There is an agreement that the word is used in different ways, so that some meanings would admit, some would exclude, atheism. Thus, to define is to decide among possible definitions.

6. The defender of the possibility of atheistic religion suggests that though nearly all religions are theistic, that belief in God is not an *essential* part of the meaning of religion.

7. One person says that Buddhism is a religion and is atheistic, but his opponent replies that if Buddhism is atheistic it *can't* be a religion; whereupon the latter arguer is accused of begging the question.

Compose a dialogue embodying the points mentioned.

II. Compose a paragraph in which several of the words you use are assigned highly unusual meanings. Provide a dictionary; e.g. salt = chair. Notice the complications in communication.

III. Invent or find in your reading an example of an argument that might be settled by careful definition of terms.

IV. Find and discuss a selection in which there is a failure to communicate precisely because of a failure to define terms.

V. Write a one page paper in which you attempt to draw upon your knowledge and research to define an ambiguous term. Suggested terms: communism, democracy, religion, duty. Notice that a definition of a complex term is often a long description and not just a concise statement.

VI. Imagine a discussion on the topic: Is a rumor necessarily untrue? One person presents a definition from a psychology book: A rumor is "A specific (or topical) proposition for belief, passed along from person to person, usually by word of mouth, without secure standards of evidence being present." (Gordon Allport and Leo Postman, *The Psychology of Rumor*. New York: Henry Holt and Company, 1947, p. ix) This definition is said by one of the disputants to "beg the question." Does it? How might this disputant redefine the term in a way more favorable to his side? Is this legitimate?

VII. What are the inadequacies of definition by exemplification? Can you think of instances in which such defining might mislead the questioner?

VIII. Look up the etymology of "ambiguity," "equivocation," "dictionary," "univocal," and "synonym." Compare the following words etymologically: "tome," "atom," "anatomy," "appendectomy." Compare "define," "definite," "finite," "final," and "finis."

IX. On each of the following arguments, use the five-step method of resolving the ambiguity:

1. I maintain as against Mr. Jevons that many of our inductive inferences have all the certainty of which human knowledge is capable. Is the law of gravitation one whit less certain than the conclusion of the 47th Proposition of the First Book of Euclid? Or is the proposition that animal and vegetable life cannot exist without moisture one whit less certain than the truths of the multiplication table? Both these physical generalisations are established by the Method of Difference, and, as *actual* Laws of Nature, admit I conceive, of no doubt. . . .

Still, Mr. Jevons, appearing not in the character of a physicist, but of a logician, tells us that "the law of gravitation itself is only probably true." It would be interesting to learn what is the exact amount of this "probability," or, if it be meant that we can only be certain that the force of gravity is acting here and now, it would be an interesting enquiry to ascertain what is the exact value of the "probability" that it is at this moment acting in Manchester as well as in Oxford, or that it will be acting at this time to-morrow as well as to-day.

If natural phenomena did indeed admit only of the same kind of study as the drawing of balls from a ballot-box, Mr. Jevons' conception of Induction would undoubtedly be the true one, and I should agree with him that "no finite number of particular verifications of a supposed law will render that law certain." But, just because we believe that the operations of Nature are conducted with an uniformity for which we seek in vain amongst the contrivances of men, do we regard ourselves as capable, in many cases, of predicting the one class of events with certainty, while the other affords only matter for more or less probable conjecture. (Thomas Fowler, *The Elements of Inductive Logic*. Oxford: At the Clarendon Press, 1876, pp. x ff. Quoted in MacKaye, *op. cit.*, pp. 140-141.)

2. David Hume in dealing with the vexed question of whether or not justice and property may be said to be natural, said: "Natural may be opposed, either to what is *unusual, miraculous* or *artificial*. In the two former senses justice and property are undoubtedly natural. But as they suppose reason, forethought, design, and a social union and confederacy among men, perhaps that epithet cannot strictly, in the last sense, be applied to them. Had men lived without society, property had never been known, and neither justice nor injustice had ever existed. But society among human creatures had been impossible without reason and forethought. Inferior animals that unite, are guided by instinct, which supplies the place of reason. But all these disputes are merely verbal." (*An Enquiry Concerning the Principles of Morals*, Appendix II.)

3. Peter: Have you ever stopped to realize that if the largest tree in the whole forest were one dark night to topple and fall, taking with it all the lesser trees in its path and smashing flat hundreds of feet of vegetation, that nevertheless all this would not make the least sound, not the least little bit, provided there were no one, no humans and no animals, within earshot?

The Wolf: I've never stopped to realize this, and I flatly don't believe it. The falling tree would make a huge noise, and it doesn't matter in the least whether there happened to be anyone there to hear it.

Peter: Don't you know there can't be any noise without ears to hear?

The Wolf: Don't you realize that noise is an objective, natural phenomenon that is studied by the physicist and has nothing to do with ears?

4. You sometimes hear people argue that all men are created equal, but this is absurd. Is the village idiot the equal of Einstein? Is the 90 pound stripling the equal of Muscles McMasters? They are not equal now and they certainly weren't created equal.

5. Aristotle taught that either God's knowledge is of himself or it is of other beings. Did he mean that if it is the first, it therefore cannot be the second?

X. Explain and defend Stendhal's remark:

"My passionate cohabitation with mathematics has left me with a violent love of good definitions, without which one arrives at nothing but approximations." (*The Life of Henri Brulard,* Catherine Alison Phillips, Trans.)

SOURCES AND ADVANCED READING

1. Richard Robinson, *Definition.* Oxford: Clarendon Press, 1950.
2. James MacKaye, *The Logic of Language.* Hanover, New Hampshire: Dartmouth College Publications, 1939. Ch. II-V.
3. John Stuart Mill, *A System of Logic.* London and New York: Longmans, Green and Company, New Impression, 1948. Book I, Ch. VIII.
4. William Ernest Johnson, *Logic.* London: Cambridge University Press, 1921. Part I, Ch. VII.
5. *Exposition, A Handbook for General Education.* Cambridge, Massachusetts: Harvard University Press, 1953. Pp. 3-31.
6. *Language ... Man ... Society,* ed. by Harold E. Briggs. New York: Rinehart and Company, Inc., 1949.

❖ VII ❖

THE USES OF LANGUAGE

The Social Setting of Language • The Magic and Morality of
Language • Language and Emotion • Attitudes • The Intent of
the Producer • Forms • Certain Prominent Types of Discourse •
The Language of Value

THE SOCIAL SETTING OF LANGUAGE

A mark on paper or a vocal sound is an instance of a word,
is a part of a language, only as it functions in such a way as to
make for a *shared meaning*. The meaning that is shared by
means of language may relate more or less urgently and
directly to some group action as in the case of the captain's
order to abandon ship or the scout's report about danger or
food or the square-dance caller's directions to the cavorters;
or the language usage may relate only indirectly and distantly
to a group action as in the case of "pure" science or literature,
but in these latter cases too, sharing, even if primarily intellectual and imaginative, is facilitated.

Every grouping within society tends to be distinguished by
a shared language. These modes of speaking vary in complexity from the secret grips and passwords of a fraternal
organization, to the argot of tramps and hoboes, to the technical jargon of learned societies, to the current slang of an
adolescent group, to national groups like Americans, to international groups like the "English-speaking world." To know
a given language is to be "in" with the group, a regular member; not to know the language is to be on the outside. The

"new kid" in a neighborhood may be as easily detected by his unfamiliarity with the prevailing idiom as the typical American in Paris may be discovered by his American accent. Even a family tends to have a small private language which visitors do not understand or employ.

A fair number of the remarks that all of us make in the course of a day have roughly the same function as our smiles and waves and handshakes. Take the following "conversation":

Hey, Tom.

Oh, hi there, Bill.

How goes it?

Can't complain. How's everything with you?

Not bad. How you been lately?

Fine, thanks. You're looking well.

Thanks. Feeling well too.

Well, I'll see you.

Yeh. Nice to have seen you. Take it easy.

O.K. So long.

Many people, sometime in their lives, take a lofty view of such trivial talk and may even go so far as to resolve to have none of it, confining themselves with puritan rigor to "important things." But a certain amount of small talk, chatter which communicates almost nothing except a certain friendliness of attitude, is an important lubricant to our social living. Though some persons may be justly criticized for hardly ever getting beyond chit-chat, it does not follow that such is altogether dispensable. The anthropologist, Malinowski, has this to say on the subject:

There is in all human beings the well-known tendency to congregate, to be together, to enjoy each other's company. Many instincts and innate trends, such as fear or pugnacity, all the types of social sentiments such as ambition, vanity, passion for power and wealth, are dependent upon and associated with the fundamental tendency which makes the mere presence of others a necessity for man. Now speech is the intimate correlate of this tendency, for, to a natural man, another man's silence is not a reassuring factor, but, on the contrary, something alarming and dangerous. The stranger who cannot speak the language is to all savage tribesmen a natural enemy ... The modern English expression, 'Nice day to-day' or the Melanesian phrase, 'Whence comest thou?' are needed to get over the strange and unpleasant tension which men feel when facing each other in silence.[1]

The young child, as we had occasion to observe in an earlier chapter is, to a larger degree than is usually recognized, non-social. He talks, makes observations, asks questions, but is surprisingly indifferent to his audience. He doesn't care much whether anyone hears his remarks or answers his questions; he seldom takes other persons into account except those he has internalized into his game. But every child learns to talk to and with his fellows. He comes to take them into account. His becoming a socialized personality himself and his learning to talk a social language are two sides of a single process. Or the point can be made by contrasting reflective human activity with the most intelligent behavior of other animals. George Herbert Mead, whose writings on this subject have been most influential, writes as follows:

We say the animal does not think. He does not put himself in a position for which he is responsible; he does not put himself in the place of the other person and say, in effect, "He will act in such a way and I will act in this way." If the individual can act in this way, and the attitude which he calls out in himself can become a stimulus to him for another act, we have meaningful conduct. Where the response of the other person is called out and becomes a stimulus to control his action, then he has the meaning of the other person's act in his own experience. That is the general mechanism of what we term "thought," for in order that thought may exist there must be symbols, vocal gestures generally, which arouse in the individual himself the response which he is calling out in the other, and such that from the point

---

[1] Bronislaw Malinowski, "Primitive Languages," in C. K. Ogden and I. A. Richards, *The Meaning of Meaning* (New York: Harcourt, Brace and Company, 7th ed., 1945), supplement.

of view of that response he is able to direct his later conduct. It involves not only communication in the sense in which birds and animals communicate with each other, but also an arousal in the individual himself of the response which he is calling out in the other individual, a taking of the role of the other, a tendency to act as the other person acts.[2]

That is fundamental for any language; if it is going to be language one has to understand what he is saying, has to affect himself as he affects others.[3]

Mead's explanations bring home the importance of language as an instrument for socializing the personality and for establishing a community. A community, after all, is a group in communication. Language must not be thought of merely as a means for expressing some preconceived thought or idea, not merely as a way of indicating the presence or nature of some object. "Meaning," John Dewey has said, "is primarily a property of behavior."

The heart of language . . . is communication; the establishment of cooperation in an activity in which there are partners, and in which the activity of each is modified and regulated by partnership. To fail to understand is to fail to come into agreement in action; to misunderstand is to set up action at cross purposes.[4]

THE MAGIC AND MORALITY OF LANGUAGE

We express *ourselves* about *things* to *people,* and we hope thereby to affect those people in certain ways. It has been widely believed that words and patterns of words have direct power over others, for instance through incantations, spells, curses, and prayers. If one only knows the right words, he supposedly can control the winds and rains and seas; he can strike down his enemy and bring blessings to his friend; he can call

---

[2] George Herbert Mead, *Mind, Self, and Society* (Chicago: University of Chicago Press, 1934), p. 73. Copyright 1934 by the University of Chicago.

[3] *Ibid*, p. 75.

[4] John Dewey, *Experience and Nature* (La Salle, Illinois: The Open Court Publishing Company, 1925), p. 179.

up demons and spirits to work for him; he can weave spells and transport himself to far-away places and become invisible or assume weird shapes. To know a person's name is to have a kind of control over him, so that some primitives will not tell their names to strangers. To know the mystic names of gods is to have fearful powers.

Primitive peoples tend to make a very close identification between word and object. A thing's name is part of the thing, never wholly separable from it, something palpable and powerful. A name in itself (and not just what it refers to) is something good or bad, right or wrong, relatively potent or relatively weak. Frazer tells of a Caffre belief that if one shouts the name of a young thief over a kettle of boiling, medicated water and then claps on the lid and lets the name soak for a few days, the criminal will be reformed.

There are always some taboo words, among primitive people and civilized people, and at times of the greatest enlightenment as well as in dark ages. Not always the same words are taboo. A Cree Indian out of respect for his sisters refuses to speak their names. A Victorian thought the word "leg" not fit for polite society and spoke, accordingly, of the limb of the chair.[5] Closely allied is the feeling that "damn" and "hell," though they may be permitted in some circumstances, are not quite proper for children and perhaps for ladies. "Darn" and "heck," though transparent imitations, are generally considered innocuous. Especially strong in our society is the prohibition (again, except in certain restricted circumstances) on words designating sexual and eliminative functions and organs; more accurately, the taboo is against not all such words—certain rather medical-sounding terms are all right—but against the oldest such words in our language, especially the so-called four-letter words. They may not be used in movies, over the radio or television, in newspapers, magazines, or books. Their use in mixed company may call down the

[5] Dickens wrote of trousers as "those manly garments which are rarely mentioned by name." (*Dombey and Son*)

severest reproaches, ending perhaps in social ostracism. Their presence even in an otherwise distinguished work of fiction may suffice to have it banned as indecent and immoral. Indeed, what better indication of the potency of this taboo than the absence of examples in this chapter?

Language habits change. Some ages are much more hidebound in their language restrictions than others. Some take pride in what they regard as the large degree of tolerance about language in our time. Others find therein signs of the decadence or the immorality of the age. The fact remains that we do have our circumlocutions and our euphemisms; almost everybody is shockable by language. Probably it will ever be so.

LANGUAGE AND EMOTION

A host of writers on language, including most prominently Ogden and Richards, have made a great deal of a basic distinction between Scientific (or Symbolic or Referential) Language and Emotive Language. In Emotive Language, or better, the Emotive Use of Language, reference to fact is either absent or is subordinated to the expression or evocation of feelings and attitudes.

The better to understand this distinction, let us discuss the *proposition*. Here are eight sentences:

(1) Baltimore is south of Boston.

(2) Mercury is heavier than lead.

(3) By 1975 there will be a medicinal cure for cancer.

(4) *The Sistine Madonna* is a beautiful painting.

(5) "God's in his heaven/All's right with the world."

(6) "Oh, to be in England/Now that April's there."

(7) Pick up your feet!

(8) Ouch!

The first three are expressions of propositions; the last two clearly are not. What is the difference? It may be answered that a proposition is that entity which is either true-or-false. (1) claims to be the report of a fact. The claim may be one

which can be "made good" or it may not. There are ways in
which we can go about checking up on this claim. We can
seek to verify it, say by consulting a United States map, and
then come away saying, "Well, that's a true proposition."
Similarly there are ways of checking up on the truth of (2),
and after a certain amount of checking we may be satisfied
that (2) is the expression of a false proposition. A false proposition is not any less a proposition than one which is true. But
that which is neither true nor false is not a real proposition.
It will be noted that we have spoken of these sentences as
expressing propositions. The sentence is not the proposition,
but the means of getting the proposition before us. There
may be two different sentences which express the same proposition. We have changed sentence (1) if we say, "Baltimore
lies south of Boston" but the altered sentence still expresses
the same proposition. A better example, perhaps, would be
afforded by translating the sentence into French: "Baltimore
est au sud de Boston." This is quite a different sentence, but
if the translation is accurate, the proposition hasn't changed.

Sentence (3) differs from the other two in one interesting
way, namely that we can't tell whether it's true or false. Still,
we know that it is (or perhaps you prefer to say that it *will be*)
one or the other. There are practical difficulties in the way of
its verification, yet we know what kind of evidence will need
to turn up in order that we may make such an assertion confidently.

But now at the end of the list, we find in (8) an exclamation which is not, at least not in any very straightforward way,
either true or false. If someone were to say, "Ouch!" and then
someone standing nearby were to ask you, "Was what he said
true or was it false?" you'd think that a pretty silly question.
You'd think the exclaimer had been misunderstood: "He only
said 'Ouch!'"

Similarly (7), a command, seems to be neither true nor
false. Those qualities seem irrelevant to it. So, probably, with
the poetic wish of (6). It may be argued that in the case of all

three of these last sentences there is what might be called a latent proposition present. Thus if hearing the "Ouch," I say, "He's hurt," what I say is either true or false. In the case of (7) the recruit may (though it's not at all likely) complain to the sergeant, "But I *wasn't* dragging my feet" thereby indicating the sergeant had asserted that he *was*. And an unfriendly critic of the poet might wryly remark, "He says he wants to be in England but he's just saying that—he really doesn't." Again this reply would be based on the implicit assertion of a proposition. Still, the wish, the command, and the exclamation are not themselves directly expressions of propositions, and this was our principal point.

What may be said of (4) and (5)?

If it were said of a painting that it was done in oils or that it measured seven feet by four feet, there would be no question but what the assertion in either case was either true or false. Or if the painting were alleged to be valuable enough to fetch upwards of $10,000 on the market, then this could be verified and the accuracy of the statement checked. Does it not seem, then, that " 'The Sistine Madonna' is a beautiful painting" is a very similar kind of sentence to " 'The Sistine Madonna' is a valuable painting"? Gramatically they are identical in form. But by those who make a sharp distinction between emotive and referential language it is said that logically the two sentences are entirely different in that whereas the latter expresses a proposition the former does not. It is often said that the first sentence illustrates the "pseudo-propositional" sentence; that is, one which gives the appearance of stating a fact, but in reality does not do so, not because it is false but because it is neither true *nor* false. It's a matter of taste, and, according to the old maxim, "There's no disputing about tastes." Still, as the answer has come, isn't it taste precisely that one does dispute about? Isn't the person who ascribes beauty to the famous painting likely to mean what he says? Won't he stoutly maintain his position? Won't he point to this or that corroborating opinion, this and the other characteristic of the artist's style, his delicate and subtle color, his splendid composition, the exquisiteness of his lines? These questions have often been answered by some more questions. Will not all of this be thought quite beside the point by the person who *feels* differently about the painting, whose emotional reaction is unfavorable or unpleasant, who dislikes rather than likes the work? In short, is not beauty *simply* a matter of somebody's feeling, so that to say "That is beautiful," is to say no more than "I like that," or "That gives me a pleasant feeling"? And of course it is a notorious fact that one man's meat is another's poison, that what is beautiful *to one person* is not at all beautiful to another. In the case of market value or size or shape and so on, there is something objective which can be consulted; but in the case of beauty and goodness and greatness and other such values, there is only a *subjective* feeling, no commonly agreed upon and shared criterion by which to judge. Consequently no verification is possible. It is not a case, as in the instance of our example (3), of there being *practical* difficulties in the way of verification; here there are *theoretical* difficulties which are insuperable. That is, among disputants there is no common ground, nothing which can be pointed to as settling the matter. One person feels one way and another feels another way, and that's the end of the matter.

An instance of emotive language, then, as thus far presented in accordance with a widely-held theory, is one in which there are expressed certain emotions of the speaker or writer. But this account needs to be supplemented. A given user of an emotive utterance *may* be even more interested in calling out in his audience a certain response than in giving vent to his own feelings. One can easily be imagined saying, "What a beautiful sonata!" in the hope of eliciting a feeling expressed in the reply, "Yes, isn't it!" It is, of course, even possible for a person to be insincere in the expression of his own feeling and yet successful in inducing the desired response from the hearer.

The story is told about a young musician who courted a girl who, though not herself musically trained, seemed to have the most sensitive and highly developed musical tastes, for she approved and disapproved in all the "right places." Every time the musician felt strongly moved by the beauty of a piece and happened to glance at his companion, her face too showed signs of great joy; but when he was annoyed or disappointed by the performance of a composition, he could detect that she too was dissatisfied. Still, sad to relate, he was of a somewhat suspicious nature, and decided to try out a hypothesis that occurred to him. The next time the two were at a concert, he deliberately reversed his own reactions, taking care to frown, though ever so slightly, when a passage pleased him and to show subtle signs of delight when something struck him as inferior. Lo and behold, the girl's reactions, too, were switched, and the hypothesis was bitterly confirmed: she had been reacting not to the music but to him, taking her cues for the "proper" reaction from his facial expressions. Her gestures, though insincere, were aimed at producing an approving response in her lover, and were, as we have seen, for a while successful.[6]

Now we may give a fuller account of the emotive use of language: it aims either at expressing the feelings of the producer or at evoking certain feelings in the interpreter or both.

But now what of the lines in (5): "God's in his heaven/All's right with the world"? This too may be interpreted as an emotive utterance, a pseudo-propositional sentence, one which seems to report a state of affairs but actually just expresses the exuberant joy of living, a feeling of confidence and sanguinity and one, too, which no doubt tends to produce such feelings in him who hears or overhears. Some (such as Ogden and Richards) would say that the fact that these are lines of poetry settles the matter, poetry being by nature emotive discourse.

Perhaps enough has been said to give a fair idea of the

---

[6] It is not recorded whether the romance was blighted.

theory which makes a basic distinction between emotive and referential use of language.

No one is likely to deny that there is a certain real plausibility to this position; nevertheless, it will not be held here for these reasons:

(1) It suggests a cleavage between emotion and referential thought which is untrue to the facts.

(2) It tends to disparage "emotive" language.

(3) It tends to encourage the relegation of difficult language to the wastebasket of "the merely emotive."

(4) It does not account for all types of language usage.

Let us elaborate these objections slightly. (1) If two lawyers are opposing each other in a trial and one of them gives a calm, well-organized, cautious, elaborately documented, precisely stated argument and the other indulges in an incoherent harangue full of abusive invective, citing no facts, but just venting his feelings and calling upon the prejudices of the jury, we will have no trouble in setting these uses of language over against one another. Or if we examine first a paper in the *Journal of Theoretical Physics* and then a voodoo chant, we will be impressed with the contrast between rational and irrational uses of language. We may be rightly impressed with the care and precision of a radio commentator's analysis of the news, but it isn't likely that he is one who has no feelings about the events he describes. In the vast amount of discourse that we encounter every day, the differences are not so impressively sharp. However much we wish to reprove the person who is carried away by his emotions, who thinks wishfully rather than objectively, we ought not to exaggerate the case. "Oh what a beautiful morning" no doubt usually expresses the delight of its speaker, but it isn't likely to be said about a January dawn which is just a cold, gray drizzle. It is surely an exaggeration to say that "The power of sentences has nothing to do with their sense or the logic of their construction." [7]

---

[7] Joseph Conrad, *Lord Jim* (New York: Modern Library, 1931), p. 75.

(2) Often the distinction between the emotive and the referential is an invidious distinction, as if to say that language highly charged with emotion is somehow necessarily bad, or at least inferior to more scientific use.[8] But there are times when cold, systematic discourse is completely inappropriate — it is easy to parody the pedantic scholar who must deliver a marriage proposal in the same manner in which he would present a learned article—just as inappropriate and regrettable as emotionalism may be under different circumstances. Yet one often encounters sneers of "merely emotive language" or "nothing but poetry."

(3) Further, the supposition that a given term or sentence or passage can automatically be labelled as either "sense" or "nonsense," as either "referential" or "emotive," easily leads to a crass dismissal of difficult or unsavory discourse as beyond the pale. Stuart Chase, in his popular and popularized book *The Tyranny of Words,* proposed that we should go through sermons and political appeals and the like and replace all of the big words of indefinite reference with the expression "blab-blab." It may be good tactics, if your aim is to win an argument at all costs, to insist that your opponent is saying nothing but "blab-blab," but it may be a very irresponsible type of argument, one which neglects real issues and refuses to deal seriously with charges and allegations. It may save trouble to pronounce as simply unintelligible whatever one does not quite understand, but trouble should not always be saved.

(4) Even if we accept a rough and ready distinction between the referential and the emotive, there seems to be a good deal of language usage which is not either one. The case for this objection will be made out in a subsequent section where a different classification is proposed.

---

[8] This is not the case with Ogden and Richards, who hold poetry, which they describe as emotive, in very high regard.

ATTITUDES

A complete act of communication establishes a bond between sign producer and sign receiver. There is meaning when someone "gets something over" to someone else: meaning is a matter of a symbol producer affecting a symbol interpreter. The meaning (in this sense) is the nature of the response thus evoked. It may be, as we have seen, strikingly cognitive, in which case the interpreter is set to analyzing, searching, inquiring and other such activities; it may be singularly emotive, in which case the interpreter is set to feeling. It may be something else. And it will in all likelihood be a complex rather than just a simple response.

What we need now notice, however briefly, is that the employment of the symbols is nearly always affected by the attitudes of the producer. The interpreter in turn tends to adjust his response to the attitude so reflected. Further, his response tends to be conditioned by his own attitudes.

Two sorts of attitudes may be distinguished: (1) those toward the other party in the communication process, both the producer's toward his audience and vice versa; (2) those of either producer or interpreter toward the subject matter or the object of the discourse. The producer's attitudes may be reflected in his choice of language, the tone of voice he employs, accompanying gestures and in other ways.

Suppose for an illustration that Mr. A desires the presence in his (Mr. A's) office of Mr. B. So he sends around a memorandum. But how is it worded?

You will report immediately.

Report immediately.

Please report right away.

Please come over as soon as you can.

Would you mind dropping in when you can make it?

Next time you're down this way, perhaps you'd drop in for a moment.

These are just a few of an indefinitely large number of

possibilities. The choice of wording obviously will depend in part upon Mr. A's attitude toward Mr. B. Of course it may well depend too on which way he thinks will be most effective, most conducive to future good relations, and so on. Whether Mr. B will tremble and obey, ignore the message, be angered by the insolence of the sender, or what, will depend in part on his attitude toward Mr. A and in part upon the way the message is conveyed and in part on other matters.

That language usage is also determined by the producer's attitude toward *what* his communication concerns, is obvious. A Republican and a Democrat will not speak in identical tones about Franklin Roosevelt. Sergeant Stripes may be referred to in quite different ways by Mrs. Stripes and Pfc. Sack.

THE INTENT OF THE PRODUCER

What we try to accomplish by means of the language we employ, why we say what we say, varies infinitely, being somewhat different for every speaker and every occasion. Nor is the problem automatically solved in the individual case by asking the speaker what he's trying to accomplish, for he is not necessarily the final authority on his own intentions. Any one of us, for instance, might be accused of using a patronizing tone on a certain occasion, and then for the first time realize that this was the case. Then, there is the famous reply of Robert Browning when asked for the meaning of a line of his own verse: "When I wrote that, God and I knew what it meant. Now God alone knows."

It has been pointed out that the attempt to divide all language usage into two such classifications as *referential* and *emotive* is ill-advised. But a three-way classification, or four-way, or sixteen-way, is not going to remove the deficiencies of oversimplification and of arbitrariness. Just as personalities cannot very comfortably and adequately be fitted inside such pigeon holes as "introverted" and "extraverted" or "melancholic" and "choleric," so language—the real language of real people—is bafflingly complex, being not just this thing or that thing but many things all at once, some of them without good names. But it is convenient for some purposes, to be able to classify personalities, and it is possible to gain in understanding of communication processes by following a scheme of language classification. Yet before presenting such a scheme let it be firmly understood that:

(1) The classification is not complete, it does not exhaust the possibilities of what language does.

(2) Instances of actual language use will seldom be *simply* classifiable.

(3) This system of classification is not final or inevitable; it is one among several actual and many possible systems.

What, then, are the principal reasons why men try to communicate with their fellows? What are they trying to do with their words? Let us try a five-fold classification.

1. *Expressive.* Possibly the most basic use of language is for purposes of expression. Expression of what? Well, of feelings, of ideas, of plans, of theories, of experiences, of problems. Expression may be *to* somebody. Sometimes somebody —even some particular somebody—seems essential to our expressive needs: we feel that what we have to say will not be quite real until it has been heard. But sometimes all we need in order to make it real is to "put it into words." People no doubt differ greatly in their expressive needs, varying from the strong and silent types to those who are covered with an intolerable itch until they have given expression to something that has occurred to them or something that has happened to them or something which they have felt. But all of us seem to have some such need some of the time. It is the need to embody in language what is just confused or inchoate within us. Sometimes it won't go and we say, "I know what I mean, but I can't say it, I can't find the words for it." And that kind of cramp, that frustration, is especially eloquent in informing us of the expressive need. Notice has already been taken of young children who are relatively indifferent to their audi-

ence, but who chatter a good deal of the time. They are playing games, expressing their wishes and their imaginings, and
if they couldn't talk about what they were doing, most of the
fun of the games would disappear. As we grow up we no
doubt lose some of the child's spontaneity of expression, but
we retain the need and to some degree retain the practice,
however we try to hide it.

2. *"Rapportive."* If our need is sometimes to get something
said, whether or not anybody is communicated with, sometimes our need is to communicate, whether or not anything
gets said. As discussed above, there is often among men the
compulsion to break silence. Only very intimate companions
can be comfortably silent with each other. Often we make
talk that does little more—but this is not unimportant—than
to make for friendly, easy relations. Interviewers are taught
that often before they can get on with business they have to
establish some bonds with the interviewee, make him feel relaxed and comfortable. Most of us cannot sit alongside a
stranger for very many miles on a bus or a train without in-
dulging in a little idle conversation. In many, many circumstances, talk, however small, helps establish rapport.

3. *Incitive.* "Speak up!" "Vote for McMurrachu!" "Buy
an extra one!" "Do your duty!" Much speech is used to pro-
mote action, to incite some particular form of behavior. From
soap box haranguing to soap opera huckstering, from legal
pleading to close order drill, from "instructions on the box"
to pulpit admonishing, from homework assignments to signs
of warning, language is used to get hearers and readers to *do*
something. The incitement may proceed by entreating, pray-
ing, commanding, threatening, suggesting, wheedling, coax-
ing, cajoling, asking, demanding—what you will. One may
even incite oneself as in saying aloud and alone: "Buck up!"
Or in leaving oneself a note: "Pick up the laundry." A supernatural force may be the receiver: "Forgive me, oh Lord" or
"Send us rain!" Moral discourse is typically incitive. Advertising, the speeches of the lover, most political speeches, many

editorials—here are just a few samples of incitement. Any kind of question (except a "rhetorical" one) may be considered incitive in being a means of provoking the kind of response which we call "answering."

If sometimes language directs very specific action, there are other times when incitement is more generalized. Margaret Mead has explained that among the Arapesh people of New Guinea communication tends to be vague:

When among the Arapesh, some event of importance occurs, a birth or death, a quarrel of proportions, the visit of a governmental patrol .., there are shouts and drumbeats from hilltop to hilltop. But all that the signals convey is that something has happened about which the listeners had better become excited. . . .

There is some slight attempt to differentiate drumbeats, but so contrary is specificity to the cultural emphasis of the Arapesh that the distinctions are always getting blurred.[9]

This is an extreme case, but it seems that in the communicative processes of all people, one of the functions of language is to incite what is at first an almost undifferentiated emotional response, which further communication may succeed in sharpening and making more specific.

4. *Evocative* (or Imaginative).

> In Xanadu did Kubla Khan
> A stately pleasure-dome decree:
> Where Alph, the sacred river, ran
> Through caverns measureless to man
> Down to a sunless sea.

What goes on here? What is the author of such a poem trying to do with his language? Surely we are not here being asked to do anything, at least nothing but *imagine*. But the words work on us, conjure up in us pictures, feelings, a mood. Something like this happens when a good storyteller gets going, whether the story ends in an explosion of laughter or in a

[9] Margaret Mead, "Some Cultural Approaches to Communications Problems," in Lyman Bryson (ed.), *The Communication of Ideas* (New York and London: Institute for Religious and Social Studies, 1948), pp. 11-12.

shudder or a knowing shake of the head; we who have heard have had a rich experience evoked in our imaginations. For purposes of evocation, the tale need not be fictional—it may be literally true—so long as the intent of the user is to create in his audience images and feelings for the sake of the images and feelings.

The term "word magic" (not to be confused with the magic which is thought to get material results) is frequently given to that use of words which creates "spells" and moods and rapt, imaginative seizures. Aldous Huxley has a character in his novel *Crome Yellow* say:

That's the test for the literary mind, the feeling of magic, the sense that words have power. The technical, verbal part of literature is simply a development of magic. Words are man's first and grandiose invention. With language he created a whole new universe; what wonder if he loved words and attributed power to them! With fitted harmonious words the magicians summoned rabbits out of empty hats and spirits from the elements. Their descendants, the literary men, still go on with the process, morticing their verbal formulas together and, before the power of the finished spell, trembling with delight and awe. Rabbits out of empty hats? No, their spells are more subtly powerful, for they evoke emotions out of empty minds. Formulated by their art the most insipid statements become enormously significant. For example, I proffer the constatation, "Black ladders lack bladders." A self-evident truth, one on which it would not have been worth while to insist, had I chosen to formulate it in such words as "Black fire-escapes have no bladders ... The creation by word-power of something out of nothing—what is that but magic? And, I may add, what is that but literature? ... And you can't appreciate words. I'm sorry for you.[10]

By the evocative use of words we have formed in us not only moods but also attitudes, ways of regarding persons and institutions and events. And attitudes, of course, prepare for action; but so far as evocation is concerned, the intent of the

[10] Aldous Huxley, *Crome Yellow* (New York: George H. Doran Company, 1922), Ch. XX. By permission of Harper & Brothers.

producer is the inducing of certain states of mind and not any possible overt behavior that grows out of such states.

5. *Informative.* It may be thought strange that only in fifth place (not that the order is particularly significant) do we encounter that use of language which some seem to consider the *real,* the true function. But quantitatively in everyday discourse, the intent to communicate facts or knowledge may bulk relatively small. As to its importance, however, there can be no question.

It has been observed in another connection that information may be considered under two headings: (a) *empirical,* reports about matters of fact or states of affairs, incorporated in synthetic sentences; and (b) *formal* statements elucidating the meanings of terms and propositions or showing what follows from given propositions, which statements are set forth in analytic sentences.[11]

Informative discourse is sometimes labelled "scientific" discourse, but this seems a mistake, for though all purely scientific use of language may be informative, many attempts to give information can scarcely be called "scientific" without great stretching of that admittedly elastic term. "The goal to which science moves," writes Charles Morris, "is a systematized body of true statements about everything which has occurred or will occur." [12] Short of that goal, however, most of the statements which we make when we give directions, tell the temperature, tell what groceries were bought, or write news of the family do not enter systematically into any body of knowledge and are not arrived at and verified by the elaborate and precise techniques that we associate with the scientific process.

Scientific discourse may be either empirical or formal and

[11] A formal sentence which tries to do the work of an empirical sentence may be insipid or villainous, but it may also be funny, intentionally or not. Thus in *Hamlet* when a grave digger is asked how the Prince had gone mad, he gravely replies, "E'en through losing his wits."

[12] Charles W. Morris, *Signs, Language and Behavior* (New York: Prentice-Hall, Inc., 1946), p. 126. Reprinted with permission of publishers.

is usually both. To the extent that it formulates laws and describes what has been observed and makes predictions, it is empirical. To the extent that it defines terms and deduces conclusions from its observations and laws, it is formal. Science typically avoids the other uses of language discussed above, tries to replace the vaguer and more indefinite commonsense words like "many," "quite a few," "several," "somewhat hotter" and the like (which expressions may be perfectly suitable and adequate for some informative occasions) by terms which express exact quantities. The body of scientific knowledge at any time consists, as Morris puts it, of "pruned, precise, and confirmed statements, systematically organized. . . ." [13]

Mathematics, so important to physics and chemistry and the other predominantly empirical sciences, is today usually thought of as the formal science, *par excellence*. To see how the statements of pure (as distinct from applied) mathematics differ from those of empirical science and empirical common sense, consider the different ways in which you would *support* your belief that, on the one hand, the square on the hypotenuse of a right-angled triangle is equal to the sum of the squares on the other two sides, and on the other hand, that equal-sized balls of lead and wood fall at approximately equal rates or that lemon juice removes ink stains from cotton cloth. In the case of the geometrical theorem, we can *prove* our conclusion by showing that it follows according to accepted laws of deduction from certain already granted propositions. Only a naïve student would think of getting out a ruler to measure a large number of hypotenuses and other sides in order to accumulate evidence. But Galileo (if we may credit the famous story about the tower of Pisa) tried to show that bodies do not accelerate according to weight, by actually dropping objects from a height and *seeing* what happened. And to the Thomas who doubts the power of lemon juice, we say, "Look here, now."

[13] *Ibid.,* p. 127.

Deductive logic is another instance of a formal science.

We will content ourselves with the five uses of language which have been discussed: Expressive, "Rapportive," Incitive, Evocative, and Informative; but this list is incomplete. For instance, one might list as a separate category, *Magic;* that is, the attempt to influence the environment directly by the employment of words, as when "abracadabra" is uttered in order to ward off diseases.[14] And there are expressions uttered without motive, like involuntary groans. But it is thought that with some squeezing and winking, most actual uses of language can be discussed in terms of the five classifications here detailed.

Linguistic success and failure will vary as intent varies. The commonest words for evaluating discourse are probably "true" and "false," but it should be clear by now that these apply only when the intent is to inform. "Correct" and "incorrect" also apply to the informative use of language. Often the words "valid" and "invalid" are employed, especially for formal language. Still, a passage may be correct, true, and valid and yet not inform, because the matter is too difficult, the receiver too dense, the language unfamiliar or for some other reason.

In the case of evocation, success may be a matter of what Tolstoi called "infectiousness," that is, the communication of a feeling, mood, or attitude, making it carry across from producer to interpreter. One incites successfully, of course, just to the extent that he promotes the action he desires. "Rapportive" language succeeds or fails as it makes or fails to make for ease and relaxation and friendliness between persons. And the expressive need is filled if what the user comes up with satisfies him as an embodiment of what goaded him to speech.

---

[14] Glendower: I can call spirits from the vasty deep.

Hotspur: Why, so can I or so can any man; but will they come when you do call for them? (Shakespeare, *Henry IV*, Part One, III, 1.)

FORMS

When we think of the informative intent, we probably think of declarative sentences such as "That dog is hungry" or "This is five per cent Uranium ore" or "Cats can be taught to be friendly to mice." When we think of the incitive intent, our minds run to imperative sentences such as "Leave the room!" or "Visit your neighborhood druggist!" Such are the commonest forms in which such intents are realized. However, if a label should say, "Connect points A and B by means of wire R" the *intent* behind the sentence might be better considered informative than incitive, in telling *how* to do something rather than in trying to get you to do it, as to which the manufacturer may be entirely indifferent. Again, if a girl in a parked car with her "date" remarks, "The moon is so bright tonight," it is possible that her intention is not really informative. Suppose one wants his companion to get up and close a window. Perhaps he'd say, "Please shut the window." But might he not say instead: "Don't you find it drafty in here?" or "I'm cold," or "Maybe I'd better put on a sweater," or something else? In short, though the very form of a sentence may be a superficial sign of the intent of its producer, it is by no means a reliable sign. In communicating with our fellows, we are, as interpreters, constantly confronted with the task of trying to determine "what he's getting at," that is, of trying to ferret out a speaker's intent. And as producers ourselves we just as constantly meet with the difficulty of choosing some linguistic means sufficient to the realization of our purposes. There are no royal roads to success in either direction, no easy ways of solving the problems. It is not much help to insist that what is required is "sensitivity to language" except in so far as that is a reminder that language is a delicate instrument, not one to be manipulated by anything so mechanical as rules.

CERTAIN PROMINENT TYPES OF DISCOURSE

Very frequently language is classified as Literary, Religious, Legal and Political, etc. rather than according to the categories listed in this chapter. We need, then, to look briefly at this rival system to see whether it can be handled in our terms.

Literary Discourse. This is the language of novels, short stories, poems, and plays. It is frequently highly ornamented language, metaphorical, strongly imagistic, rhythmic. What purposes of authors does it fulfill? The answer has to be: Many. The so-called propagandistic writer may use his novel as a way of fomenting revolution or counter-revolution. A poet like Lucretius may, in a long poem, give exposition to a scientific philosophical system. But most literary works must be understood as chiefly expressive and evocative. Authors differ as to the relative importance of these two: some seem little interested in publication, so long as they have been able to satisfy themselves; others do not feel fulfilled unless they have communicated, in the sense of arousing in others' imaginations the total experiences which have formed in their own minds.

Religious Discourse. This is the language employed by prophets, by revealers and interpreters of divine guidance, by theologians, by priests and ministers, and by worshippers. To the extent that religions prescribe certain ways of behavior, religious discourse may be considered as principally incitive: in describing what is right and what is wrong, what is commanded and what is forbidden, what one ought and what one ought not to do, what one's duties and obligations are, the aim is typically to control the behavior of a group. Theologically, religious language intends to be informative, that is, to describe the nature of God or the gods, the origin of the world and of man, man's ultimate fate, and the like. The rituals of religion may be importantly evocative, with close affinities to art. The supplicant is of course directly incitive, while the worshipper in adoration may be purely expressive, wanting above all else to give utterance to his feelings.

Legal and Political Discourse. "Legal discourse designates the punishments which an organized community empowers itself to employ if certain actions are or are not performed, and its aim is to cause individuals to perform or not to perform the actions in question." [15] The informative and incitive elements are here nicely fused. Certain actions are promoted and certain actions are inhibited by the description of what happens if.... The language of Political Science, like that of any science, is mainly informative; but the language employed by candidates for office and their supporters and by advocates and opponents of bills and rulings, is typically incitive.

THE LANGUAGE OF VALUE

There is a special problem that arises in conection with sentences containing "value" words. How are we going to classify sentences such as the following?

1. I am especially fond of French apple pie.
2. He admires Tschaikowsky excessively.
3. TVA has been a signal success in social engineering.
4. The British health plan is a mixed blessing.
5. The Buchenwald tortures were among the most horrible crimes ever committed.
6. Even so, she ought to be faithful to him.
7. A teacher's moral responsibility is to teach the principles of democracy.

Probably most people think of value judgments as not essentially different from factual judgments. "That is red" accordingly would be considered a similar kind of statement to "That is pretty." However, as we have seen above, many semanticists insist that value judgments are altogether different, their difference lying in their unverifiability. Accord-

15 Charles Morris, *op. cit.,* p. 130.

ing to this extreme view, expressions of evaluations ought to be counted as merely expressive or "emotive."

This problem has, as yet, no entirely satisfactory resolution. However, some clarification is available.

It is certainly true that a great many evaluations, if considered as attempts to convey information, must be counted as vague and ambiguous in the extreme. Not many persons who speak about *good* music, *bad* coffee, *duty,* what one *ought* to do, can give a clear explanation of the meaning of the value-terms they employ. But this is not to say that the terms never have and cannot have any intelligible meaning. For instance, it might be possible to state sentence (1) as follows: "It can be observed in my behavior in bakery shops, with restaurant waiters when it is time to order dessert, and with my wife as I make requests for dinner, that I often ask for French apple pie." Again, it might be discovered that I have some motive for lying about my taste for French apple pie; but the fact that I *may* be lying is an indication that there must be some informative character to the assertion.

Suppose Jack says to Tom: "You ought to see the movie at the Bijou." His sentence can perhaps be translated as follows: "If, as I suppose, you like 'Westerns' with much hard riding and sharpshooting, you can spend a pleasant two hours seeing such and such a film." Jack may be wrong in saying this; Tom having seen the film, may complain that he was utterly bored; but, as this proved the evaluation mistaken, it likewise proved that the evaluation had an informational content.

Again, sentences containing "ought" can often be satisfactorily replaced by more clear-cut statements: "If he wants 'x', 'y' is an attested effective means to achieve it."

"Badness" of a governmental administration can often be spelled out in terms of matters of fact such as numbers of unemployed, amount of public debt, officials convicted of crime, etc. Such clarifications do not ultimately remove the "subjectivity" of value judgments. This is illustrated by considering sentence 5; even after you have clarified it by stating the mode of execution, the numbers killed, the official reasons for these actions, it is still *possible* for somone to express a liking for and an approval of the Buchenwald activities.

Very often, of course, value sentences are incitive. Advertising is the obvious example, but there are many others. The statement about TVA (sentence 3) may be in a given context an invitation to support a particular candidate. In general when one person says, "Y is good," he will very likely be saying at least these two things: "I like Y" (partly expressive, partly informative) and "You should like Y also" (incitive).[16]

PROBLEMS FOR DISCUSSION

A. Five uses of language have been distinguished. Obviously there is overlapping here, but it is useful to be able to determine whether a given bit of discourse has this or that purpose. In the following, show how the context or the voice inflection might determine the proper classification of the passage:

1. The polls are open until 9:00 P.M.
2. His political program is radically Socialistic.
3. More than 90 per cent of the American people are proponents of a capitalistic economy.
4. She is six feet tall and weighs 170 pounds.
5. He is a novelist who aims at complete realism, even to the point of reproducing the raciest kind of Army speech.
6. Either you are an American or not an American!
7. It is inconsistent to profess a belief both in the equality of men and the inequality of races of men.
8. Enchiladas are highly seasoned with peppers and other spices.
9. This year nearly all coeds will wear their hair two to three inches longer.

---

16 For a technical but very important elaboration of this position, see C. L. Stevenson, *Ethics and Language* (New Haven: Yale University Press, 1944).

10. President Truman unquestionably followed the New Deal pattern.

11. Hallelujah!

12. Ouch!

B. What intentions might the producer have in asserting the following sentences?

1. T.N.T. explodes when detonated.

2. Oh what a beautiful morning!

3. It costs $2000 to make this saddle.

4. My black horse is easily worth two of your best goats.

5. Freedom is everybody's business.

6. Make your pile first!

7. You can always learn.

8. Your license must be revoked, if a court finds you guilty of manslaughter while driving.

9. Diamonds are cheap this year.

10. At 30 miles per hour one travels more than 30 feet (2 car lengths) before one starts to brake.

11. Motorists who drive at reasonable speeds may operate an automobile for many years without having an accident.

12. The speed limit is 20 miles per hour.

13. The Tax Commission maintains a record of every driver in the state.

14. Your mother is back from Iowa.

15. 'Bubbles' is a new washing miracle and leaves your hands snow white.

16. In the Sign of the Cross, I shall conquer.

17. She's not bad!

18. Fire!

19. 'Nasty' is a nasty word.

20. Americans spend so much time making money that they lose little time spending it.

21. The uniform Act Regulating Traffic on Highways writes into the law the rules of courtesy and common sense.

22. If the car does not keep running, pull the dashboard knob marked "Choke."

23. The material world is lovely.

24. *Othello* is a better play than *Hamlet* because it better observes the unities of place and time.

C. The telephone book is almost purely informative. Can you think of other types of publications which exhibit one or another of the language uses listed in this chapter?

D. With what accuracy might music be called a language limited to non-informative uses?

E. Explain: A wife complained to her lawyer, "When I ask Charles if he loves me, he acts as if I were asking for information."

F. Read and re-read the following passages until you believe you understand their meaning and attain to a proper emotional reaction. Then explain what it seems to you the author in each case was trying to do in writing as he did. What means did he employ? How well did he succeed?

But howsoever these things are thus in men's depraved judgments and affections, yet truth, which only doth judge itself, teacheth that the inquiry of truth, which is the love-making or wooing of it; the knowledge of truth, which is the presence of it; and the belief of truth, which is the enjoying of it—is the sovereign good of human nature. (Francis Bacon, "Of Truth.")

Remember also thy Creator in the days of thy youth, before the evil days come, and the years draw nigh, when thou shalt say, I have no pleasure in them; before the sun, and the light, and the moon, and the stars, are darkened, and the clouds return after the rain; in the day when the keepers of the house shall tremble, and the strong men shall bow themselves, and the grinders cease because they are few, and those that look out of the windows shall be darkened, and the doors shall be shut in the street. . . . (Ecclesiastes.)

This day, my sons, ye shall quit you like men. By the memory of your father's wrongs, by the hope of your children's rights! Tyranny impends in red wrath: help for you is none, if not in your own right hands. This day ye must do or die. (Thomas Carlyle, *The French Revolution.*)

Allowed to look once upon the wonderful spectacle, which is to repeat itself in the world forever, we should look and admire, for tomorrow we die; we should eat, drink, and be merry, but moderately and with much art, lest we die miserably and die today. (George Santayana, *Three Philosophical Poets.*)

Education, enlarging as it does our horizon and perspective, is a means of multiplying our ideals, of bringing new ones into view. And your college professor, with a starched shirt and spectacles, would, if a stock of ideals were all alone by itself enough to render a life significant, be the most absolutely and deeply significant of men. Tolstoy would be completely blind in despising him for a prig, a pedant and a parody; and all our new insight into the divinity of muscular labor would be altogether off the track of truth. (William James, "What Makes a Life Significant.")

Touchstone: Then learn this of me: to have, is to have; for it is a figure in rhetoric, that drink, being poured out of a cup into a glass, by filling the one doth empty the other; for all your writers consent that *ipse* is he; now, you are not *ipse*, for I am he.

William: Which he, sir?

Touchstone: He, sir, that must marry this woman. Therefore, you clown, abandon,—which is in the vulgar, leave—the society, which in the boorish is, company,—of this female,—which in the common is, woman; which together is, abandon the society of this female, or, clown thou perishest; or to thy better understanding, diest; or, to wit, I kill thee, make thee away, translate thy life into death, thy liberty into bondage. I will deal in poison with thee, or in bastinado, or in steel; I will bandy with thee in faction; I will o'errun thee with policy; I will kill thee a hundred and fifty ways: therefore tremble, and depart. (Shakespeare, *As You Like It.*)

EXERCISES

I. Find examples in newspapers or magazines to illustrate each of the following. Mount your clippings on half sheets of paper and write in a short explanation of your classifications.

1. Informative usage, incitive in form.

2. Incitive usage, informative in form.

3. Informative usage, informative in form.

II. Write a dialogue in which you employ *all* of the different language usages, with as much variety in form of expression as possible. Label in the margin each usage. Make your dialogue as interesting and meaty as you can. Suggested length: 500 words.

III. Find and quote three instances of tautologies disguised as facts. Give your interpretation of the quotations.

IV. Analyze each of the instances of evaluation given in the last section. To what degree is each informative? In so far as it is informative, what meaning is to be given to the vague and ambiguous words?

V. What sometimes "objectionable" word is replaced by each of the following euphemisms?

1. cuspidor	5. inexpensive or popular-priced
2. tonsorial parlor	6. hired help
3. dental surgeon	7. custodian
4. paying-guest	8. ill

VI. What euphemisms are used for the following?

1. drunk	5. dead
2. insane	6. fat
3. to tell a lie	7. sweat
4. stupid	8. hell

VII. Very often the choice of words will reveal hostility and antagonism on the part of the user. Thus an editorial writer for a certain type of newspaper might call a professor who has been brought in as a governmental consultant "an egg-head" or a "brain-truster." Give five other examples of words which typically betray aggressiveness, along with their more neutral synonyms.

VIII. "We must pass over a part of Mrs. Rebecca Crawley's biography with that lightness and delicacy which the world demands—the moral world, that has, perhaps, no particular objection to vice, but an insuperable repugnance to hearing vice called by its proper name. There are things we do and know perfectly well in Vanity Fair, though we never speak

of them—as the Ahrimanians worship the devil, but don't
mention him; and a polite public will no more bear to read
an authentic description of vice than a truly refined English
or American female will permit the word 'breeches' to be
pronounced in her chaste hearing. And yet, Madam, both
are walking the world before our faces every day, without much shocking us. If you were to blush every time they
went by, what complexions you would have! It is only when
their naughty names are called out that your modesty has
any occasion to show alarm or sense of outrage, and it has
been the wish of the present writer, all through this story,
deferentially to submit to the fashion at present prevailing,
and only to hint at the existence of wickedness, in a light,
easy, and agreeable manner, so that nobody's fine feelings
may be offended." (W. M. Thackeray, *Vanity Fair,* Chapter
LXIV.)

Support Thackeray's statement with some examples not
given in this chapter.

IX.   Nietzsche wrote "Words relating to values are merely ban-
ners planted on those spots where a new blessedness was
discovered—a new feeling." Interpret and discuss.

X.   In *Roughing It,* Mark Twain sets down a dialogue between
a minister, "a fragile, gentle, spiritual new fledgling from
an Eastern theological seminary," and Scotty Briggs, a
miner trying to arrange a funeral for his recently deceased
friend:

"Are you the duck that runs the gospel-mill next door?"

"Am I the—pardon me, I believe I do not understand?"

With another sigh and a half-sob, Scotty rejoined:

"Why you see we are in a bit of trouble, and the boys
thought maybe you would give us a lift, if we'd tackle you—
that is, if I've got the rights of it and you are the head clerk
of the doxology-works next door."

"I am the shepherd in charge of the flock whose fold is
next door."

"The which?"

"The spiritual adviser of the little company of believers
whose sanctuary adjoins these premises."

Scotty scratched his head, reflected a moment, and then
said:

"You ruther hold over me, pard. I reckon I can't call that hand. Ante and pass the buck."

"How? I beg pardon. What did I understand you to say?"

"Well, you've ruther got the bulge on me. Or maybe we've both got the bulge, somehow. You don't smoke me and I don't smoke you. You see, one of the boys has passed in his checks, and we want to give him a good send-off, and so the thing I'm on now is to roust out somebody to jerk a little chin-music for us and waltz him through handsome."

"My friend, I seem to grow more and more bewildered. Your observations are wholly incomprehensible to me. Cannot you simplify them in some way? At first I thought perhaps I understood you, but I grope now. Would it not expedite matters if you restricted yourself to categorical statements of fact unencumbered with obstructing accumulations of metaphor and allegory?"

"I'll have to pass, I judge."

"How?"

"You've raised me out, pard."

"I still fail to catch your meaning."

"Why, that last lead of yourn is too many for me—that's the idea. I can't neither trump nor follow suit."

The clergyman sank back in his chair perplexed. Scotty leaned his head on his hand and gave himself up to thought. Presently his face came up, sorrowful but confident.

"I've got it now, so's you can savvy," he said. "What we want is a gospel-sharp. See?"

"A what?"

"Gospel-sharp. Parson."

"Oh! Why did you not say so before? I am a clergyman—a parson."

"Now you talk! You see my blind and straddle it like a man. Put it there!"—extending a brawny paw, which closed over the minister's small hand and gave it a shake indicative of fraternal sympathy and fervent gratification.

"Now we're all right, pard. Let's start fresh. Don't you mind my snuffling a little—becuz we're in a power of trouble. You see, one of the boys has gone up the flume—"

"Gone where?"

"Up the flume—throwed up the sponge, you understand."

"Ah—has departed to that mysterious country from whose bourne no traveler returns."

"Return! I reckon not. Why, pard, he's *dead!*"

"Yes, I understand."

"Oh, you do? Well I thought maybe you might be getting tangled some more...."

Compose another dialogue, of similar length, exhibiting two persons not speaking "the same language."

XI. Semiotics, the over-all science of signs, has been divided by Charles Morris into three distinct fields: syntactics, semantics, and pragmatics. The first has to do with syntax, the ways in which signs are combined; it is roughly equivalent to the study of grammar, but broader. Semantics has to do with all the various modes in which signs signify; it is the study of signs in relation to what they are about. Pragmatics concerns itself with the users and interpreters of signs, or, as Morris puts it, "studying the origin, uses, and effects of signs within the total behavior of the interpreters of signs." (Charles Morris, *op. cit.*, p. 219.)

A chart will summarize these points, though by oversimplifying them.

Semantics   signs ←——————————→ signified
Syntactics   signs ←——————————→ other signs
Pragmatics   sign producer ←————————→ sign receiver

There is a characteristic use of the word "meaning" within each of these fields. For Semantics, a sign has meaning when there is some feature of the total environment which it does in fact signify or which it might signify if the environment were altered in an ordered way. For Syntactics, a sign is meaningfully employed to the extent that it is combined with other signs according to certain established rules of syntax. For Pragmatics, there is meaning when someone "gets something over" to someone else; two persons enter into communication.

QUESTION: Is this classification consistent with the doctrine of the present book?

XII. It has been said that "a convenient way to describe an act of communication is to answer the following questions:

Who
Says what
In which channel
To whom
With what effect?"

(Harold D. Lasswell, "The Structure and Function of Communication in Society," in *The Communication of Ideas,* p. 37.)

Describe why it is sometimes difficult to answer one or another of these questions.

SOURCES AND ADVANCED READING

1. Charles Morris, *Signs, Language and Behavior.* New York: Prentice-Hall, Inc., 1946. Chs. IV and V.

2. George Herbert Mead, *Mind, Self and Society.* Chicago: University of Chicago Press, 1934. Part II, Chs. 8-11; Part III, Chs. 20-21.

3. C. K. Ogden and I. A. Richards, *The Meaning of Meaning.* New York: Harcourt Brace and Company, 7th ed., 1945. Ch. X.

4. John Dewey, *Experience and Nature.* La Salle, Illinois: The Open Court Publishing Company, 1925. Ch. V.

5. *The Language of Value,* ed. by Ray Lepley. New York: Columbia University Press, 1956.

6. *The Communication of Ideas,* ed. by Lyman Bryson. New York and London: Institute for Religious and Social Studies, 1948.

→ VIII ←

METAPHORICAL LANGUAGE

ἀερίων ἐπέων ἄρχομαι ἀλλ᾽ ὀνάτων.—Σαπφώ
(The words are of air but they are good.—SAPPHO)

Metaphor Essential to Language • Poetry • Symbolism • Analogy

---

METAPHOR ESSENTIAL TO LANGUAGE

One thing that literature would be greatly the better for
  Would be a more restricted employment by authors of simile
    and metaphor
Authors of all races, be they Greeks, Teutons, or Celts,
Can't seem just to say that anything is the thing it is, but have to
  go out of their way to say that it is like something else.

(Ogden Nash.)

Ogden Nash's whimsical lines summarize a recurrent attack upon the employment of figurative language. Listen to a debater say, "Strip the rhetorical flourishes from my opponent's arguments and what it comes to is..." Then, like as not, he will paraphrase his rival in language every bit as figurative as the original. Deny a political orator the phrases "ship of state," "vistas of the future," "our own fifth column," and the like, and you have tied his hands behind his back—figuratively speaking. "Come," we say to him, "speak plainly. Never mind all the embellishments and high-flown talk. Just what do you mean?" But is it as easy as all that?

We will try to show that figurative language as such is not

the enemy of clarity. The real enemy is the careless or irresponsible or obtuse use of figurative language. In fact, if one wanted to fight against all employment of non-literal language, he would be engaging in a losing battle, for the very existence of language seems to be dependent upon metaphor.

As we have already noticed, the actual origins of language are heavily veiled, so that it is difficult to achieve any but the slightest verification for speculations as to their nature. Ernst Cassirer tried to show that there are two quite distinguishable forces operative in the growth of language, myth and logic. But among primitive peoples it seems impossible to separate the tendency to mythologize and the tendency to extend vocabulary by metaphorical means; so we might revise our statement to speak about the *logical* and the *mythical-metaphorical*.

Now, it is important not to over-rationalize the genesis of language. We may easily be misled by taking as our model for language growth the deliberate coining of names for new gadgets or newly observed plants or animals, even where the naming is metaphorical; for instance, the giving to a new bleach the brand name "Clouds," or to a flower with a round, inverted blossom and a prominent stamen, "Carillon." In such cases, one has a clear idea of the qualities of two objects, finds an overlap, and makes a transfer of names. But it is instructive to consider the "magic of analogy." To sprinkle the ground in a drought in order to make rain betokens an identification between the natural and the artificial watering: the sprinkling *is* raining. This mythical activity is genuinely indistinguishable from primitive, undeliberate, metaphorical naming. Any *likeness* whatsoever may lead to an extension of the denotation of a name. One can virtually open a dictionary at random and by consulting etymologies find metaphorical word origins which seem to us highly far-fetched. "Tragedy" arises from a word meaning "goat" and a word meaning "song." And it doesn't entirely clarify the matter if one learns that among the Greeks serious plays were probably first performed at religious ceremonies which featured the sacrifice of goats. Certain very old Indo-European riddles suggest a highly metaphorical cosmology coming into being. "What are a dozen cypresses with thirty boughs on each?" The answer is: the twelve moons of the year, each with thirty days. "What two horses, one black and one white, chase each other continually but in vain?" Answer: the night and the day. Or consider the activity of classification. Some Indians classify butterflies as birds, which strikes us as bad taxonomy only because we are not sufficiently impressed with the fact that both are flying animals.

Careful and purposeful classification suggests the rise of logic, that is, of the deliberate, systematic, consistent ordering of discourse. Aristotle could not be satisfied with thinking of a tragedy as a goat-song; he had to *define* the term, which is to say, include it within a genus and clearly differentiate it from the other species within the same genus: "Tragedy is an imitation of an action that is complete, serious . . . and of a certain magnitude . . . through pity and fear effecting the proper purgation of these emotions."

The logician's work illustrates an extraordinarily self-conscious effort to limit and stabilize meanings of symbols and thus to gain conceptual precision. The physicist cannot tolerate a concept of weight which suggests burdensomeness, importance, seriousness, oppression, etc., but must nail down a single operational meaning—for instance, by defining weight as a pointer reading on a certain kind of scale. The achievement of a relatively un-figurative language in the writings of exact scientists is a deliberate and systematic suppression of many of the resources of language; and it is no more the case that all language ought to be so literal than it is that we ought to use language exclusively for informative purposes. Furthermore, it is by no means clear that even for purposes of informative communication, figurative language is dispensable. I. A. Richards has written, "Metaphor is the omnipresent principle of language. . . . Even in the rigid language of the settled sciences we do not eliminate or prevent it without great difficulty."[1] Consider, for instance, such scientific and philosophical analogies as "flow of electricity," "stream of consciousness," and "mind as *tabula rasa*."

Metaphorical thought can be fruitfully considered not only in the context of mythologizing, but also in our own every-day attempts to understand. It is quite as true for us today as for ancient man that there is immense difficulty in attending to the unnamed. We could say that the unnamed is the unnoticed, the unorganized. One of the basic principles of thought is that we explore the unknown by means of the known. When we come across something new—an idea, a machine, a person, a flower, a landscape—we inevitably try to understand it in terms of what we already know. A traveler in northern Spain says to himself, "These mountains are so like the Rockies." A banqueter tries a minestrone against his palate and pronounces it in the same class with his wife's vegetable soup. A Philosophy student frets about Kant's dictum, "So act that the maxim of your action can be willed to be a universal law," until he detects a certain resemblance of this command to the more familiar Golden Rule. Charles Morris has written that

A sign is *metaphorical* if in a particular instance of its occurrence it is used to denote an object which it does not literally denote in virtue of its signification, but which has some of the properties which its genuine denotata have. To call an automobile a beetle, or to call a picture of a man a man is to use 'beetle' and 'man' metaphorically. Since an automobile is not literally a beetle, to call it a beetle forces the interpreter to attend with special care to the automobile in order to determine in what sense the automobile is like (and unlike) a beetle.[2]

So it is with the words we employ. How often we will connect two thoughts by means of a single word or phrase. "Don't

[1] I. A. Richards, *Philosophy of Rhetoric* (London: Oxford University Press, 1936), p. 92.
[2] Charles Morris, *op. cit.*, pp. 136-137.

be catty." "What a corny song!" "My mind was as blank as a clean sheet of paper." Notice the force of the faddish indication of anger: "He blew his top!"

The last example points to a familiar phenomenon which we can call, "the rigidifying of metaphor." That is, striking, picturesque figures often gain such wide currency and familiarity that their figurative force is dissipated and they become mere synonymous expressions for more strictly literal words. Probably few of us now think of the accumulation of steam pressure to the point of explosion when we say or hear "He blew his top!" but we merely use this saying as a rather flat and usual way of indicating a violent expression of anger. We are surprised to hear a foreigner find delight in the word, "skyscraper," which for us is no more interesting than "tall building." Etymology reveals countless instances of this phenomenon. For example: the root meaning of "Philosophy" is "love of wisdom." "Pecuniary" originally had to do with property in cattle. Literally, bitter food is food which when bitten, bites back.

With metaphors that have grown stale and rigid it is especially easy to commit the rhetorical blunder of "mixing" metaphors. Somebody writes: "But underneath his piety there is an undercurrent of keen, dry humor which crops out occasionally and makes his talk sparkle." If we are reading carefully (and not reading the way that sentence was written) we cannot help being puzzled and perhaps unintentionally amused to try to think of an *undercurrent* of *dry* humor *cropping out* to make talk *sparkle*. Even the best poets become glib and suffer their attention to lapse. Dr. Johnson, for instance, criticized Pope for thinking that woes can be *painted* by being well sung in the lines:

> The well-sung woes shall soothe my pensive ghost;
> He best can paint them who shall feel them most.

In his essay "Politics and the English Language," George Orwell says:

By using stale metaphors, similes and idioms, you save much mental effort, at the cost of leaving your meaning vague, not only for your reader but for yourself. This is the significance of mixed metaphors. The sole aim of a metaphor is to call up a visual image. When these images clash—as in the Fascist octopus has sung its swan song, the jackboot is thrown into the melting pot— it can be taken as certain that the writer is not seeing a mental image of the objects he is naming. . . .[3]

It is sometimes useful to translate a metaphorical passage into as nearly literal language as possible in order to "de-sensitize" the language so that one may not be misled by vague and ambiguous usage. Thus if an orator spoke of "modern finance capitalism" as "the mere dead ashes of an imperialistic conflagration that has devastated the virgin natural resources of a mighty continent," the hearer might feel that he could better evaluate the position if he translated and interpreted somewhat as follows: The speaker regards modern finance capitalism as ineffective and outmoded, as the system which has resulted from an expansionist period in economic history, during which time there was a relatively unrestricted utilization and consequent depletion of natural resources on the North American continent.

Nevertheless, it would be vain and silly to attempt to carry out such a program consistently. We seldom want our language to be purely and simply designative, we speak not only about something but to someone, and this someone we often want to impress, to persuade, to incite. As we have continually insisted, language has a multitude of uses and values. We can hardly imagine a time when men did not find delight in fresh and striking language. Still, it would be quite misleading to separate, as some literary critics and logicians have done, the value of *delighting* from the values of *informing* or *evaluating*. What we frequently call *style* is seldom a mere superflu-

[3] George Orwell, *Shooting an Elephant* (New York: Harcourt, Brace and Company, 1950), pp. 85-86.

ous *addition* to the content or sense of what is said. Style is not a husk, or even a dress. In the communicative context, it is not the same to speak of "a conscientious student" and "a grind," not the same to call a professor "verbose" and to call him "long-winded," not the same to speak of a class now as "easy," now as "a snap." Translation, even within one language, is always only partial. Something propositional and intellectual changes in the process, along with the tone.

POETRY

Poetry is especially marked by its employment of metaphor (although some poetry is not heavily metaphorical) and is, partly for this reason, least translatable. Many persons have difficulty in reading poetry precisely because they have not learned to subject themselves to the complexities of live metaphorical expression. Often as a rationalization of their own trouble they will accuse the poetry of "beating around the bush," of using two words where one would do, of ornamenting and embellishing language to the point of attaining nonsense. No doubt such accusations are sometimes justifiable: there is more poor poetry than good poetry. Persons sensitive to great poetry are unanimous, however, in insisting that through figurative language some things are said which can be said no other way, quite as in music one despairs of using words to tell someone how the tones sounded.

The poet Robert Frost has well said:

Poetry begins in trivial metaphors, pretty metaphors, "grace metaphors," and goes on to the profoundest thinking that we have. . . . Unless you are at home in the metaphor . . . you are not safe anywhere. Because you are not at ease with figurative values: you don't know the metaphor in its strength and its weakness. . . . The metaphor whose manage we are best taught in poetry—that is all there is of thinking.[4]

[4] Robert Frost, "Education by Poetry: a Meditative Monologue," *Amherst Graduates' Quarterly*, Vol. XX (February 1931), pp. 77-82.

Probably it is too much to say "That is all there is of think-ing," but the exaggeration underlines the place of metaphor in our most creative intellectual processes.

This is not to say that paraphrase (a rather free and usu-ally prosaic rendering) is not useful, but only that it is not an adequate synonymous substitute.

We have already noticed that as we trace back the history of language, we come to a point where metaphor merges with myth. Now we should observe that there seems likewise to be a primal identification of art and myth.

Children in our culture are helped to understand that when they read of Zeus's being a great god who hurled thunderbolts, this is only a "story" and it is not to be con-fused with the accounts of God's answering Job out of a whirlwind. That is to say, we are brought to appreciate a myth as an entertaining tale, as an engrossing legend, as a picturesque and dramatic anecdote. We may even be charmed by the Aztec account of the sun as a God who periodically requires the strengthening nourishment of human sacrifice. By the person for whom the sun *is* god, the *aesthetic* appeal is not abstracted and separately savored. Even the very sophis-ticated Plato urged the banning of Homer's epics from the well-ordered state on the grounds that the gods were therein falsely represented. (Plato, to be sure, was mainly interested in the harm that might be done children and thus the state through the representation of the gods, presumably paragons of virtue, as carousers.) And Soviet authorities, on parallel grounds, castigate music which represents bourgeois ideology. We know that "distance" is required in order that a distinctly aesthetic response be evoked; that is, we must not be *too* closely linked, by belief or by personal ties, with the object.

Language is a parallel case. We have to learn to see the beauty of figures of speech; at first they are just functional to our understanding—indeed it would not be too much to say that they constitute our understanding. "Apollo, the far-darter" named a reality, and a sometimes menacing one, but *we* commend the vivid imagery of the epithet.

But literary art is not trivial, and something may be lost in separating the logical from the beautiful and the evocative. Plato knew this. Sometimes in his endeavor to express in precise, purified language a profound insight into reality, he would despair and say, "But let me construct a myth that will suggest something like the truth." There is a deep sense in which the poet tries to recapture in his language something of the fullness and warmth that is missing in "coldly" logical language.

Cassirer has written:

What poetry expresses is neither the mythic word-picture of gods and daemons, nor the logical truth of abstract determinations and relations. The world of poetry stands apart from both, as a world of illusion and fantasy—but it is just in this mode of illusion that the realm of pure feeling can find utterance, and can therewith attain its full and concrete actualization.[5]

But instead of just discussing poetry, let us examine Shakespeare's 73rd Sonnet:

That time of year thou may'st in me behold
When yellow leaves, or none, or few, do hang
Upon those boughs which shake against the cold,
Bare ruin'd choirs, where late the sweet birds sang.
In me thou seest the twilight of such day
As after sunset fadeth in the west;
Which by and by black night doth take away,
Death's second self, that seals up all in rest.
In me thou seest the glowing of such fire,
That on the ashes of his youth doth lie,
As the death-bed whereon it must expire,
Consum'd with that which it was nourish'd by.
   This thou perceiv'st, which makes thy love more strong,
   To love that well which thou must leave ere long.

[5] Ernst Cassirer, *Language and Myth*, Susanne K. Langer, Trans. (New York and London: Harper & Brothers, 1946), p. 99.

One exclusively used to prose would be struck with some strangeness of language here. There are some archaic words such as *may'st, doth, thou, seest;* and some spelling that is not ours: *ruin'd, consum'd,* etc. But these are, of course, more indicative of the period when the words were written than of any distinction between poetry and prose. There is, next, the fact that every line begins with a capital letter, but this will soon be seen to signify little more than that this is a poem and should be so read in order to emphasize its rhythm. Perhaps more difficulty is presented by some of the syntax. Thus a word order more normal to prose would be: "Thou may'st behold in me that time of year..." And we would probably say (in place of line 2) "When a few yellow leaves or none at all." Still again, we may at first be bothered in lines 7 and 8 with the delayed appositive: "Death's second self," stands in apposition to "black night."

The matter of rhythm is more complex. Prose, though not without rhythm, has no definitely patterned sound. But if one notices the alternation of stressed and unstressed syllables in an oral reading of the poem, he will find a regular (though not unvarying) pattern, like this: ta-TA ta-TA ta-TA ta-TA ta-TA. If the question is asked, "Why do poets employ metrical language?" two points may be made by way of answer. There seems to be in the human animal a very deep-seated satisfaction in rhythm. The child delights in "Diddle diddle dumpling, my son John," not for the meaning, obviously, but for the patterned sound. There are probably few people who fail to be attracted even to untuned clicks and taps and booms, castanets, tom-toms, drums. (The parents of a three-year-old could probably be included among the few!) And there is the further fact that even without intent, language tends to become rhythmical during emotional states: mark the keening of a bereaved woman, the well-spaced periods of the orator stung in debate, even the cursing of an enraged top-sergeant. This suggests that the rhythmical is somehow intimately *expressive* of feeling as well as strongly *evocative* of feeling; hence if, as we have maintained, the language of poetry is set over against (in some respects, but not in all) the cold language of logic and science, we are better prepared to recognize the importance of the rhythmical character of poetry.

Not all poetry is rhymed, of course, but when it is, the presence of the rhyme raises a question as to its purpose, for here is a language feature seldom encountered in non-literary discourse. If a child inadvertently rhymes, he will say,

> I'm a poet
> And don't know it.

It is to be observed that there is a scheme to the rhymes of our sonnet's fourteen lines, which may be symbolized thus:
A B A B C D C D E F E F G G. (This scheme has come to be listed as a characteristic of the "Shakespearian sonnet.") Now, looking at the pattern we observe three quatrains (four-line units) and a couplet. If with this in mind we return to the poem, we will have no trouble in discovering that there is also a certain division of the "sense" into these four parts. Thus, the rhyme helps establish these sub-divisions, the likeness in sound binding the lines together.

If it seems that we have digressed far from figurative language, we intend to show that there is a genuine relevance to all this. Thus, just as the rhyme scheme establishes four parts within the poem, so are these parts distinguished by certain ruling figures of speech.

In the first line we see a comparison set up between the aging of a man and the passing of the seasons — a common enough metaphor; and, as the poem progresses, the seasons are measured by the drooping of foliage and the departure of the birds. We are led thus to ask the question: In human aging, what corresponds to these familiar phenomena of wintering? Immediately we think of the loss of the "bloom" of youth, the depletion and graying of hair, the growing incapacity and unwillingness to sing, and—as extensions of the literal meaning of "sing"—to cavort, to be carefree, romantic, joyous, etc. The phrase, "Bare, ruin'd choirs" may give us a little pause until we see the shift in meaning of "choirs" away from choral groups to the *place* of their singing— actually an old meaning of the word—so that we are led to think of the branches of the tree as a choir loft, now bare, and ruined, that is, deprived of leaves and birds, dilapidated, despoiled.

In the second quatrain, the figure shifts. Now old age is compared to twilight and death to night. Death is especially related to night by calling the latter "Death's second self," and furthermore, the darkness of night calls to mind the darkness of the tomb in the phrase "seals up all in rest."

In the final four-line unit we have a rather complicated figure of a fire. Old age is likened to glowing embers, the loss of youth to the ashes underneath. Soon this bed of coals is to be a cold bed, a death-bed; the ashes of youth which have served as foundation to the coals will themselves take over and all will be ashes.

The couplet which ends the poem is still different, relatively forthright and direct, except for the irony involved in the counsel to the poet's mistress, to make her love strong— this contrasting with the previous twelve lines, all of which have pointed to decay, weakening, and death.

If now, with this paraphrase before us, we seriously ask the question whether the prose-substitute is adequate, nearly everyone will reply in the negative. There is that in the poem which is by no means captured in the prosy explanation: not alone rhythm and rhyme, but the metaphors themselves, which function, it should be noticed, not just as dispensable ornaments or baubles on the essential tree but as genuine instruments for the revealing of meaning. This controverts the authority of Alexander Pope:

> True wit is nature to advantage dressed,
> What oft was thought, but ne'er so well expressed.

True wit, true poetry, true metaphorical thinking are by
their advantageous expression what many have tried to think
of but never before quite succeeded in capturing. In "Upon
those boughs which shake against the cold," the reader gets
a forcible visual image and gets the feel of the spectator who
sympathetically and concomitantly also shakes against the
cold—who, that is, gets a full-qualitied emotional experience,
especially as one thinks not only of a tree but also of an aging
lover. And in that metaphor which compares life to a many-
layered fire, reducing to glowing coals and finally to cold
ashes, by virtue of the comparison, something is said about
life that cannot be quite duplicated in any statement which
disposes of the metaphor.

Thus, three characteristics of a successful metaphor may be
noted. First, it is arresting: it seizes our attention by compar-
ing those things which we had not thought to compare before,
or not in just this kind of way. Second, it gives us the *feel* of
the experience communicated: probably vivid imagery is
established and there is induced in us, the reader, an emotional accompaniment to the intellectual processes involved.
Finally, the metaphor is a device for saying something, a
way of pointing to certain qualities or properties or characteristics of an object or an event or a process by a direct likening
of it to something which we already know.

Although in great poetry we find, no doubt, the richest
source of metaphor, the use of metaphor, as we have repeatedly said, is as wide as language itself. Knowing about metaphor is important, not only in order that we may understand
it when it is employed by an artist, but also that we may ourselves make more effective use of it, in our own writing and
speaking. Mention was made above of "dead metaphor,"
expressions which are implicitly metaphorical but which have
through usage become so familiar as to cease to operate
figuratively. Alongside dead metaphors we ought to place
dying metaphors, that is, those figures which have been so
used that the comparison invoked, though real, is weak, un-

vivid. If it should happen that on a rainy day, the first five persons you met commented, "Nice weather for ducks," you might have difficulty in being polite to the last one. To anyone properly discriminating in language usage, the presence of slang (treated here because it is so frequently metaphorical) in writing or conversation is not, as such, either booed or applauded. One who studiously avoids slang expressions is likely to impress most people as pedantic and stuffy. Some slang is lively and colorful, two important qualities for language. Furthermore, use of slang serves, upon occasion, a rather important ceremonial purpose. A child who has moved into a new neighborhood or a new section of the country, feels ill at ease until he fits his language comfortably into the prevailing slang patterns. A raw recruit in the army or a freshman at college will typically make some effort to talk as those around him talk. Nevertheless, too great an employment of dead and dying metaphors means dead thinking and lifeless communication. Often, overuse makes one appear ridiculous; Ring Lardner achieves many of his humorous effects by letting his characters expose themselves through their language, slangy or provincial. For instance, in "Some Like It Cold," Mr. Lewis, the song-writer, writes his girl friend that "N. Y. is the Mecca for a man that has got the musical gift." And his correspondent, not to be outdone, tells about her own cleanliness. "Edie often says she cannot see how I always look like I had just stepped out of a band box. She also calls me a fish (jokingly) because I spend so much time in the water." She concludes coyly: "Will you write a song about me some time? I would be thrilled to death!"

SYMBOLISM

It is common to encounter discussion of the "symbolism" of art, myth, and dream, where "symbol" and "symbolism" have a special meaning. Thus we hear of the symbolism in Medieval painting, of the symbolic character of religious ritual, and of the literary group called "Symbolists," who staged a revolt against the Naturalists, arguing that literature should not *depict* but *suggest,* and suggest not obvious things but the evanescent, the subtle, the mysterious, the ineffable. The *Encyclopaedia Britannica* defines "symbol" (in our new sense) as "a visible object representing to the mind the semblance of something which is not shown but realized in association with it." There is, for instance, a rich symbolism of Christianity: a ship representing the Church; a Lamb, a Hound, and a Shepherd representing Christ; a Phoenix, immortality; a serpent, Satan; a dove, the Holy Ghost; and so on. In *Pilgrim's Progress* we recognize that not only does the word "Christian" symbolize a certain fictional character, but that the character symbolizes every Christian man trying to achieve salvation. In the ancient fable of the fox and the grapes, a human failing is symbolized. The parable of the sower in the fourth chapter of the Gospel according to Mark is a profound illustration of this kind of symbolism. Jesus is there represented as saying to his followers:

Behold, there went out a sower to sow: And it came to pass, as he sowed, some fell by the way side, and the fowls of the air came and devoured it up. And some fell on stony ground, where it had not much earth; and immediately it sprang up, because it had no depth of earth. But when the sun was up, it was scorched; and because it had no root, it withered away. And some fell among thorns, and the thorns grew up, and choked it, and it yielded no fruit. And other fell on good ground, and did yield fruit that sprang up and increased; and brought forth, some thirty, and some sixty, and some an hundred. And he said unto them, He that hath ears to hear, let him hear. And when he was alone, they that were about him with the twelve asked of him the parable. And he said unto them, Unto you it is given to know the mystery of the kingdom of God: but unto them that are without, all these things are done in parables; that seeing they may see, and not perceive; and hearing they may hear, and not understand.... And he said unto them, Know ye not this parable? and how then will you know all parables? The sower soweth the word. And these are they by the way side, where the word is sown; but when they have heard, Satan cometh immediately, and taketh away the word that was sown in their hearts. And these are they likewise which are sown on stony ground; who when they have heard the word, immediately receive it with gladness; And have no root in themselves, and so endure but for a time: afterward, when affliction or persecution ariseth for the word's sake, immediately they are offended. And these are they which are sown among thorns; such as hear the word, and the cares of this world, and the deceitfulness of riches, and the lusts of other things entering in, choke the word, and it becometh unfruitful. And these are they which are sown on good ground; such as hear the word, and receive it, and bring forth fruit, some thirtyfold, some sixty, and some an hundred.

Here is an extended symbolic passage: the words we read tell a literal story and that story in turn symbolizes the moral meaning of the anecdote.

Anyone may have ears and yet hear not—not be able to interpret the symbolism. In a recent, highly interesting book, *The Forgotten Language: An Introduction to the Understanding of Dreams, Fairy Tales and Myths,* the psychoanalyst Erich Fromm has argued that there is a universal symbolic language which operates according to a different logic from that of daytime and science, a language which most of us know but dimly (though we all employ it), but which we would do well to learn or—it might better be said—to remember.

It is a language symbolic in the last of the three senses of "symbol" which he distinguishes. There are *conventional* symbols, whereby, say, the word "rug" stands for a floor covering not by virtue of any special connection between the name and the thing except the agreement, as it were, so to call floor coverings. Next there are *accidental,* or what might be called "associational" symbols, illustrated by the fact that the mention of Lake Michigan might bring to a certain person's mind a happy beach party he once enjoyed on its shores. Finally, there are *universal* symbols. Universal symbolic language "is a language in which the world outside is a symbol of the world inside, a symbol for our souls and our minds." [6] The relationship between the "sensory experience of a deserted, strange, poor environment" and "a mood of lostness and anxiety" is not conventional or accidental; it is an "intrinsic" relationship. Again:

We express our moods by our facial expressions and our attitudes and feelings by movements and gestures so precise that others recognize them more accurately from our gestures than from our words. Indeed, the body is a symbol—and not an allegory—of the mind. Deeply and genuinely felt emotion, and even any genuinely felt thought, is expressed in our whole organism. In the case of the universal symbol, we find the same connection between mental and physical experience. Certain physical phenomena suggest by their very nature certain emotional and mental experiences, and we express emotional experiences in the language of physical experiences, that is to say, symbolically. [7]

In common with all psychoanalytic theorists Fromm believes that dreams are universally symbolic of inner states, there being the same sort of relationship between the story or the picture of a dream and the dreamer's fears and desires as there is between the plot of a parable and its moral.

To venture further into this difficult and highly controversial subject would be as inappropriate, in an elementary book, as to neglect entirely a kind of symbolism which is deservedly receiving more attention with each passing year.

ANALOGY

Huygens, the great Dutch physicist of the seventeenth century, once wrote that light

spreads as sound does, by spherical surfaces and waves; for I call them waves from resemblances to those which are seen to be

---

[6] Erich Fromm, *The Forgotten Language: An Introduction to the Understanding of Dreams, Fairy Tales and Myths* (New York: Rinehart and Company, Inc., 1951), p. 12.

[7] *Ibid.*, p. 17. Notice that the word "attitude" has a double meaning: we "strike an attitude" which is symbolic of our attitude as a state of mind.

formed in water when a stone is thrown into it, and which present a successive spreading as circles. . . .[8]

This is an analogy, which may be simply defined as an extended metaphor. This particular comparison turned out to be a very fruitful one in the history of science. It enabled men to think about and to investigate light phenomena in more adequate ways than had been possible before.

But here is another analogy from another seventeenth century writer, an argument against discoveries newly made by Galileo:

There are seven windows in the head, two nostrils, two eyes, two ears, and a mouth; so in the heavens there are two favourable stars, two unpropitious, two luminaries, and Mercury alone undecided and indifferent. From which and many other similar phenomena of nature, such as the seven metals, etc., which it were tedious to enumerate, we gather that the number of planets is necessarily seven.[9]

Of course this strikes us as ridiculous, and we are likely to say, "That's what comes of employing analogies." But then, remembering Huygens' analogy, we might add: "at least we've got to be careful of *bad* analogies." But what is a bad analogy, and what a good one? What are analogies good for? What are the limits of their usefulness?

We can make a beginning by noticing that a very great deal of knowing and discovering consists in finding resemblances. Because these symptoms are very like the symptoms in a hundred other cases, the physician makes his diagnosis and his prognosis. By virtue of their having a similar bone structure, a group of animals are said to be "vertebrates." We try to decide whether Franco Spain is sufficiently similar to Mussolini Italy to be called a fascist state. And so on.

---

[8] Quoted by Philip Wheelwright, *The Way of Philosophy* (New York: The Odyssey Press, 1954), p. 149.

[9] Quoted in Susan Stebbing, *A Modern Introduction to Logic* (London: Methuen & Co., Ltd., 1930), p. 251.

Normally, however, we do not use the word "analogy" for that resemblance between objects or events that lumps them together as members of a single class, but reserve the word for the resemblance in certain attributes or relations between things which are quite definitely different in kind, as when we work out an analogy between wisdom and light or between life and a journey or between sub-atomic structure and the solar system.

For cognitive purposes, as we have seen, analogies may be leading or misleading, fruitful or barren, helpful or actually harmful. Analogies may be profitably employed (1) for explanation and (2) for suggesting hypotheses and providing tentative beliefs. They may be unprofitably employed when they are used (3) to establish or prove a point.

(1) Imagine a third grade teacher trying to think of a way of explaining to her class the meaning of "splitting the atom." Finally an analogy occurs to her and she says, "Splitting the atom is something like cracking an egg. If we want to use the energy which the egg contains, if we want to eat the egg so that it will nourish us, we must crack the shell. Well, the atom too has energy inside it and this energy can be released and used only when the atom is cracked or split." It may not be a very good analogy; still, for that age level the explanation might help. Its use is simply in communicating an idea difficult or impossible to get across by more literal explanation. On a more sophisticated level, an example may be taken from the physicist, Arthur S. Eddington, a master at popular exposition of difficult matter. In the course of urging that it is easy to exaggerate the extent to which scientific laws describe reality, he employs the analogy of an aged college bursar, whose only knowledge of the college consists of what he can infer from the debits and credits of his ledger books. We on the outside, of course, think that he can't learn very much in that way, certainly not much about courses and text

books and professors and students, but he is highly impressed with his neat and elegant accounts.[10]

Does the analogy end there? It can, if the reader can be counted on to supply the missing half, likening the bursar to the scientist, the entries in the account books to the comparisons explicitly made. An analogy *is* an analogy only if something is compared to something else, but the degree to which the analogues and their relations require spelling out will vary with the communicative situation.

(2) Forming analogies is a useful process not only for explaining knowledge already acquired, but also for facilitating the very acquisition of knowledge. Suppose it to occur to an anthropologist, meditating upon the nature of a certain matriarchal society, that it bears certain resemblances to a colony of ants. This analogy then opens up the *possibility* of further points of comparison; for instance, are there "drones" in the human group? Or one can imagine an ancient astronomer deciding that, since the planets are similar in their relation to the sun, they might well be similar in other respects too, such as each having a satellite like that of the earth. Again, a historian of the arts who had noticed a certain parallel in the development of painting and music, might be led to inquire whether there is any movement in music to correspond with surrealism. Now the point to notice in all this is that these are *hypotheses* suggested by observed resemblances. Whether the hypotheses are to be held true depends upon the ensuing verification. For a long while it was assumed that if light acts like waves in water, there must be some medium corresponding to water for the light to travel in. The notion of ether was invented. But a famous and crucial experiment by Michelson and Morley convinced most scientists that there is no such ether-medium. The hypothesis was a brilliant one, but in time it was disallowed by experimental trial.

10 See A. S. Eddington, *The Nature of the Physical World* (London: Cambridge University Press, 1928).

(3) This immediately suggests the fallacy of "*proof* from analogy." Analogies do not prove; they only suggest, more or less strongly. Thus, in the analogy which compares the planets with the "windows" of the head, the writer concluded that "the number of planets is necessarily seven." The "necessarily" is entirely unwarranted, not merely because this particular inference is false, but because from observed likenesses it never necessarily follows that there are further unobserved likenesses.

Of course, sometimes the necessary observations, the verification, is not easily effected, and yet even pending further investigation, we may feel that some analogies are stronger than others. What makes an analogy strong? In his *Dialogues Concerning Natural Religion*,[11] David Hume examined in great detail what is perhaps the most famous argument from analogy, the so-called teleological argument for the existence of a divinity. One of the characters expresses the argument as follows:

Look round the world: contemplate the whole and every part of it: you will find it to be nothing but one great machine, subdivided into an infinite number of lesser machines, which again admit of subdivisions, to a degree beyond what human sense and faculties can trace and explain. All these various machines, and even their most minute parts, are adjusted to each other with an accuracy, which ravishes into admiration all men who have ever contemplated them. The curious adapting of means to ends, throughout all nature, resembles exactly, though it much exceeds the productions of human contrivance; of human design, thought, wisdom, and intelligence. Since therefore the effects resemble each other, we are led to infer, by all the rules of analogy, that the causes also resemble; and that the Author of Nature is somewhat similar to the mind of men; though possessed of much larger faculties, proportioned to the grandeur of the work, which he has executed.

[11] David Hume *Dialogues Concerning Natural Religion* (New York: Oxford University Press, 1935).

Another character in the dialogue enters the dispute by discoursing on the nature of analogical argument:

That all inferences ... concerning fact, are founded on experience, and that all experimental reasonings are founded on the supposition that similar causes prove similar effects, and similar effects similar cause; I shall not, at present, much dispute with you. But observe, I entreat you, with what extreme caution all just reasoners proceed in the transferring of experiments to similar cases. Unless the cases be exactly similar, they repose no perfect confidence in applying their past observation to any particular phenomenon. Every alteration of circumstances occasions a doubt concerning the event; and it requires new experiments to prove certainly, that the new circumstances are of no moment or importance. A change in bulk, situation, arrangement, age, disposition of the air, or surrounding bodies; any of these particulars may be attended with the most unexpected consequences: And unless the objects be quite familiar to us, it is the highest temerity to expect with assurance, after any of these changes, an event similar to that which before fell under our observation. The slow and deliberate steps of philosophers, here, if anywhere, are distinguished from the precipitate march of the vulgar, who, hurried on by the smallest similitudes, are incapable of all discernment or consideration.

The disputants disagree, finally, not about the nature of argument from analogy, but about the impressiveness, the strength, of this particular analogy. And, of course the argument did not begin or end in the eighteenth century. Today there is still considerable disagreement about how strong this analogy is.

It is perhaps wise to make a distinction between the *quantity* and the *quality* of similarity in an analogy. We say, in general, that the *more* points of similarity there are between analogues, the better our inference that they are similar in other respects too. Still, two objects may be alike in a great many ways and different in only a few, where, nevertheless, the few are important and the many unimportant. Importance is partly a matter of relevance, that is, relevance of the observed similarities to the inferred similarities. This may be put schematically. Suppose we are arguing that since A and B are alike in respects p, q, r, and s, they are probably alike also in respect t. The argument will not be very strong if p, q, r, and s, are qualities *very* different from quality t; the similarities may be largely irrelevant to the point at issue. Here is a concrete example. If a Martian visitor having inspected an Abyssinian and an Eskimo, was so impressed with the observed fact that they both had but a single head with hair on top, both had two legs, two arms, and a great number of other anatomical features in common, went on to conclude that therefore there was a high probability that they both spoke the same language and enjoyed the same diet, we would object that language and diet, being acquired habits, have very little to do with gross anatomy. If on the other hand the Martian had concluded that there was a strong likelihood of the two persons' having similar internal organs, we would be more impressed with his scientific acumen, for aspects of anatomy are much more relevant to other aspects of anatomy than they are to something non-anatomical.

Our conclusion, then, is that analogies do not *prove* but that they may certainly suggest and explain. When they are employed persuasively, it is sometimes necessary to answer them persuasively. Brief mention may be made of four means of countering analogical arguments. First, it may be shown that the differences between the assumed analogues are even more extensive than the likenesses. Second, it may be shown that the displayed likenesses are not important or relevant to the assumed likenesses. Third, the analogy may be "turned." That is, it may be shown to have implications distinctly unfavorable to the purposes of its original employer. Thus, consider someone arguing as does a character in Plato's dialogue "Phaedo" that the soul of man may be likened to musical harmony, and in being thus immaterial, is immortal. But now an opponent may answer: "Don't you see that harmony is always dependent upon a musical instrument and if the instrument is broken, the harmony vanishes; in the same way, when the body dies the soul must die too." Finally an analogy may be met with another analogy which has contradictory implications. This latter device may be illustrated by a political debate. Suppose that one orator declares:

Electing Zilch would be like entrusting a battleship to a child in rompers. He has not had the training, the experience, the sheer know-how to do the job.

His opponent, of course, counters:

Putting Zilch into office will be like letting the fresh sea breezes into the foul and stagnant air of a building long occupied by a self-perpetuating, decaying gang.

Or, on a somewhat more serious level, there is the reply to Huygens' comparison of light to the waves in the water, that light is rather more like bullets being shot from a gun.

PROBLEMS FOR DISCUSSION

A. What are the grounds for saying that metaphor is essential to language?
B. Do you agree with Orwell that "The sole aim of a metaphor is to call up a visual image"? Explain.
C. Interpret and evaluate the several parts of R. P. Blackmur's statement about great poetry:
> The words sound with music, make images which are visual, seem solid like sculpture and spacious like architecture, repeat themselves like the movements in a dance, call for a kind of mummery in the voice when read, and turn upon themselves like nothing but the written word. (*Language As Gesture*, p. 12)
D. How effective are the figures in the following peroration: "We Americans have got to keep our eye on the ball, our shoulders to the wheel, our noses to the grindstone, and our feet on the ground, while with a stiff upper lip we swallow defeats and hitch our wagon to a star—come hell or high water, and let the chips fall where they may." Why? Explain each metaphor.

E. A society is like a ship, and a taut ship is a happy ship. Develop the analogy, and then discuss its merits and its limitations.

F. In the following sonnet of John Keats, which words are used in a non-literal sense? Are there any 'border-line cases'?

> CAT! who has pass'd thy grand climacteric,
>> How many mice and rats hast in thy days
>> Destroy'd?—How many tit bits stolen? Gaze
> With those bright languid segments green, and prick
> Those velvet ears—but pr'ythee do not stick
>> Thy latent talons in me—and upraise
>> Thy gentle mew—and tell me all thy frays
> Of fish and mice, and rats and tender chick.
> Nay, look not down, nor lick thy dainty wrists—
>> For all the wheezy asthma,—and for all
> Thy tail's tip is nick'd off—and though the fists
>> Of many a maid have given thee many a maul,
> Still is that fur as soft as when the lists
>> In youth thou enter'dst on glass bottled wall.

EXERCISES

I. Explain the point of the metaphorical usages in the following phrases by expanding the comparison intended.
1. a bestial act. (Note pronunciation.)
2. the right end snagged the pass.
3. get into a stew.
4. on thin ice.
5. being touchy.
6. thick-skinned.
7. numb-skull.
8. the turf of the gridiron.
9. in his cups.
10. dog days.
11. highly touted dancer.
12. ambidextrous.
13. heel.
14. independent as a hog on ice.
15. as fast as a scalded dog.

II.   Compose a paragraph in which you make use of an extended figure of speech for purposes of argument (e.g., the state as a ship with its political leader as a pilot at the helm running the shoals, etc.).

III.   Comment in detail on the metaphors, in the following, indicating the reasons for their effectiveness as against more literal language.

A VALEDICTION: FORBIDDING MOURNING

by John Donne

As virtuous men pass mildly away,
    And whisper to their souls, to go,
Whilst some of their sad friends do say,
    The breath goes now, and some say, no:

So let us melt, and make no noise,
    No tear-floods, nor sigh-tempests move,
T'were prophanation of our joys
    To tell the laity our love.

Moving of th'earth brings harms and fears,
    Men reckon what it did and meant,
But trepidation of the spheres,
    Though greater far, is innocent.

Dull sublunary lovers love
    (Whose soul is sense) cannot admit
Absence, because it doth remove
    Those things which elemented it.

But we by a love, so much refined,
    That ourselves know not what it is,
Inter-assured of the mind,
    Care less, eyes, lips and hands to miss.

Our two souls therefore, which are one
    Though I must go, endure not yet
A breach, but an expansion,
    Like gold to airy thinness beat.

If they be two, they are two so,
  As stiff twin compasses are two,
Thy soul, the fixed foot, makes no show
  To move, but doth, if th'other do.

And though it in the center sit,
  Yet when the other far doth roam,
It leans and hearkens after it,
  And grows erect, as that comes home.

Such wilt thou be to me, who must
  Like th'other foot, obliquely run;
Thy firmness draws my circle just,
  And makes me end, where I begun.

IV. Locate, transcribe, and analyze one example each of the following:
1. a needlessly figurative, misleading passage.
2. a prose passage in which the use of metaphor is commendable.

V. Thomas de Quincey has written:

There arises a case. . . . where the style cannot be regarded as a *dress* or alien covering, but where style becomes the *incarnation* of the thoughts. . . . Imagery is sometimes not the mere alien apparelling of a thought, and of a nature to be detached from the thought, but is the coefficient that, being superadded to something else, absolutely *makes* the thought.

Find one case in which it seems to you that this is so and explain why you think so, by indicating what in the thought would be lost if the style were to be changed.

VI. What is lost by the rewriting of these lines of poetry? Give as full an answer as possible.

I met a traveler from an antique land
Who said: Two vast and trunkless legs of stone
Stand in the desert. Near them, on the sand,
Half sunk a shattered visage lies, whose frown,
And wrinkled lip, and sneer of cold command,

Tell that its sculptor well those passions read
Which yet survive, stamped on these lifeless things,
The hand that mocked them and the heart that fed;
And on the pedestal these words appear:
"My name is Ozymandias, king of kings;
Look on my works, ye Mighty, and despair!"
Nothing beside remains. Round the decay
Of that colossal wreck, boundless and bare
The lone and level sands stretch far away. (Shelley.)

I ran into a tourist from overseas.
"A couple of big stony legs," he said,
"Are in the desert. On the ground near these
Is a half-buried, broken, frowning head
Whose dry, sneering lip says coldly, 'Please
Know that my chiseler knew the hate,
The expression, that lasts on these dead things.
His hand that teased, my heart that ate.'
And on the base these words are written:
'I am Ozymandias, best of kings,
See what I've done, you Great, and be smitten.'
There's not much more, except that around
Those big old stones, so weather-bitten
There's nothing but sand all over the ground."

VII. George Santayana has said that the poet is a "goldsmith in words." Explain his meaning.

VIII. How effective is the following argument?

Let me illustrate this with a simple metaphor. Let the child of low intelligence and weak natural endowments be represented by a pint container; and the child of extremely high endowments and intelligence, by a gallon container. According to the democratic concept of education, you must put into the pint container whatever kind of liquid you put into the gallon container, even though only one pint can go here and a gallon there. It will not do to put cream into the gallon container and, say, water—dirty water, at that—into the pint container. Vocational education is the dirty water we are now pouring into our pint containers. Liberal education is the cream we are giving the few. (from a lecture on Adult Education by Mortimer Adler.)

IX. Prepare a report on dream symbolism, either from folklore or from scientific psychological sources.

X. Is the following analogy effective? "Hunters do not shoot at large game with small cartridges. Do not hunt for a job without a large knowledge of the words of the English language." (Advertisement for a correspondence course.)

XI. Evaluate the several metaphors in Lafcadio Hearn's insistence that

words have colour, form, character. They have faces, parts, manners, gesticulations; they have moods, humours, eccentricities; they have tints, tones, personalities. I write for beloved friends who can see colour in words, can smell the perfume of syllables in blossom, can be shocked with the fine elfish eccentricity of words. And in the eternal order of things, words will eventually have their rights recognized by the people.

XII. John Mason Brown once said in a lecture:

The language is an instrument far older and mightier than any Stradivarius. It is forever at the disposal of those who can handle it, and in each age and in the hands of every writer who has mastered it, it has produced a very special and individual melody. ("The Apes and the Angels," *Saturday Review of Literature,* July 3, 1954.)

Try to devise another figure as effective as this one for revealing the power of language.

XIII. Consult a dictionary for the meanings of "fable," "apologue," "allegory," "analogy," "parable," "simile," "hyperbole," "metonymy," and "synecdoche."

XIV. Margaret Schlauch in *The Gift of Tongues* writes at length of "semantic rejuvenation" about which she says: ". . . some of the most abstract terms in the language are really faded metaphors. On examination it turns out that an earlier meaning, now forgotten, is often lively in the extreme. Hence an obvious means of invigorating our jejune vocabulary is to fall back on those lively older meanings." From the following examples of hers, look up the word italicized in each passage, and tell what older meaning or meanings the writer seems here to be rejuvenating.

1. Essential oils are wrung;
   The attar from the rose
   Is not *expressed* by suns alone
   It is the gift of screws. (Emily Dickinson)

2. "Season thy *admiration* for a while with an attent ear." (Shakespeare)

3. "Thou hast no *speculation* in those eyes." (Shakespeare)

4. "Streets that follow like a tedious argument
   Of *insidious intent*
   To lead you to an overwhelming question." (T. S. Eliot)

SOURCES AND ADVANCED READING

1. Ernst Cassirer, *Language and Myth*. New York and London: Harper Brothers, 1946.
2. Monroe C. Beardsley, *Thinking Straight*. New York: Prentice-Hall, Inc., 1950. Ch. IV.
3. Cleanth Brooks and Robert Penn Warren, *Modern Rhetoric*. New York: Harcourt, Brace and Company, 1949. Ch. XI.
4. Robert H. Thouless, *Straight and Crooked Thinking*. New York: Simon and Schuster, 1932. Ch. XII.
5. I. A. Richards, *Philosophy of Rhetoric*. London: Oxford University Press, 1936.
6. L. Susan Stebbing, *A Modern Introduction to Logic*. London: Methuen & Co., Ltd., 1930.
7. R. P. Blackmur, *Language As Gesture*. New York: Harcourt, Brace and Company, 1952.
8. Margaret Schlauch, *The Gift of Tongues*. New York: Modern Age Books, 1942.

IX

THE LANGUAGE

OF CONCERTED ACTION

Reasons for Belief and Argued Persuasion • What Attitude Shall We Take toward Persuasion? • Persuasive Language • Some Persuasive Fallacies

---

REASONS FOR BELIEF AND ARGUED PERSUASION

Ideas or propositions may be *entertained, asserted,* or *argued.* To entertain a proposition is merely to notice it, to hold it before one, to consider it. To be able to entertain an idea independent of belief is one of the marks of the educated man. To assert a proposition is to affirm or to deny its truth. To argue it is to assert it with reasons. Simple illustrations are:

> That it is going to rain. (Entertained.)
> It is going to rain. (Asserted.)
> It is going to rain because the
>   barometer is falling. (Argued.)

Persuasion may be argued or unargued. By "unargued persuasion" is here meant that which advances no reasons. The gangster's blackjack is sometimes, with grim humor, called "the silent persuader." And there are many other types of forceful persuasion where the "Do this!" or "Believe that!" is backed up by power. Wheedling—the child's "Oh, come on ... n ... n ... n"—in all of its variants is unargued persuasion too. A great deal of advertising and political campaigning proceeds without the show of reasons: "Try Doxall!" "Vote straight Republicrat!" Still another kind of unargued persuasion is the claim to self-evidence. To be sure, if a proposition is seen to be self-evident, its persuasive power is irresistible, but there is a long history of doctrines which have appeared to some people as self-evident and to others not only as lacking self-evidence but as downright false. Even the geometric axioms of Euclid have been taken by many mathematicians of the last hundred years not as obvious truths but only as postulates—that is, as propositions *assumed* for certain purposes to be true.

In logic, the word "argument" means, not as it sometimes does in common parlance a quarrel or even a disagreement, but only an assertion backed up by reasons. There are good and bad arguments, measured both in terms of sheer effectiveness and in terms of the objective adequacy of the reasons, but reasons of some sort there must be. Argued persuasion, then, is the attempt to induce belief by means of assertions and their supporting reasons.

(1) *Appeal to Authority.* Here the reasons cited for belief are that such and such respected persons or institutions endorse the given assertion. A great many of the beliefs of every one of us are based on the testimony of authorities. The following list is only a sampling suggestive of the variety of authorities to which appeal is commonly made:

Webster's New International Dictionary makes the "a" short in "inanity."

Robert Montgomery says, "I smoke Luckies because they taste better."

Einstein taught that the velocity of light is constant.

The Gallup Poll recently revealed that fewer than one quarter of American adults can name even one prophet mentioned in the Old Testament.

The Bible tells us that the meek will inherit the earth.

Shakespeare said, "The play's the thing."

The New York Drama Critics Circle voted Tennessee Williams'
play the best of the season.

Of course, the respected authorities may not be famous;
the testimony of a parent, teacher, elder, employer, or friend
may be impressive in certain cases.

What can be said about the logical worth of appeal to
authority? Perhaps the best answer can be made out by a
series of questions:

(a) Is the authority rightly quoted? It was not Shakespeare
in his own person, but his character Hamlet who said, "The
play's the thing...." and what he said was "The play's the
thing/Wherein I'll catch the conscience of the king."

(b) Is the authority testifying in a field where he is
genuinely competent? Einstein in discussing light was, of
course, entirely within the area of his special ability; on
politics his opinions would not necessarily have the same
weight. Robert Montgomery may be a fine judge of acting
ability without thereby qualifying as an expert on tobacco.

(c) Is the authority supported by other authorities in the
same field, especially recent ones? Galen was doubtless a
great physician for his time, but his advocacy of bloodletting
is not substantiated by the findings of modern medical
authorities. The psychologist Carl Jung may be cited in
behalf of a belief in "racial memories," but other psychologists sharply disagree.

(d) Does the authority have a record of success and recognized achievement? Sometimes we are rightly suspicious of
the "pedigree" of someone quoted as an authority: "eminent
skin specialist," "internationally recognized consultant," "a
man who has appeared before the crowned heads of Europe"
—and other such vague identifications scarcely establish the
prestige of an authority. On the other hand, one would be
inclined to repose much confidence in a judgment within his
own field of a person known to be a Professor of Astronomy

at Harvard University or the head of a research laboratory of General Electric.

Of course, the testimony of the best established expert in the world does not constitute a guarantee of the truth of a given assertion, but since we must take some matters on authority, we try to choose our authorities with the best possible discrimination.

(2) *Commonsensical Experience.* The second of the types of reason which may be persuasively urged in behalf of a belief need not long detain us. It differs from authority in being direct experience; it differs from science in being "everyday," ordinary. It consists in testimony based upon personal observation:

I saw the movie myself and it's a good one.
Don't forget that I spent two years in Germany, so I know what
    I'm talking about.
Seeing is believing.
I'm from Missouri: show me!

Of course when I ask another person to accept my observations, I am asking him to accept me as an authority, but when it is a question of forming my own beliefs, my own experience is likely to count very heavily. Still, it is part of reasonableness to recognize one's own capacity for distortion, prejudice, hasty generalization. What each of us sees is to an important degree determined by what we already believe, a sobering truth long in the possession of homely wisdom, but impressively documented by recent social psychology. What we have ourselves experienced may, nevertheless, not have happened, or not have happened as we supposed. After all, Chicken Little thought the sky was falling and strongly testified: "I saw it with my eyes, I heard it with my ears, and a piece of it fell on my tail!"

(3) *Scientific Induction.* Without any serious doubt, one of the chief differences between this and previous ages consists in the scientific predisposition today of so large a proportion

of the population. It is not meant by this that most persons are themselves practicing scientists, but only that even laymen tend to withhold their belief from propositions which they consider inadequately based on scientific grounds. More and more we want to know what the evidence is and how it was acquired. In fields where, only yesterday, rumor, gossip, and everyday observation held sway, there are today masses of ordered and quantified data.

It is here impossible to do more than very briefly indicate some of the principal features of scientific induction. Four such features may be noted:

(a) *Public Empirical Verification.* The scientist forms hypotheses, that is tentative answers to his problems, which he then subjects to carefully controlled tests by experiment and observation. Always his claim is that his answers are objective in the sense that they do not reflect the personality of the investigator but only the nature of the facts. Any other competent observer would get like results in like circumstances.

(b) *Fallibility.* Although some scientific laws are supported by such a great quantity of evidence that it strains the imagination to think of their ever being wholly supplanted, it remains a characteristic of all scientific knowledge that it makes no claim to being absolute and final. Always it is subject to correction and even overthrow when new evidence arises. Another way of saying this is that the sciences tend to be less "self-protective" and "defensive" than other ways of knowing; scientific advances are made not only by substantiating new theories, but also by upsetting old ones.

(c) *Quantification.* The sciences typically aim at exact measurement, quantification, statistical treatment of the data, and the employment of mathematical formulae for expressing relationships.

(d) *Abstractness and Systematization.* Scientists are always uneasy at the possession of merely *odd* facts, or results which, however well substantiated themselves, do not find a place within some larger whole. The scientist typically pushes toward more and more comprehensive laws and systems within which all his special results can be accommodated.

When propositions advanced for our acceptance are scientifically backed, we, in this great age of science, are likely to be impressed and persuaded. Still, anything with so much prestige is almost certain to be exploited: not all that comes bearing the label "scientific" *is* scientific, not all scientific "truth" is true. And, unless the word "science" is defined in an implausibly broad way, by no means is all knowledge scientific.

(4) *Rational Deduction.* Sometimes we are asked to believe a proposition not so much because it agrees with observed facts about the world, but because it *follows from* accepted truths. If lead is heavier than gold and gold is heavier than aluminum, then it follows that lead is heavier than aluminum. If the library is always closed on Sunday and if this is Sunday, it follows that the library is closed today. If in arithmetical addition the order of the integers is insignificant, then $3+5 = 5+3$.

In pure rational deduction, the premises are taken as *given,* that is as not themselves in question within this context. Then the deductive question is: on the assumption that these premises are true, what else can be concluded? Even if it happens that the premises are untrue, still there may be logical consequences. If butter costs a nickel a pound and if Mrs. Jones buys three pounds, we can without great labor decide how much she has to spend, even though all the while something in us whispers that butter is not that cheap. If all swans are white and if all white birds are mammals, then it may be inferred that all swans are mammals; the inference is logically sound, even though both premises are false. It is not the case, as is sometimes thought, that if the premises are false, the conclusion logically drawn from them will always be false also. From the two false propositions, Dwight Eisenhower is an admiral and all admirals are Republicans, there follows by strict logic the true proposition that Dwight Eisenhower is a Republican. But if the premises are true and the logical deduction is sound, the conclusion will also be true; on this rule rests the whole claim to rational knowledge.

WHAT ATTITUDE SHALL WE TAKE TOWARD PERSUASION?

We live under an almost constant barrage of persuasion, some of it professional, ranging in import from the most trivial gossip to life-or-death matters. No one utterly fails to evaluate incitements; no one is fooled all the time and no one fails to be fooled some of the time. But it does not follow from this that everyone is equally gullible or equally rational or equally cynical. Indeed we all make distinctions among our acquaintances: some are easy marks, forever being "taken in," susceptible to every new inducement, showing themselves to be "suckers," lacking in sales resistance; others are doubting Thomases, "hard nuts to crack," suspicious of all claims, skeptical of the motivations of anyone who indulges in persuasion. There is a third group: those who are hard to convince, those who in important matters examine the evidence, those who are willing to replace an initial skepticism with conviction, as support for a position increases. But again, any one person tends to differ in his degree of rationality with respect to different subjects. The tough-minded astronomer may be irrational in religious argument; the scrupulous logician may be incurably prejudiced on questions of racial superiority; the hard-headed business man may be a "sucker" for any appeal to the sanctity of the home. And there is no panacea for these kinds of ills, no set of rules which guarantee rationality, and no assurance apart from rationality that Truth will prevail.

But to speak of possible responses to persuasion—rational or otherwise—is, of course, to stress the passive side, the role of the listener. Let us not belittle the positive side nor miss the creative function of persuasion in human society. First comes doing, and then come evaluation and criticism. Who will board the Ferris wheel of leadership? Who will take the world on his shoulders? Or like the Prophets, tell it which way is good, and which evil?

For if working together is important, then persuasion is also. The fact is that we men live no more by the grace of nature than we do by the grace of our fellow men. We have expressive and rapportive needs, and a need for information about how to eke out our existence. But the more important fact, if we may be permitted a philosophical and socio-logical observation, is that institutions are social—and in the end they consist of *attitudes of mind* of individual persons. Property, for example, is an institution, and it rests on a voluntary but enforceable determination by all people except the owner not to trespass. Human attitudes are more sub-stantial and enduring than stone walls: it is not the wall alone, but the jailer, that keeps the prisoner in his cell. Reflect on these matters, and then you will grasp the really profound importance of persuasion.

It is not so surprising that, statistically, a great deal of our talking and writing should be persuasive in aim. The child begins wheedling before he is out of the cradle. We are forever trying to get somebody to do or refrain from doing something or at least to do it our way. One may even have to give himself a good talking to now and then, or so formulate his task in words that it will look bearable and feasible. The reader's attention is drawn again in this connection to what was said about language as social in Chapters III and VII. The dynamic forms of human life are penetrated through and through with linguistic structure. From the rough marching songs of infantrymen and the soulful work-chants of boatmen and gandy dancers to the careful transmission of information in a laboratory of microbiology, language enables or assists enterprise to be thoroughly *joint* enterprise.

Reciprocity and mutual dependence have climaxed in the division of labor, or 'complex cooperation,' of the present day. Human actions are analyzed, dissected, mechanized, and then transferred to machines that are electronically self-controlled. Language becomes specialized, technical, esoteric; but still it is required to perform social and economic functions that are ever more difficult and abstruse. In the industrialized urban community, nothing can be left to chance; in contemporary human relationships, little can be taken for granted; communication is no longer stable, instinctive, and implicit, but everything has to be explicit and *said*.[1] Communicative procedures must be clearly and distinctly stated, and read and understood. How do you say it? How can we get them to understand it? To see it our way? To do it?

Now where so much activity is both reasoned and cooperative, where the individual is counted upon for spontaneous performance and initiative, as in modern society, there persuasion is at once imperative and hard and subtle. "Persuasion is the civilized substitute for harsh authority and ruthless force."[2] If the individual is not to be forced, he will need to be persuaded on his own terms and in his own tongue; and *his* tongue reflects his trade and skill, his interests, and his prestige and position in the social hierarchy. The individual will be free to resist, too, and he will on occasion take his turn at persuading you, the persuader. Ideally, communication is close to work and people and is reciprocal; "the essence of the open atmosphere of communication is frequent face-to-face contact."[3] A good communicator is democratic to the core; he is well-informed; and he is imaginative, especially in the sense that he can quickly grasp another man's point of view. In such a communicator, persuasiveness is hardly distinguishable from listening, replying, and helping.

[1] See the contrast of urban with small community relationships and communications in Baker Brownell, *The College and the Community* (New York: Harper & Bros., 1952), Ch. XII, "Contacts and Communications."

[2] Robert T. Oliver, *Persuasive Speaking, Principles and Methods* (New York: Longmans, Green and Co., 1950), p. 1.

[3] Edmund P. Learned, David N. Ulrich, and Donald R. Booz, *Executive Action* (Boston: Harvard University, Graduate School of Business Administration, 1951), p. 114.

So great is the practical importance of concerted action, that persuasion overflows all the usual forms of discourse. The use of non-incitive forms of discourse to persuade is not only legitimate but even inevitable. The listener ought therefore to be cautious and critical but not hypercritical. Every man should know the devices of rhetoric from the inside out, and the forms that persuasion can take, both in order to get along well with other people and work for the right as he sees it, and in order to understand better that which he listens to, and the motives behind it.

PERSUASIVE LANGUAGE

Persuasion may be couched in any form whatsoever: questions, exclamations, commands, declarations; elegant, polite, vernacular, or vulgar discourse; language highly rational or blatantly emotional. Its outward dress may be not only incitive, but rapportive, informative, expressive, or evocative.

(1) There are, of course, sentences in typically incitive form, the pure persuasive discourse of signs like "Verboten!" or "No Spitting!" and the commands of drill instructors. The child's "Gimme," and "Gimme that," and "Stop," and his pleading "Please, oh, please. ..." These openly incitive forms are effective on certain kinds of occasions, for example, in formal situations like "Come in" in response to a knock on the door, or like "Don't feed the animals" in the zoo; or in sudden emergencies, like "Cheese it, the cops!" or, wherever repetition of the expression is frequent. This third sort of incitive discourse is common in advertising ("Drink Coke!" "Eat Wheaties!") where its effectiveness rests less on its being said than on its being said again and again. For it is true to a limited extent that if you do not succeed in persuading at once, you should try it again, and you may then say it in the same words (exact repetition), or in different words (restatement).

The imperative or incitive form is used with great frequency, but we may sometimes question whether it is very successful. Is it not used more often to commence, to cue, to summarize, or even to command, than to persuade? Persuasion lies *behind* these "imperatives"—in authority or force —rather than *in* them. In itself, "See America first," may be no more persuasive than "See Tasmania first"; but the former summarizes a "patriotic" creed, while the latter is flat or even evokes the sadness of distance. The incitive form in itself is, in the point of view of persuasion, nothing more than the device of *direct suggestion*. Unless couched in loaded words, a direct suggestion is no more reason for doing something than the child's "just because," and it can appear arbitrary or even arrogant. "The more *indirect* the suggestion, the more it can be made to be an original determination or plan or conclusion on the part of the listener, the greater its dynamic power." [4]

(2) "Rapportive" language is essential to persuasion. Everyone is acquainted with stereotyped pictures of the politician hand-shaking, back-slapping, and baby-kissing, and of the college president smiling, awarding honorary degrees, and all the time trying to win money for his institution. But rapport in communication is much more justifiable than some criticism would allow. To succeed in establishing rapport or really to be ingratiating requires sensitivity and the ability to seize on the hearer's perspective. But the power to take the perspective of the listener cannot be achieved without sedulous cultivation; it is a major achievement and certainly a rare one.

"Rapportive" language is important in connection with persuasion because rapport is important. Identification of interest and of fundamental purpose and outlook is essential to cooperation. "A suggestion that can be phrased so as to be congruent with the need of people to identify with or be in harmony with other people will be more readily accepted

[4] H. L. Hollingworth, *The Psychology of the Audience* (New York: American Book Company, 1935), p. 142. Italics added.

than one that neglects these considerations.[5] Naturally, a suasive speaker is expected to establish bonds between himself and his listener, and a suasive writer between himself and his reader. The very choice of expressions to be used may be affected by considerations of rapport. Groups of all kinds treasure and guard their characteristic modes of expression. The Boy Scouts, the Girl Scouts, the Marines, and M.D.'s, all take a certain pride in their special, esoteric language. Members of the VFW find a wry pleasure in calling one another "Comrade," and if someone by error thought it sounded bolshevik, the joke would be on him. So when you address the convention of a labor organization, it is proper to speak the language of laboring people. You may speak there, not of temerity, but of guts; on the other hand, before an organization of middle-class women, your language would have to be more "discreet."

(3) Language that purports to be expressive may intend to persuade. The casual expression of scorn, for example, is a well-worn way of directing children away from undesirable places and actions. The expression of confidence is a way of cheering your neighbors; confidence begets confidence. Men who have positive personalities speak in an honest, earnest way and carry us with them. Such men are rare, even among major executives. "The only exceptions will be those few men, or perhaps the single man, at the top, who have so well consolidated their own position, in terms of prestige and operating autonomy, that they feel profoundly sure they can no longer be budged." [6] *They* express confidence.

(4)   I never saw a wild thing
        sorry for itself.
        A small bird will drop frozen dead from a bough
        without ever having felt sorry for itself.[7]

[5] David Krech and Richard S. Crutchfield, *Theory and Problems of Social Psychology* (New York: McGraw-Hill Book Company, 1948), p. 363.

[6] Learned, Ulrich, and Booz, *op. cit.*, p. 58.

[7] D. H. Lawrence, "Self-Pity," in *Pansies: Poems* (New York: Alfred A. Knopf, 1929), p. 64.

There is a sense, then, in which the poet is persuasive, deeply persuasive. There are even those who hold the extreme view that the literal function of the arts is to persuade. The effects of Zola's novels and of *Uncle Tom's Cabin* are often mentioned. The typical atrocity story—to sink to a still lower literary level—seeks to evoke a picture that will lead to action. But D. H. Lawrence said: "The essential function of art is moral. Not aesthetic, not decorative, not pastime and recreation. But moral. The essential function of art is moral. . . . A morality which changes the blood rather than the mind. Changes the blood first." [8]

Evocative or imaginative forms are effective because they change the blood first. "For to be eloquent," wrote Quintillian a long time ago, "is to be nothing else than able to set forth all the lively images you have conceived in your mind, and to convey them to the hearers with the same rich coloring, without which all precepts we have given are useless like a sword concealed and kept hidden in the scabbard." [9]

Where actual instances or samples cannot be exhibited, imaginative presentation may furnish a good substitute—or may be much better than the actual instances. The advent of TV permits an approximation to direct and dramatic presentation. The satisfaction of the smoker can be seen on his face on the screen.

The magazine advertisements of the tourist agencies of foreign countries aim to evoke a landscape, or a picture of life over there. The point is to arouse a dream, a desire, where argumentative persuasion would seem irrelevant and perhaps dull or annoying.

Dramatization of ideas is the technique of casting abstract ideas into vivid, concrete forms, turning them into *people* who depict them in sensory form and make them act and clash. The Polio Foundation every year appeals to our sym-

[8] D. H. Lawrence, *Studies in Classic American Literature* (New York: Albert & Charles Boni, 1930), p. 254.
[9] *Institutes of the Orator*, Vol. II, Bk. 8.

pathy, for example, by choosing some child to symbolize the rich, human results of our contribution.

Then there is the famous and successful advertisement:

THEY LAUGHED WHEN I SAT DOWN
AT THE PIANO
BUT WHEN I STARTED TO PLAY!—

Arthur had just played "The Rosary."

The room rang with applause. I decided that this would be a dramatic moment for me to make my debut. To the amazement of all my friends, I strode confidently over to the piano and sat down.

"Jack is up to his old tricks," somebody chuckled. The crowd laughed. They were certain that I couldn't play a note.

"Can he really play?" I heard a girl whisper to Arthur.

"Heavens, no," Arthur exclaimed. "He never played a note in all his life. . . ."

I decided to make the most of the situation. With mock dignity I drew out a silk handkerchief and lightly dusted off the piano keys. Then I rose and gave the revolving piano stool a quarter of a turn as I had seen an imitator of Paderewski do in a vaudeville sketch.

"What do you think of his execution?" called a voice from the rear.

"We're in favor of it!" came back the answer, and the crowd rocked with laughter.

Then I started to play.

Instantly a tense silence fell on the guests. The laughter died on their lips as if by magic. I played through the first few bars of Beethoven's immortal "Moonlight Sonata." I heard gasps of amazement. My friends sat breathless— spellbound.

I played on, and as I played, I forgot the people around me. I forgot the hour, the place, the breathless listeners. The little world I lived in seemed to fade—seemed to grow dim— unreal. Only the music was real. Only the music and visions it brought me. Visions as beautiful and as changing as the wind-blown clouds and drifting moonlight that long ago inspired the master composer.

At this point it is a strong man indeed who can resist the charm of the "Ten easy lessons" clincher.

Perhaps the evocation of the HERO—inviting identification—explains the success of the following famous box advertisement in pulling answers from all over England:

Men wanted for Hazardous Journey. Small wages, bitter cold, long months of complete darkness, constant danger, safe return doubtful. Honor and recognition in case of success.—Sir Ernest Shackleton.[10]

Since character and psychology enter so manifestly into persuasion both as means and as ends, or targets, the persuader is one of the best customers of the psychologist. He is interested in fixing and changing belief and in the whole psychology of conviction. It was Lew Sarett who said in his classes that "Persuasion is the study of the methods whereby a speaker may induce an individual or an audience to do a thing by *implanting a wish* to do it by driving at some deep hunger, instincts, emotions or habits or by making use of any psychological force to intensify that wish." We should not allow ourselves to be biased or deluded by the fact that the present book is about language and the logic of meaning. Persuasion is *not* just language and logic. Persuasion bears on beliefs and on the actions that derive from beliefs; it naturally involves us in psychology, sociology, literature, and other studies of human nature.

The persuader should be deeply respectful of the subtlety and depth of human personality, both in himself and in his audience. The persuader as such has no arbitrary authority. He moves his audience by the arousal of desire, the evocation of nobility and intelligence, and the manifestation of character. As the copy in the piano playing ad indicates, *character* may be even more impelling than social success;

[10] Advertisement appearing in the London *Times* in 1900. Requoted—as is the one above—from Robert L. Heilbroner, "Where are the ads of yesteryear?" *Harper's Magazine*, Vol. 206 (June, 1953), pp. 93 and 95.

for the piano player finally makes an easy ascension and transcends the everyday world of praise and social reward altogether.

There are famous cases of individual power over mobs and crowds: Spinoza calmly greeting and subduing the mob which came to lynch him, Melvin Traylor, President of the First National Bank of Chicago, speaking from the balcony to stop a run on the Bank. We repeat a tale from the *Autobiography* of John Stuart Mill. When Mill ran for Parliament from Westminster, with backing from labor, an opponent had a placard printed of a quotation from Mill's pamphlet, "Thoughts on Parliamentary Reform." The quoted passage was to the effect that "the working classes in England, though differing from those of some other countries, in being ashamed of lying, are yet generally liars." The placard was handed to Mill at a meeting chiefly composed of workers, and Mill was asked whether he had written and published it.

I at once answered, 'I did.' Scarcely were these two words out of my mouth, when vehement applause resounded through the whole meeting. It was evident that the working people were so accustomed to expect equivocation and evasion from those who sought their suffrages, that when they found, instead of that, a direct avowal of what was likely to be disagreeable to them, instead of being affronted, they concluded at once that this was a person whom they could trust.[11]

The confidence of the audience is what every speaker, writer, and journalist most wants. If the abiding confidence of his audience is once won, then time can be saved in putting across 'subordinate' points. The expert *is* evidence for a proposition. As everyone knows, people tend to make up their minds in blanket fashion as to what kind of policy to follow; then they buy, for example, the daily newspaper that follows that policy. This loyal following—this monopoly over a segment of public opinion—is the secret wish of every publisher.

[11] *Autobiography*, Ch. VII.

Before we altogether leave the topic of evocation, we should remark that evocation may serve the interests of science and scientific method. Why should we prefer the scientific method over the methods of intuition and authority? The American philosopher Charles Peirce answered by evoking the picture of a chivalrous bridegroom:

The genius of a man's logical method should be loved and reverenced as his bride, whom he has chosen from all the world. He need not condemn the others; on the contrary, he may honour them deeply, and in doing so he only honours her the more. But she is the one he has chosen, and he knows that he was right in making that choice. And having made it, he will work and fight for her, and will not complain that there are blows to take, hoping that there may be as many and as hard to give, and will strive to be the worthy knight and champion of her from the blaze of whose splendours he draws his inspiration and his courage.[12]

And to be fully honest, we must yet add that "science" in turn can serve the persuasive use of evocation. Scientific advance and wide acceptance of scientific method in modern industry, plus the transfer of laboratory principles to education, have helped create the stereotype of "the educated man" as a thorough, methodical problem-solver. This inclusion of reasoning power at the heart of our "educated man" concept is termed by some authors the "idealization of the rational."[13] Since most people prefer to think of themselves as reasonable and critical, you can flatter (or compliment) an audience by allowing it to identify itself with the "educated man" stereotype.

(5) Most people are very firmly convinced that informative discourse is inherently superior to incitive and evocative discourse.

The feeling against persuasion and the devices of rhetoric

[12] Charles Sanders Peirce, "The Fixation of Belief." Originally published in *Popular Science Monthly* in 1877.

[13] Winston Lamont Brembeck and William Smiley Howell, *Persuasion, A Means of Social Control* (New York: Prentice-Hall, Inc., 1952), p. 128.

is ancient. At his trial, Socrates scorned (or *said* he scorned) to use any non-informative language in defending himself. "One who has reached my years, and who has a name for wisdom ought not to demean himself." [14] He said that the duty of the judge was not to make a present of justice, but to give judgment; and Socrates would not stoop to begging and crying, and producing his children in court.

Montaigne called rhetoric "a tool invented for handling and stirring up a mob and an unruly community; and it is a tool," he said, "that is only employed for sick states, like medicine. . . ." [15]

David Hume's description of the role of eloquence in human affairs is so cool that some will find it cynical.

Disputes are multiplied, as if everything was uncertain, and these disputes are managed with the greatest warmth, as if everything was certain. Amidst all this bustle 'tis not reason which gains the prize but eloquence; and no man need ever despair of gaining proselytes to the most extravagant hypothesis, who has art enough to represent it in any favourable colours. The victory is not gained by the men at arms, who manage the pike and sword; but by the trumpeters, drummers, and musicians of the army.[16]

Plato and Socrates were willing to admit the eloquence inherent in truth. A man must be able to know and define and denote the subjects of which he is speaking, and to discern the natures of those whom he is addressing. But then the persuader is more than rhetorician; and we read, near the end of the *Phaedrus:*

Socrates: And now the play is played out; and of rhetoric enough. Go and tell Lysias that we went down to the fountain and school of the Nymphs, and were bidden by them to convey a message to him and to other composers of speeches—to Homer and other writers of poems, whether set to music or not; and to Solon and

14 Plato, *Apology.* Jowett translation.
15 "Of the Vanity of Words."
16 David Hume, *Treatise of Human Nature,* Introduction. The truth of the last quoted sentence is actualized in psychological warfare.

others who have composed writings in the form of political discourses which they would term laws—to all of them we are to say
that if their compositions are based on knowledge of the truth,
and they can defend or prove them, when they are put to the
test, by spoken arguments, which leave their writings poor in
comparison of them, then they are to be called, not only poets,
orators, legislators, but are worthy of a higher name, befitting the
serious pursuit of their life.

Phaedrus: What name would you assign to them?

Socrates: Wise, I may not call them; for that is a great name
which belongs to God alone,—lovers of wisdom or philosophers
is their modest and befitting title.[17]

Our own view, like that of Aristotle, is that fair-minded
and intelligent men owe it to themselves and to society to
understand and use persuasion. A good case could be made
out for the opinion that Socrates himself was far from neglectful of rhetoric. Socrates' persuasion is often on a metaphysical
level—but it is still persuasion, and his metaphysical truth
is sometimes—in our eyes—an expression of his sense of
values rather than the absolute which he believes it to be.
It could be compared in this respect with the "scientific"
dialectic of Karl Marx, which now appears more rhetorical
than scientific; the word "scientific" is laudatory and serves
goals of suasion.

Some of those who today would model other discourse on
the language of science seem to forget that the latter has been
deliberately sterilized and specialized, and hence is by no
means adaptable to every human purpose. Scientific language
is deliberately rendered colorless in order to express un-
colored kinds of truth. But the vernacular is venerable and
colorful—the language of working and living together. The
vernacular can hardly fail to incite, whatever forms it may
superficially assume: it has grown with and from our daily
practical activities. One reason why incitement does so often
appear in informative dress is that in the activities of the

---

[17] Plato, *Phaedrus*. Jowett translation (adapted).

tribe, *instruction, challenge,* and *doing* are all taking place together.

The fact is that the main function of language is not to express thought, not to duplicate mental processes, but rather to play an active pragmatic part in human behavior. Thus in its primary function it is one of the chief cultural forces and an adjunct to bodily activities. Indeed, it is an indispensable ingredient of all concerted human action.[18]

Appeals to the heart, to custom, and to our better judgment are often only analytically distinguishable. People are not quite so confused and gullible as Holden Caulfield thought: "All you have to do is say something nobody understands and they'll do practically anything you want them to." Neither are people intellectual machines entirely determined on rational grounds. But sometimes a plain old sound argument may be very effective persuasively. Brembeck and Howell relate a student testimonial. When beginning to study persuasion, the student had little faith in the persuasive powers of reasoned discourse. But later on he said, "I am amazed to find that when you advance primarily emotional appeal you have to keep 'pushing' it all the time, but if you do a good job of building a logical argument you can sit back and relax; it will stand by itself!" [19]

According to Dean McBurney, the changing pattern of communication in America

is characterized by a growing emphasis on logical values in place of high pressure mumbo-jumbo: by simple, direct statement rather than verbal obfuscation; and by a sense of relativity in language usage in place of arbitrary, dogmatic assertion. These changes are inevitable in a democratic society which is becoming more conscious of the processes of communication and more sophisticated in their use.[20]

---

[18] Bronislaw Malinowski, *Coral Gardens and Their Magic* (New York: American Book Company, 1935), Vol. II, p. 7.

[19] Brembeck and Howell, *op. cit.*, p. 130.

[20] James H. McBurney, "The Plight of the Conservative in Public Discussion." *The Quarterly Journal of Speech.* Vol. 36, No. 2 (April, 1950), p. 167.

SOME PERSUASIVE FALLACIES

Mention has been made in passing of such spurious persuasive devices as the citation of dubious authorities, the over-reliance upon personal experience, the disguising of superstition as science, and the exaggeration of most claims to "self-evidence." Without attempting to give a complete catalogue of fallacious persuasion, mention may be made of five other common forms of persuading by deception: the Loaded Question, the All-or-none Statement, the True-because-not-disproved Claim, Rationalization, and Redundant Argument.

(1) Suppose a politician affirmed, "Many people are dissatisfied with the present administration." How many people are "many"? How dissatisfied is "dissatisfied"? Partly because of this kind of vagueness and partly because of the opaque relationship that holds between what people do and what they say, election pollsters must be ever so careful in framing their questions. The pollsters need to know the extent of dissatisfaction among the voters.

In *The Art of Asking Questions,* Stanley L. Payne [21] reports replies as follow to the question, "Do you think most manufacturing companies that lay off workers during slack periods could arrange things to avoid layoffs and give steady work right through the year?"

> 63% said companies could avoid layoffs,
> 22% said companies could not avoid layoffs, while
> 15% had no opinion.

But when the alternative was stated explicitly, and not just implied, "Do you think most manufacturing companies that lay off workers in slack periods could avoid layoffs and provide steady work right through the year, or do you think layoffs are unavoidable?"

[21] Stanley L. Payne, *The Art of Asking Questions* (Princeton: Princeton University Press, 1951), pp. 7-8. Notice that persuasion *may* here be double barrelled: first the answerers are persuaded by the loaded question and then by the results of the poll used persuasively by a politician.

35% said companies could avoid layoffs,
41% said layoffs are unavoidable, and
24% had no opinion.

Consider then the naïvete and looseness of questions like "Does he like to read?" "Does he like to argue?" "Is he moral?" These questions albeit vague still invite yes or no answers. If they receive them, then a double wrong has been committed. The questions are too vague to warrant answers. The answers, if taken to mean anything at all, contain the All or Nothing Fallacy.

(2) The All-or-Nothing Fallacy lies in insistence on contradictories or contraries where less stringent contrasts are in order. To insist that an object is black or white is to overlook gray and the entire color range between white and black. The Fallacy is committed or elicited in expressions such as the following:

You are either for us or against us.
Business is business.
Make up your mind right now.
It's a smear.

How easy to say "Jack is stupid!" or "Jim is intelligent." We sharply divide the members of our fraternity and even of our own family into the intelligent and the unintelligent without corresponding clarity of meaning. Yet many expert examiners in universities and elsewhere say, "All an IQ tells you is what score someone made on a certain test." In general, the more expert one is in testing and judging capabilities, the more skeptical he is in respect to the scope and significance of intelligence measurement. A simple bifurcation of mankind into intelligent and unintelligent is hasty nonsense. And in fact the man in the street does not use the word "intelligent" to signify the same qualities in blacksmiths, card sharks, accountants, entrepreneurs, chorus girls, jockeys, and preachers. Common contraries of intelligence include slowness to absorb intellectual content, insensitivity to beauty, insensibility to human pain and pleasure, inability to care for one's self in minor, practical ways, absence of a habit of thrift or of saving, provincialism (or cosmopolitanism), awkwardness, etc. In declaring someone to be intelligent, therefore, I say nothing very precise about him, unless the reader knows my basic valuations and attitudes and hence also what "intelligent" stands for in my "personal vocabulary."

It is better to leave open questions open, except to that degree that pressure of decision requires temporary, practical commitment. Some areas permit of less precision than others. As Aristotle said, "Precision is not to be sought for alike in all discussions, any more than in all the products of the crafts. . . . It is the mark of an educated man to look for precision in each class of things just so far as the nature of the subject admits." [22]

(3) Suppose someone revives the old story about Adolf Hitler's being alive, residing somewhere in South America, and the story meets with a skeptical response. The story teller might then challenge: "Can you prove that it's untrue? No? Well then. . . ." Or a politician might say of his opponent, "Two years ago I publicly declared that he was guilty of falsifying his income tax return, and he has never sued me for perjury. Is this not an open admission of my charges?"

But of course, the onus of *proving* generally lies upon the one who makes the assertion. Nothing is established as true simply by virtue of its not being shown false. No one has demonstrated that the other side of the moon does not contain an exact duplicate of the Grand Canyon, but there is not the slightest reason to believe that it does. There may be many reasons why a perjurer is not *sued* for his perjury: he may have been protected by congressional immunity, his victim may have wanted to avoid the notoriety and expense of a trial, and so on. Perhaps the advertiser's claim that there

[22] *Ethics,* 1094b, W. D. Ross, Trans.

is great significance in his having been able to give a money-back guarantee for his product is sometimes a subtle employment of this fallacy. "Money-back guarantees" are sometimes not what they seem on the surface to be, but even more important is the apparent fact that very few consumers will go to the trouble of returning and proclaiming their dissatisfaction with a relatively inexpensive product. Their inaction is no real endorsement of the product.

(4) "Rationalization" has been characterized as the finding of good reasons rather than real reasons. It is the attempt to put a false rational front on a prejudice or any other belief held irrationally.

(5) A Redundant Argument is not an argument at all but only an assertion manipulated to resemble an argument. Here is an example from a student paper:

The belief in immortality because people strive for it is very weak. Even though people believe that there is a hereafter, this doesn't necessarily prove anything. However many people want immortality and act like it's real, it still is a question of whether it is. It may be possible for there to be immortality but it isn't proved, and so isn't necessarily true. In short, immortality is possible, but isn't proved in any way sufficient to allow us with confidence to say that there is or isn't such a thing, however desirable it may seem to all of us.

The careful reader will notice that this "argument" scarcely gets beyond saying that a certain belief is weak, though it makes this assertion over and over. By contrast the genuine argument has the form: This deserves to be believed because.... "This" symbolizes the assertion, and what follows the "because" are the reasons. Of course actual arguments are not always so explicit. Frequently, much interpretation is left to the reader or hearer.

PROBLEMS FOR DISCUSSION

A. The allegation was recently made that a man had at one time said:

> I believe that communism should be taught in our schools by communists and students allowed to make up their own minds about it.

and at another time said:

> I am deeply opposed to communism as a political and economic position and to the habitual communist distortion of truth.

He was accused of inconsistency. Was he accused justly?

B. Wherein is Garibaldi's speech, made after failure to defend Rome, persuasive?

> Let those who wish to continue the war against the stranger come with me. I offer neither pay nor quarters nor provisions. I offer hunger, thirst, forced marches, battles, and death.

C. "DEMOCRACY has become a sacred word in Russia, where it was often criticized before 1929. In the Western democracies it was a sacred word throughout the past half-century. At the turn of the century it was, and it is now, virtually always judged favorably. In Germany, on the other hand, this word, which had been approved under Weimar, became a term of abuse under the Nazis." (Pool, Ithiel de Sola et al, *Symbols of Democracy*. Stanford: Stanford University Press, 1952, p. 71.)

Name half a dozen other "sacred" words—words which carry a strong persuasive power—in present day America.

D. We quoted Professor Oliver to the effect that persuasion is a civilized substitute for force and harsh authority. Can you think of any instances of persuasion which are harsh and ruthless?

E. Scientists, professors of science, and laboratory assistants are patently objective while working in the laboratory, and they pursue a highly impersonal, well-worked out method there. Is it your impression that this objectivity and method transfer to other areas of these scientists' lives? Are these people more objective than others in respect to politics, economic doctrine, religion, art? Discuss.

F. There is a Fallacy which we may appropriately name "The Fallacy of Always Hunting a Fallacy." Illustrate it.

G. Speaker Rayburn is said to have said, "If you want to be a Congressman, the first thing to do is to get yourself elected." Discuss pro and con.

H. Read to the class and comment on the military propaganda written by Benjamin Franklin, reproduced on page 207 of W. Hummel and K. Huntress, *The Analysis of Propaganda.* New York: William Sloane Associates, Inc., 1949.

I. What real difference is there between an Office of Propaganda on the one hand and Public Relations or Information Services on the other? Discuss.

J. Distinguish between *being rational* and *rationalizing.*

K. Explicate the meaning and assess the persuasive force of the following expressions:

"He gave a demonstration of a man who denounces nudism while taking his clothes off."

"Pastime in the country is crime in the city."

"Congress: A man gets up to speak and says nothing. Nobody listens—and then everybody disagrees." A foreign visitor's description, quoted in A. Wiley, *Laughing with Congress.*

L. Analyze the persuasive techniques of Tom Sawyer in the whitewashing of the fence story and of Marc Anthony in the well-known speech in *Julius Caesar.* Or substitute less worked-over literary instances.

M. What are some other words besides "because" which frequently indicate that what follows will be reasons for a certain assertion?

N. " 'Show me the man who says anything against women, as women, and I boldly declare he is not a man.' And Mr. Snodgrass took his cigar from his mouth, and struck the table violently with his clenched fist.

" 'That's a good sound argument,' said the placid man."

(Charles Dickens, *Pickwick Papers,* Ch. XIV.)

Do you agree with the placid man's evaluation? Why?

EXERCISES

I.   "Get out!" is an imperative. Make a list of ten expressions that are equivalent to it in meaning. Arrange them in order of degree of politeness.

II.   In the same way as in I above, compose and arrange five sentences recommending discretion.

III. Apologize to the owner in two effective sentences for breaking a very costly goblet belonging to
      1. your boss (or)
      2. your professor
      3. your father
      4. your servant
      5. your girl (or boy) friend's parent.

IV.   Write a brief bit of persuasive discourse: a proposal of marriage or an application for a job.—See James C. Worthy, *What Employers Want.* Chicago: Science Research Associates, Inc., 1950.

V.   Write a letter to the forum of your local paper (or to your congressman) urging action on a current, local issue. Address and actually post the letter.

VI.   "Rapportive" language and human relations: Politely state the following propositions:
      1. You smell bad.
      2. Your slip is showing.
      3. You will be late.
      4. You are not correctly educating your daughter.
      5. Your complexion is terrible.
      6. You cannot be hired by us because your references are weak.
      7. You will not get far; better not continue a Liberal Arts program.
      8. Your wife was just arrested.
      9. Your return ticket is invalid by ten minutes.
      10. You should give up playing the piano altogether.

VII. Wherein are the following polite and delicate (or wherein do they fail to be?)
      1. Ushers will seat those who were detained. (In church.)

2. Mrs. Thomas Vernon, your mother, passed away an hour ago. Her last words were of you.

3. The successors of Ben Hill, Inc. hope that they may be of service to you in the manner of the Hill Company.

4. You need nothing but your genius and still a little time and practice.

VIII. List six expressions commonly used at parting.

IX. Write a 500 word essay about terms that are alleged to be emotionally neutral.

X. Briefly describe some new science and tell wherein it is truly a science.

XI. Make a short speech (three minutes) on one of the following topics:

1. In favor of small towns
2. Go-getters
3. English literature and personal culture
4. The good in isolationism

XII. Describe a fallacy in each of the following:

1. "The Duke yet lives that Henry shall depose."
2. Twice two and three.
3. Either the alarm clock does not ring when no one is present or sound is not a something heard.
4. John and Mary are whittling and sewing.
5. KILLER SAYS DEAD MAN WAS CHASING HIM WITH DRAWN RAZOR.
6. Laws are legislated; there are laws of nature; therefore there must be a legislator of nature.
7. Loosely wrapped in a newspaper she carried three dresses.
8. To kill is to murder; wartime military service may require killing; therefore, wartime military service may require murdering.
9. GIANT BABY NEEDS SALE.
10. Kiwis are practically extinct; this bird is a kiwi and is therefore practically extinct.
11. The doctrines of Dadaism being heretical ought to be condemned.
12. One who opposes war is a coward, for he is not willing to die for his country.

13. "When it rains, it pours."

14. Aristotle must have been a man of extraordinary industry; for only such a man could have produced his works.

15. "The bourgeois sees in his wife a mere instrument of production. He hears that the instruments of production are to be exploited in common, and, naturally, can come to no other conclusion than that the lot of being common to all will likewise fall to the women." (From the *Communist Manifesto*.)

16. The prosperity of England is owing to its national character, just as the sad condition of India is owing to the absence of national character.

17. Nothing is better than wisdom; home brew is better than nothing; therefore home brew is better than wisdom.

18. The Navy is stiff-necked, therefore Admiral Marc A. Mitscher must have been stiff-necked.

19. "There is no real difference between poetry and science. Science measures and discovers quantity; poetry measures and discovers quality. But as there is no quality without quantity, the poet depends on the scientist, and poetry and science complete each other." (From Francis Scarfe: *Auden and After*. George Routledge and Sons, Ltd., London, 1942, p. 188.)

20. ACTRESS REFUSES TO TELL BROTHER WHOM SHE MARRIED.

21. It is not unusual to find a boy who likes a dog better than his father.

22. It is my duty to discourage sin. Usury is a sin. So I shall not pay the money back.

XIII. Analyze the following positions:

1. Science is properly defined as: "the persistent, careful use of the mind." Now, everybody knows that Physics is a science and that Poetry is an art, not a science. All our reliance should be upon science so far as we are concerned to become better acquainted with the world around us. Thus, to hope to gain anything besides pleasure from the poets is to hope in vain.

2. My opponent has constantly used the most belligerent language. He is forever talking of declaring war against poverty and disease, of doing battle with treasonable elements, of fighting monopoly and inflation. But I have been taught to believe: "Blessed are the peacemakers."

3. I believe in Freedom, but there is a difference between Freedom and License. To allow professors unappreciative of the fruits of American Free Enterprise to continue in their jobs is not Freedom but License. Therefore, "Academic Freedom" is a misnomer.

4. The only evidence that anything is visible is that someone sees it. The only evidence that anything is audible is that someone hears it. Thus the only evidence that anything is desirable is that somebody desires it.

XIV. Attack the following statements by exposing in each some logical fallacy.

1. Since the state can do no wrong, no laws should be repealed.

2. The entire history of the human race is nothing but a grand struggle between Liberty and Authority.

3. Our democratic courts are inevitably corrupt. Have you ever met a judge, or any other man, who was not very desirous indeed of increasing his income?

4. In order to maintain our objectivity, we ought to call the Communists not "Reds," but "Purples," "Grays," "Whites," or by the name of some other more *neutral* color.

5. The poor will always be with us, and so I should not advise you to waste time helping that old woman.

XV. In the following passages, distinguish the mere assertions from the arguments. In the case of the arguments, show which words advance the *reasons*. Do you find any "redundant arguments"?

1. It is not fair that colleges should require students to take certain courses. Students should be allowed to elect whichever classes they prefer. The system of free election is the only really defensible one.

2. Brando is a fine actor.

3. Science has proved that tar water is good for you when taken according to the directions on the label.

4. There are three major objections to the United Nations: It reduces the sovereignty of nations; it is not truly more powerful than the League of Nations; it assumes that even Communist countries can work cooperatively with other nations.

5. Since *The Power of Positive Thinking* led the best-seller lists for many months, it must be a book well worth reading.

SOURCES AND ADVANCED READING

1. Baker Brownell, *The Human Community,* New York: Harper and Brothers, 1950.

2. Samuel A. Stouffer, *Communism, Conformity, and Civil Liberties.* New York: Doubleday & Co., 1955.

3. Irving J. Lee, *How to Talk With People.* New York: Harper and Brothers, 1952. Foreword and Ch. I.

4. "Communications in Today's World," *Northwestern University Information,* Vol. XX, No. 25 (1952). Read the talks by Professors Roethlisberger and Rogers now reprinted in S. I. Hayakawa, (ed.), *Language, Meaning and Maturity.* New York: Harper and Brothers, 1954.

5. Robert T. Oliver, *Persuasive Speaking, Principles and Methods.* New York and London: Longmans, Green and Co., 1950.

6. Winston Lamont Brembeck, and William Smiley Howell, *Persuasion, A Means of Social Control.* New York: Prentice-Hall, Inc., 1952.

7. John Stuart Mill, *A System of Logic.* London and New York: Longmans, Green and Co., New Impression, 1948. Book V, "On Fallacies."

8. R. W. Jepson, *Clear Thinking.* London and New York: Longmans, Green and Company, 1948. Ch. III.

9. Robert H. Thouless, *How to Think Straight.* New York: Simon and Schuster, 1948.

10. Charles L. Stevenson, *Ethics and Language.* New Haven: Yale University Press, 1944. Chapters VI and IX, "Persuasion," and ". . . Persuasive Definitions."

X

PROPAGANDA

Definition of "Propaganda" • Example and Analysis
of Propaganda • Propaganda and Control • Propaganda and
Prejudice • Analysis • Elements of Propaganda

DEFINITION OF "PROPAGANDA"

Propaganda may be defined as organized persuasion by a group in order to fulfill objectives of the group. We make the definition persuasive, and the term pejorative, by adding that propaganda is organized persuasion in the composition of which truth is subordinated to effectiveness.

The best way to become acquainted with some devices of propaganda is perhaps to read, write, and analyze some recurrent types. The evaluation of effective persuasive appeals is a difficult enterprise, and successful criticism calls for experience and subtlety. Such analysis plus good luck along with eternal vigilance may help us raise our score for rationality and insight.

EXAMPLE AND ANALYSIS OF PROPAGANDA

Let us examine a propaganda leaflet. At the top is a picture of a man we identify as a physician. He has on a white, short-sleeved gown over his suit, a stethoscope around his neck. He is leaning forward across his desk, as if talking to a patient. In looks he is distinguished, intelligent, firm, and yet friendly and kindly. He says to us:

My business is health and disease, and I want to talk about my business. It's what I know most about. Since I was a kid and played at doctoring my kid sister's dolls (with her acting as nurse), my chief concern in life has been to help people who are sick to get well and people who are well to stay that way. It was in order to equip myself for this business that I went to college and medical school, stoking furnaces around the neighborhood to support myself in the dormitory. And after graduation and two years of interning in a hospital I borrowed a thousand dollars to buy a little equipment, and pay a month's advance rent on an office where I could practice. I've spent just over thirty-one years in this business of doctoring.

Now, I've always been proud of the practice I've developed and proud of the profession to which I belong. But today I'm alarmed—alarmed at a proposal some people in Washington are making which aims a dagger right at the heart of American Medicine. It is a scheme known by different names: "National Health Insurance," "Federal Health Plan," and so on, but the real name for which is *socialized medicine*. (I suppose it is part of my training to be blunt and "call a spade a spade.")

Fortunately, we live in a democracy, a government "of the people, by the people, and for the people." Lincoln, the author of those great words, knew the price of freedom. He knew that there are different kinds of slaves and different kinds of slave-owners. Today there are those who would make all of us slaves to a vast federal bureaucracy. *Socialized medicine* supporters want to enslave the doctors and the nurses and the patients and make them all do the goose-step to the orders of a corrupt political appointee armed with a wad of government forms in one hand and a great pile of taxpayers' money in the other. *Socialized medicine* supporters are apparently admirers of Red Russia, where their pet scheme has had such a long and notorious career. Or they are worshippers of pink England where more and more ordinary people are stumbling through a pile of red tape to the consulting room of some doctor who has been appointed by the politicians to hold "sick call." Who is it in fact that is making all the noise about the wonders of *socialized medicine*? It is some left-wing labor leaders (not the rank-and-file members who are better than 76 per cent opposed to tampering with the American system); some ne'er-do-wells who beat the drum for any thing contrary to the established ways of our forefathers; and some misguided "intellectuals" who because of their blindness to practical realities are trying to sell their country down the river. Harry Bridges of course supports the plan. But where stand the people whom Americans trust? What about the great industrialists, the church leaders, the lawyers, the Women's Clubs, the American Legion, the chambers of commerce? What about the insurance men? (Ask them about the phony health "insurance".) Finally, what about doctors, who in speaking about matters of health, are speaking about what they know? Ask your own physician. He knows and he will tell you. He is the one you want to go to about health, not the politician.

Mr. Harold Stassen, former President of the University of Pennsylvania and one of our most honored statesmen, after an intensive, scholarly study of *socialized medicine* in England reports that the quality of medical care there has gone down at about the same rate that costs have gone up. British doctors are alarmed at what they believe will be the ultimate effects on the health of the populace. One prominent London dentist explained that his own practice, under government supervision, had become like a slot machine—utterly impersonal and mechanical. That is the result when you exchange democracy for socialism.

Compare the records of Free American Medicine and the Politicians. While American doctors have in fifty years raised life expectancy from 49 to 68 years, the politicians have raised taxes from 6 cents to 25.3 cents out of every dollar of income. Do you want to trade scientific success for even more political failure? HELP STRIKE A BLOW FOR AMERICAN FREEDOM!

Yours sincerely,

John T. Stover, M. D.

This bit of propaganda has for our purposes the virtue of displaying a number of the typical sorts of appeal encountered in political, economic, and social persuasion, and in advertising. We may proceed by paragraphs:

(a) The persuasive writer is always in danger of evoking

the *wrong* response. Lest he be supposed a "mere propagandist" he must establish, if he can, confidence, rapport.
Here the method is that of appearing at once a highly trained
and thoroughly experienced expert and yet a man of humble
or ordinary origins. If he said directly, "I am a man of
eminence but even I played dolls with my sister and helped
work my way through college just as you readers did," the
arrogance would be a bit too pronounced to be effective in
setting the right tone. Haughtiness is here avoided; in its
place we perhaps get the self-assurance of a man who has
known what it is to feel the pinch of poverty, a man whose
concern, however, is not with making money so much as with
helping others. Such a man can be trusted in what he is about
to say.

(b) Now the man becomes identified with his profession
(unquestionably one which most people are already kindly
disposed to). He states the problem in terms of a threat to
this profession rather than to himself. The tempo steps up
and inflammatory expressions come in: "aims a dagger right
at the heart of American Medicine" (the medical profession
is American and has a heart); "scheme"; "Some people in
Washington" (vaguely insidious group). Not only is the unpopular term "Socialized" coupled with the enemy-plan, but
its "disguises" are revealed. Again the writer manifests his
forthrightness, this time a scientific forthrightness, as he calls
the scheme by its *right* name. The use of the "spade" saying
at once reveals the author's colloquial attitude and trades on
the general acceptance of the maxim.

(c) Here we see an alignment of the sides, the forces of
light and the forces of darkness. Democracy, people's government, Lincoln, freedom, doctors and nurses, our forefathers,
practicality, common working men, great industrialists, veterans, clerics, women, business men and civic boosters are set
over against the horrifying array of slave-owners, fascist-
militarists, Red Russia, federal bureaucracy, left-wing labor
leaders, ne'er-do-wells, intellectuals, Harry Bridges, malcon-

tents, aliens, English Socialism, etc. There is a use of statistics, with the corresponding scientific, factual aura, though entirely vague as to its source. And there is the telling argument that since physicians are specialists in healing, they must be specialists in the social matter of the best way of conducting medical practice.

(d) "Let us get down to the facts" is an implicit introduction to this paragraph. Mr. Stassen's respectability as a public figure in a high academic post (and therefore a scholar) is invoked to bless the vague allegations made about "Socialized Medicine" in England (already smeared as "pink"). The negative testimony does not actually materialize on a factual basis, but perhaps one gets the impression of having read an objective, detailed account of the failure of the plan in Britain. Again the present system is linked with Democracy, the proposed system with "Socialism."

(e) Now that the opposition is taken care of, what about the advantages of the defended way of medical practice? This system is credited with the extension of life expectancy, whereas, the politicians (unpopular word) who are associated with the opposed scheme are blamed for raising the taxes. Again there is a neat pseudo-scientific paralleling of quantities. Now it is Science (a good thing) against politics (a bad thing).

(f) Here is a militant slogan as a summary-incitement. The final touch is the dignified and authoritative "M.D."

We may say by way of summary that among the standard weapons of the propagandist illustrated in Dr. Stover's letter are devices for *securing confidence* in the writer and other devices for *destroying* not only the position but the very *credibility* of his opponents.

The confidence of anyone reading the letter is sought by means of displays both of authority and humility, by using old saws and slogans, by associating one's own cause with popular movements, groups, and actual persons, and by giving the impression (at least) of scientific factuality in reporting the advantages and promises of the supported idea.

The reader's disapproval of opponents of our propagandist is kindled by using inflammatory language, by associating the opponents with unpopular movements, groups, and actual persons, and by giving the impression of scientific factuality in the report of the faults and dangers of the opposed idea.

PROPAGANDA AND CONTROL

The aim of the propagandist is to govern. Propagandizing and advertising are ways of directing and controlling human behavior. The propagandist seeks to guide men by arguing, conditioning, exhibiting, picturing, praising, condemning, exaggerating, and de-emphasizing. His final objective, through all kinds of maneuver, is to manipulate beliefs and desires, and hence acts. His attention is always on attitudes of mind. Things, and the truth about things, are for him instrumental. Sometimes, the actual fact will be on his side. His objective is to sway and steer people.

The propagandist, of course, may also manipulate things: he has his "props." The television staff arranges and illuminates apples, and pulls the camera close for an appealing, realistic effect. But it is this effect, inciting people to *buy* apples, that counts. The "realism" of the close-up is just one way among others of affecting attitudes of mind. The propagandist's stakes are on the somewhat pliant convictions of the viewer. To the advertiser, then, the physical realities are a secondary consideration; he will be glad to arrange and re-arrange physical realities if only he can affect attitudes and actions. His stock-in-trade is the semblance of factuality, something which he now brilliantly, now laboriously, constructs. At the risk of seeming cynical, we observe that even the honest propagandist is paid (and ought to be paid) for the effectiveness of his activities, not for his "scientific factuality."

Honest or dishonest, propaganda is not used just for the purpose of selling a little cheese and a little soap. The advertiser wants to secure his customer's trade once and for all, if he can. The political, religious, economic, and social propagandist wants also to win his man. The great battle of our time is among total ideologies and modes of living, no one of which is completely consistent or inconsistent. In the spheres of politics and economics, the propagandist is out to win full confidence in, or even fanatical adherence for, his position; and he's out to damage the credibility of his opponents. The propagandist knows what he is doing. Most of us do *not*, in fact, hear both sides indefinitely; we are committed, for example, to read the *Tribune* or the *Sun-Times,* but not both, or the *Herald Tribune* and the *Times,* but then not the *Mirror* and the *News*

Propaganda may consist of the whole truth, or of some part of the truth. Partial truth is more characteristic of propaganda, and it may be either pertinent or irrelevant. An automobile manufacturer may find that true information about the chassis and engine in his product is less effective in advertising than true pictorial information about the glorious highways of New England. Since his aim is to sell his cars, he will then advertise by telling you the truth about the glorious highways. Even if it pays him to advertise pertinent information, it may be very one-sided information. Husbands have been heard to complain that their wives are 'taken in' by a salesman's emphasis on pretty details: "What a beautiful dashboard! What shiny chrome! What convenient ashtrays!" All the while *he* is seriously concerned to know about horsepower and speed. But he can see for himself that everything the salesman says is true.

Propaganda may even transcend partial and irrelevant truth and be a direct lie. The technique of the big lie has flourished in our own era. Some psychologists are convinced that a big lie will succeed where a little one would fail. The composite photo technique has been used with some success:

a political candidate may be ruined by showing him in conversation with a leading communist he may not even know.

At the other extreme, propaganda may be neither true nor false but just suggestive or entertaining. If entertaining, it is in the tradition of patter—the silly but amusing dialogue of vaudeville. If suggestive, it may be of any degree of subtlety: there are the deBeers landscapes that help sell diamonds, the pictures of Coca-Cola embedded in ice, the mansions behind hard-top convertibles. Especially where the intelligence of the audience is low, propaganda may suggest information while affirming nothing at all.

An advertiser may create a pleasurable association with his product by sponsoring a radio program—and perhaps also create a feeling of obligation to buy.

PROPAGANDA AND PREJUDICE

A first task of the advertiser is to find out *what people want*. Then he can direct himself to his audience. Every major advertising agency includes a division of market research, the primary job of which is to find out the size and nature of the market and how it can be reached psychologically. The appeal ought to fit the audience as the punishment fits the crime. Then, by transfer, the audience is brought from its present likings to a liking for the advertiser's wares. Advertising is catering.

Perhaps this suggests why the public retains an inveterate prejudice against propaganda, why the American public has not wanted a Ministry of Propaganda, or Department of Propaganda. In the merchandising of wares, huckstering is traditional. But political, economic, and military propaganda caters to present interest and prejudice in an often degrading way. Propaganda is objected to, not because it's persuasive discourse, but because it's slanted. It reports in color and, instead of inciting us to face and learn the hard facts, it tells us what we want to know while using us to achieve another's aims. It at once confirms and uses prejudice.

And what is prejudice? It is the ignorance of our own ignorance, the false conviction that we know the facts and recognize the comparative values in a given situation. It's simply a failure of self-criticism.

Most of us are willing enough to admit that we do not know many things. The engineer is quick to confess his ignorance of sewing. The merchant need not know anything about nuclear physics. The plumber is frankly ignorant of Chinese music. In these respects, we would say that the people are, for better or worse, ignorant; but we would not call them prejudiced. The prejudiced person is ignorant of something which matters, concerning which he feels strongly; and he falsely supposes that he knows all about it.

Why won't we recognize and admit ignorance in certain cases while we are perfectly willing to in others? The answer lies in the *feeling* which in the former case has become attached—or always was attached (for us)—to the opinion held. There may be not only a feeling but a commitment, perhaps an open one, so that people will laugh at us or lose confidence in our consistency, if we back away. Other things being equal, we'd rather be wrong than fickle. Besides, if the prejudice is a really deeply rooted one, if it is one that we have always had, owing to "the accident of birth," then we seem to feel that in giving it up we lose too much face: even something of our very existence.

Yet we may have even more to lose if, when real information is needed as the ground of policy decision, we substitute prejudice. Prejudice is, for example, the death of military intelligence. To some extent, we can afford, as a matter of politics, to hate the State Department, the Central Intelligence Agency, Army Intelligence, and the like. *We* can be prejudiced against them. But we count on *them* to remain objective and factual. In order to fight your enemy successfully, you must *know* him; but mere prejudice is not knowledge. Of course, prejudice may feed morale; and it is no part of our thesis that knowledge is the sole value worth striving for.

The causes of prejudice are numerous, of course. The "accident of birth" at a certain time and place — being reared in Maine rather than in Mississippi — is one which can be transcended by travel and the reading of history. But pride and the habit of keeping up with the Joneses are involved, and not so easily transcended. There is a natural disposition, moreover, to ease and stationariness; and this disposition sustains prejudice. Among ancestor worshippers, there is even something sacrilegious in the frank, deliberate casting-off of tradition. Reference to custom and tradition—"the Chinese argument," Bentham called it—is a device likely to be favored by demagogues.

There is an opposite cause of prejudice. Opposed to the enchantment lent by distance and the lovely distortion that memory has worked upon the golden years, there are also curiosity and pride in new things; the prejudice against old-fashioned things; the scientific cult, the love to hear and repeat the latest word.

ANALYSIS

To conquer prejudice, to find and hold the correct orientation and stance in respect to propaganda, to be skeptical but not cynical, these are no easy objectives. But there are some questions that we can ask ourselves about items of propaganda, when the issue seems important and we have the time. As the railroad warning signs used to admonish: STOP, LOOK, LISTEN! Ask (1) Just what am I being asked to do? (2) Just what am I asked to believe as reasons for acting? (3) How well attested are the claims I am asked to believe in? (4) Are the reasons relevant, are they reasons for the actions indicated?

We can ask questions about the various elements in the

situation, and then ask questions about the devices and techniques. Propaganda situations are sign situations. The propagandist produces or reproduces signs for his own purposes, but he aims to establish in the mind and feeling of the hearer, or interpreter, an association between some sign and a meaning, or among signs. We can ask, Is the relation between the sign and this meaning a factual one? We can ask, Do these linguistic symbols convey any information, or are they merely affective? We can ask questions about the motivation of the propaganda producer, and how his motives manifest themselves. Or we can ask about the nature of the audience, the receiver, — for example, about his pre-existent associations. To generalize and summarize: we may direct our questions towards hearer, producer, signs, and meanings conveyed; and we can ask about the relations existent or possible among any two of these.

Then sometimes it pays to look carefully at the propagandist's devices and techniques. Certain devices have been much attended to and publicized: we make short shrift of them, since they are, most of them, illustrated elsewhere in this Chapter. A familiar and powerful one is the Either-Or argument which states a position so extremely that you seem to have only two alternatives, even if there is no end to alternatives. The Either-Or passes over subtleties and shadings; and, unless it lies at an extreme, truth is passed over too. "Either you favor U. S. foreign policy or you execrate it," "Either you will stand up and fight or you are a slacker," "A student either works hard and is a good student, or he shouldn't be in college," or perhaps "A Physics teacher either is an exciting lecturer or he ought to go work for the AEC." The Either-Or aims to force your hand by leaving you no respectable alternative.

The elimination of really desirable alternatives is evident also in the use of smear. By name-calling, we blacken an alternative. By praising, we can raise one alternative high above its rivals. The carefully built question — another device — can

stack the cards against a whole range of answers: "How are
the public utilities of the United States developed on such a
sound foundation that they excel those of all other countries?"

Transfer is a psychological phenomenon of great importance
in propaganda. One strives to associate his client with the
right people and events at any cost, to keep him on the right
side of the fence, wearing the right amount of suntan. This
has been done with a deliberate touch of humor in headline
type: THE HOUSE OF SEAGRAM CONGRATULATES
RAY MILLAND ON HIS MAGNIFICENT PERFORM-
ANCE IN "THE LOST WEEKEND."

Transfer shades off into plain folks and plain-spoken folks.
Remember how Dr. Stover showed himself to be at once
eminent and yet a plain old guy who worked his way through
school?

A favorite device of the communists — a device which extends far back into their underlying philosophy of economics
and history — is the Band Wagon. This device takes off from
the fact that no one wants to be an old fogey, creeping along
far behind the main body. Everyone prefers to be on the
winning side. The communist ideology maintains that capitalism has internal contradictions which necessitate that it
move on toward depression, monopoly, collapse, revolution,
and so to (Marxist) socialism. A tendency for the capitalist to
accumulate a larger and larger share of the total wealth is,
according to communist doctrine, one side of the picture; the
other side is the reduction of all other elements of the population to proletarian status. Thus the extreme wealth of a very
few contrasts more and more with the extreme poverty of
the masses: an internal contradiction for the capitalistic system. Cut from the same cloth is the communist expropriation
of the word "progressive." Not that the illusion of victory-
bound-to-come is now fostered for the first time in Russia:
The Czarist government in World War I instructed the
official Petrograd Telegraph Agency:

All our military and naval success must be published, our losses and unsuccessful operations must not be mentioned or talked about, the number of prisoners taken must always be exaggerated, raids of enemy air forces must never be published.

ELEMENTS OF PROPAGANDA

The U. S. Department of Defense has distinguished five elements, or aspects, of propaganda: objective or mission, source, timing, audience, and subject.[1]

1. What are the objectives (to continue our example) of communist propaganda? The long-term objective is domination of world policy by the communists. The short-term objective is the isolation of the United States and the incitement of dissension among the United States and its allies. Long-term and short-term objectives are scrambled together, as is usually the case with propaganda objectives; nor are the military and political objectives kept distinct in practice. In view of their doctrine of "the final struggle," all their foreign propaganda may be classified as military propaganda. "Military propaganda" may be defined as follows: "The planned use of any form of communication to disseminate information or pretended information designed to affect the minds, emotions, or actions of a given group with the aim of encouraging friendly forces and defeating enemy forces." It is applied together with such other operational measures of a military, economic, or political nature as may be required to influence people's thoughts and actions in a specific desired way.

2. The second element in propaganda is the source. Source may be white, gray, or black. A white source is an acknowledged source, like the Community Chest, comprised of specified philanthropic agencies, appealing for funds. Advertisements have a white source, when they are signed by the party who pays for them.

---

1 *Armed Forces Talk* No. 424. Office of Armed Forces Information and Education, Department of Defense, Washington 25, D. C.

A black source is one that positively falsifies itself. Some of the recent "popular fronts" and "peace movements" have been instances of black propaganda, since communist policy concealed itself behind them. An enemy uses a black source if it broadcasts what falsely purports to be a quotation from a friendly colonel.

A gray source is a masked source. Gray source propaganda does not even pretend to be signed: it has emerged from the mists. Gray propaganda is difficult to prepare, naturally, since it must sway its audience by *what* it says alone, without reference to any authority. Here everything depends on internal evidence, on the convincingness of the copy itself. Of course, there are borderline cases: If you quote "a higher authority in the government," is the source white, gray, or black?

3. The third element is the audience. The audience of military propaganda is *all* the troops and civilians. Favorite targets of communist propaganda have been the poor and the unemployed, minority groups, laboring groups, women, and youth. They are not all sought through the same media. "In carrying out its world-wide propaganda campaign, the Kremlin does not fire its guns indiscriminately in the hope of hitting a target." [2] Communists try especially to reach Poles, for example, and other minority elements with relatives in satellite countries: there are various ways of attacking these people that are not feasible in the case of people of English or Irish stock.

4. Timing is the fourth element. Every propaganda maneuver should be timed for maximum effectiveness. In World War II, the Nazis liked to plant a rumor that the boys were about to be sent home in a U. S. division just before it was committed to battle. Observe that if the Nazis guessed wrong, and the boys were sent home, the Nazis had nothing to lose.

The old-fashioned huckster and medicine man has often been a master of timing, like his counterpart the vaudeville actor. The first woman who extends a dollar bill to buy Chad-

[2] *Armed Forces Talk* 401, p. 9.

wick Cure-All is flatly turned down. She is told to wait her turn. When the crowd has grown larger, the medicine man announces that Chadwick Cure-All is rationed, and, turning to that importunate woman, asks how large her family is, and then calculates how large a bottle it is fair to sell her. The timing is a factor in the construction of suspense, and suspense brings the deal to a close. The huckster "keeps the ball." A Congressional investigator need not be crestfallen because of the collapse of an attack: he can begin a new one, arranging his press release at exactly the right time to hit the next edition's headlines. The big-time propagandists are concerned with time in another sense, too. They are trying to make history, to determine the course of events in their own favor. The heaviest blow must be timed, therefore, to secure a knock-out. And then the issue is as quickly dropped, and the attention of the public diverted to new issues.

5. And so we come to the fifth and most obvious element in propaganda, the subject-matter. On second thought, however, subject-matter in propaganda is anything but obvious and easy, and this is just why skilled copy writers draw fabulous salaries.

Objective, source, timing, or audience may in one way or another make the choice and development of subject-matter delicate and difficult. Despite a popular belief to the contrary, saccharine advertising and politicking are not always the most effectual.

What *is* subject-matter, in this connection? Taken narrowly, it is the content actually chosen for publication: the copy, the illustration, the metaphor or comparison presented to the audience by the available or preferred media. In a broader sense, subject-matter means the entire problem of topic, including its selection, ways of treating it, the choice or rejection of illustration, together with aiming or slanting it to achieve objectives.

Propagandizing is sometimes called "uphill," if the perspective, the topic, or the side the propagandist finds himself on is unpopular. In uphill propagandizing, nothing is so compelling as the frankest assertion of "blood, sweat, and tears." Do you remember the notice about a Hazardous Journey? At the end of one of his famous speeches, before he was Reich Chancellor, Hitler commanded, "For once forget your vocation, your class; for once forget your origin, your sectarianism, and think once of that which was here before you and will be here after you—of Germany!" [3] The old Marxist slogan, "Religion is the opiate of the people," is an uphill effort designed to wake the drowsiest. But even the lowly advertising agency hack from Madison Avenue knows that the first things to achieve through subject matter are attention and a hard core of fanatical support. When a new razor blade is put on the market, for example, it may at first be sold at ten cents a blade. After a few articulate supporters have been drummed up at this inflated price, the price is lowered and the market broadened. There is lots of room for talent and even genius in this game.

Downhill propaganda brings problems of a different kind. How can you *retain* so much support, from so many conflicting sources and agencies? How can we keep the people loving old Mr. Rockefeller? (If not with millions, then with dimes.) And so there is a major upheaval in our own day through the revolutionary rise to power of the press agent and the public and industrial relations professionals whose job is to ensure continuing and increasing support from the public for persons and institutions. Downhill propaganda is often well financed: mistakes must be avoided, for nothing is so abhorrent in public relations and advertising as a boomerang.

But even fairly clever propaganda can boomerang, if the timing is a little off, or if for any reason the audience once begins to laugh. When Axis Sally talked about "what your sweetheart was doing back home," the troops gave ribald

[3] "Einmal vergessen Sie Ihren Beruf, einmal Ihren Stand, einmal Ihre Herkunft, einmal Ihre Konfession, einmal denken Sie an das, was vor Ihnen war und nach uns sein muss, an Deutschland!"

replies aplenty. Tokyo Rose was a favorite of U. S. troops, but because she made them laugh, and so instead of their morale's being lowered, it was raised.

In our day, some propaganda is like war and some is part of war. Such warlike propaganda aims to discredit completely every opposing force. Thus, the communist press strives to trace every event and policy in capitalist countries back to Wall Street and Wall Street interests.[4] In the eyes of communism and communist propaganda, you are Either . . . or . . . ! Unfortunately some anti-communists are all too quick to think and feel on communist terms: quick to reject moderate alternatives, quick to use smear tactics, and just as quick to whitewash crooked patrioteers, quick to jump to the wildest conclusions, quick to blur ancient symbols. In efforts to tighten our defense against anti-capitalist ideologies, let us therefore not fall into the totalitarian trap.

PROBLEMS FOR DISCUSSION

A. See *1984*, by George Orwell, and report on the Appendix, "The Principles of Newspeak."

B. Read the comic strips for some examples of indirect propaganda. Report your findings.

C. Plato insisted that 'right belief' is not enough for the rational person; we must believe rightly and for the right reasons. What defense can you offer for this assertion? Can you oppose it?

D. Press agents for theaters and stadiums specify that "a few choice seats are still available." State fully why they do not admit to an empty house.

E. Can you discover any propaganda in this book, apart from that which is an injunction to think straight? If so, locate it and analyze it.

F. Examine some issues of the publications of "Consumer Union" or "Consumer Research." How effective are such

---

[4] By way of counterpropaganda, the *New Yorker* once suggested changing the name "Wall Street" to "Stalin Street."

reports as antidotes to advertising-propaganda? Does the advertiser have a service to render the consumer?

G. Record on a tape recorder differing news comments by, say, Fulton Lewis, Jr., Elmer Davis, H. V. Kaltenborn, and Frank Edwards. Analyze them.

H. Are there some situations in which it is good to be prejudiced? Biased?

I. Examine magazines or newspapers of very different policy for differing accounts of some one event or person. What persuasive devices are employed?

J. Which propaganda media are most important? Why?

K. What language skills would you cultivate, if your ambition were to become an expert propagandist? How would you go about cultivating them?

L. Attack the following:

1. The State can do no wrong.

2. Science proves the eternal truth of these laws.

3. Invention of the cotton gin was entirely due to the demand for the cotton of the Old South.

4. The kind of religion which any generation will believe in depends altogether on the modes of production prevailing at the time.

5. The entire history of the human race is nothing but a grand struggle between Liberty and Authority.

6. There is nothing in the original U. S. Constitution which cannot be fully understood in terms of the economic motives of the signers.

7. Our democratic courts are inevitably corrupt. Have you ever met a judge, or any other man, who was not very desirous indeed of increasing his income?

8. Senator Snort is running for office in the only honest way and should be reëlected: he has made no campaign speeches whatever.

9. "Mr. Duffle is a forward-looking, solid Midwesterner who keeps both feet on the ground and at all times knows what the score is."

10. "Jones is a cold, calculating, self-seeking politician."

11. Technocracy is the wave of the future!

12. Whatever a southerner may say, his real motives are concealed.

13. The jury should ignore the testimony of the defendant, since, after all, he is on trial for perjury.

EXERCISES

I. Search editorials for uses where you take the following symbols to be used approvingly, disapprovingly, or neutrally:

Communism	Security
Economy	Labor
Defense	Management

II. Find a news story that seems fair. Re-write it so as to slant it. Be as subtle as you can.

III. Comment in writing on the credibility of the following:

1. "Continuing pressure of the veterans lobby during the last twenty years has increased the number of veterans' hospitals from 71 to the present 169!"

2. "The right *not* to listen ought to be more stringently exercised and protected; all public amplifier systems, sound trucks, and the like should be ruled illegal."

3. "A vast amount of money—including contributions from many who can ill afford to waste their funds—is spent on losing candidates for public office. Some of them run on the ticket of splinter parties without a mentionable chance. Something should be done to eliminate this nonsense and to cut down the dissension and waste."

4. "One of the paramount evils of propaganda is that through it the public is made to judge emotively in terms of slogans rather than to study meanings and evidence reflectively. To decrease this tendency to 'tabloid thinking,' propagandists could be required to use no expressions of *less* than twenty words length."

5. "The individual citizen is the mere tool of well-fed propagandists."

IV. Write a public letter in reply to Dr. Stover. Address it to the 24 or less per cent of rank-and-file union members who, Dr. Stover conceded, are not opposed to "socialized medicine." ("Down hill propaganda.")

Write a short letter which will be as effective all round as you can make it on behalf of "socialized medicine," addressed to those who abhor it. ("Up hill propaganda.")

V. Reveal the propaganda devices in the following:

1. "Hydrodip is guaranteed better than less efficient soaps."

2. "El-Abjullah is either a great prophet of God or he is a scheming vicious liar, the most contemptible liar in the whole of history. But look my brothers on the lovely countenance of our leader and tell me whether you have it in your hearts to say he is such a villain."

3. "Republicanism is not conservatism; it is reaction. It is the forerunner of Nazism, of Hitlerism. Free enterprise is the banner under which the Republican NAMers will lead us into the concentration camps."

4. "Stripped of the lure of profit by which to induce our people to follow their false leadership, they have resorted to exhortations, pleading tearfully for restored confidence. They know only the rules of a generation of self-seekers. They have no vision, and when there is no vision the people perish. The money changers have fled from their high seats in the temple of our civilization. We may now restore that temple to the ancient truths." (F. D. Roosevelt, First Inaugural Address.)

5. "Unless we play our part as an Imperial race there is nothing but disaster in front of the human race. With the effervescence that is going on in the world today, the only force to my mind which can maintain the ideal of ordered freedom is the 65,000,000, there or thereabouts, of the German Empire, and the 11,000,000 German-speaking members of the Austrian Empire. These 76,000,000 people, speaking the German tongue, reading the German Bible and the German Goethe—these people with a common background of *Kultur* have to share the responsibility for maintaining civilization among the 1800 or 1900 million people on the globe." (From Kaiser Wilhelm II)

VI. Harold Lasswell ("Attention Structure and Social Structure," *The Communication of Ideas,* ed. by Lyman Bryson. Previously cited) has said that in Communist Russia such words as "bourgeoisie," "capitalism," "plutocracy," "God," "Church," "religion," "imperialism," and "idealism" have a *negative* meaning; whereas "proletariat," "world revolution," "collectivism," "masses," "people," and "dialectical materialism" have a *positive* meaning. Draw up corresponding lists for (1) the United States, (2) a social group you know well.

SOURCES AND ADVANCED READING

1. R. W. Jepson, *Clear Thinking*. London and New York: Longmans, Green and Company, 1948. Ch. 4.

2. Leonard W. Doob, *Public Opinion and Propaganda*. New York: Henry Holt and Company, 1948. Ch. 12.

3. Edgar Allan Poe, "Diddling." No. 30 in *The Complete Tales and Poems of Edgar Allan Poe*, Modern Library Giant. New York: Random House.

4. Ralph Barton Perry, *The Citizen Decides*. Bloomington: Indiana University Press, 1951. Ch. XII.

5. Edwin Leavitt Clarke, *The Art of Straight Thinking*. New York, London: D. Appleton-Century Company, 1929. Ch. XIII.

6. Alfred McClung Lee, *How to Understand Propaganda*. New York: Rinehart & Co., 1952.

7. Leo Lowenthal and Norbert Guterman, *Prophets of Deceit*. New York: Harper and Brothers, 1949.

8. *Public Opinion and Propaganda* (readings), ed. by Daniel Katz, Dorwin Cartwright, Samuel Eldersveld, and Alfred McClung Lee for the Society for the Psychological Study of Social Issues. New York: Dryden Press, 1954.

XI

COMMUNICATION

FOR INDIVIDUAL AND SOCIETY

Communication and Mental Health ● Communication and
Democracy

COMMUNICATION AND MENTAL HEALTH

It is widely recognized that one of the heaviest of all
punishments is solitary confinement. Schoolboys sometimes
cruelly send one of their fellows to Coventry, not speaking to
him, appearing not to hear him, and in general acting as if
he were absent. Everybody knows the extreme annoyance of
"blocking" on a word, of not being able quite to think of
it; or of not being able to say something which one "has
in mind," not being able to make somebody else understand;
or of failing, even after repeated attempts, to "get" what
somebody else is saying. Our need to communicate with our
fellows is not less basic to human nature than our need for
food and shelter.

Someone has estimated that in our culture we spend, on
the average, 70 per cent of our waking day talking or listening, reading or writing, though of course we differ among
ourselves in being more or less talkative or quiet. But quality
is more important than quantity. The man who talks the
most is not necessarily the best communicator—everybody
knows that. There is the type of person who speaks sparingly
but, as we say, "when he speaks, people sit up and take

notice." But the gabby type and the strong-silent type are both *types;* a more fully individualized person is flexible in assuming roles. At times he talks much, at other times, little. Sometimes his language will be formal, sometimes informal, sometimes considered and precise, and at other times relaxed and chatty. He will take into account those with whom he is in communication as well as the subject matter of the discourse, and adjust his language accordingly. All of us at times are guilty of inappropriateness, but some people seem to be chronically so.

Knowing oneself and knowing others are not two quite independent processes, but are so intertwined as to be inseparable; both may be said to be matters of communication. The well-integrated person may be likened to a smooth functioning net of communication, where messages are accurately and easily coded and decoded, with no breakdowns in transmission and no areas left isolated and incommunicado. But the communication net is not satisfactory unless it makes available long-distance as well as local calls; we must be able to get over to our fellows and to enable them to get over to us. Too much "noise" in the system signalizes a failure, a breakdown in communication, and hence an impairing of understanding.

A communication breakdown, if it is something more than a temporary jamming, is just another name for a psychic disorder, either social or individual. The psychiatrist Ruesch has put it this way:

If the ability to communicate successfully becomes synonymous with being mentally healthy ... it is obvious that people are mentally healthy only when their means of communication permit them to manage their surroundings successfully.[1]

He goes on to say:

The condition which the psychiatrist labels "psychosis" is essen-

---

[1] J. Ruesch and G. Bateson, *Communication: The Social Matrix of Psychiatry* (New York: W. W. Norton and Co., Inc., 1951), p. 87.

tially the result of the patient's misinterpretation of messages received; and the condition which we commonly label "neurosis" is the result of unfortunate attempts of a patient to manipulate social situations with the purpose of creating a stage to convey messages to others, and the result is frustration for the patient. Then the patient is forced to develop ways of handling the frustration, which procedure further distorts the processes of communication.[2]

The extreme case is the schizophrenic, who finds himself unable to interpret the messages he receives, unable to correct his errors, and unable to get across to others; he retreats into a world of his own where his communication is with wraiths.

Just as mental disease can be considered as a communication breakdown, so can the cure for such illness be appropriately thought of as a re-establishment of lines of communication, permitting the patient to open up areas of himself which had become hidden from view and so ineffable, isolated, blocked off; and to re-establish the give-and-take of converse with the outside world.

Carl R. Rogers, writing from a different psychological point of view, comes to a very similar conclusion. He goes so far as to say, "The whole task of psychotherapy is the task of dealing with a failure in communication."[3]

This brief digression into abnormal psychology has as its purpose a clearer insight into the absolutely fundamental importance of clear communication for a healthy, full life for the individual human being. Its importance is no less for society as a whole.

COMMUNICATION AND DEMOCRACY

No society can survive without means of communication. The very idea of a society implies the exchange of feelings

2 *Ibid.*, p. 88.

3 Carl R. Rogers and F. J. Roethlisberger, "Barriers and Gateways to Communication," *Harvard Business Review*, Vol. XXX, no. 4 (July-August, 1952), p. 28.

and ideas for the purposes of group action. But in many societies the communication has been one-way, with regularly marked off channels regulating the flow. There can be a society in which the man at the top speaks and the Word then is disseminated down to the lowest; there can be a society in which the Lowells speak only to the Cabots and the Cabots speak only to God. But this is not democratic society, for in a democratic society everybody speaks to everybody and is spoken to in return.

A democracy is rooted in freedom, and the primary freedom is the freedom to *do*. Rabelais wrote of a wonderful new-type monastery where the slogan written over the gate was: Do What Thou Wilt. That was, so far, a democracy. To speak of freedom *from* fear and freedom *from* want is to emphasize the ultimate dependence of freedom to act upon a certain security: the man who is hungry and with no prospect of a meal, the man who must live in dread of powerful enemies, may still be free, but his freedom is hollow. Nevertheless, most believers in the ideal of democracy mean, when they speak of freedom, freedom of action, including worshipping and voting and reading, writing, listening, and speaking. A democracy is rooted in the belief that no one has all the answers and even that no one has very many of the answers. This being so, everybody needs all the help he can get from everybody else in reaching decisions on matters of public policy. Answers, or what look like answers, can come from the strangest places, from the humble and inexpert as well as from the high-placed and authoritative. To be undemocratically unfree is to run the risk of cutting somebody off from those unexpected sources of wisdom.

A democracy *is* a democracy just to the extent that there is *flow* back and forth among its constituents. However large or small the group, democracy obtains when there is plentiful opportunity to speak up, to make one's voice heard, to be in on the decisions. There is reason to believe that finally a democracy is even the most *efficient* type of group, however much haggling and debating and compromising it may tolerate and encourage.

Of course freedom to communicate with one's fellows is a far more meaningful privilege for the articulate and the literate than for the inarticulate and the illiterate. Education of a populace which has attained to some mastery over the tools of communication is of central importance in the type of society which depends upon the whole populace for its ultimate policy decisions. There are many ways in which a democracy may founder and die. One way is through the gradual deterioration of the communicative processes. Suppose a society like that pictured by George Orwell in *1984,* where the whole of the people, all but a tiny élite, lost the power of dissent by the most thoroughgoing thought-control. Orwell's thesis was that if a people were deprived of their very vocabulary of dissent they would lose thereby their capacity to *think* dissent. Similarly a society in which most of the people forgot how to write and speak except in crude slogans, forgot how to listen and read with critical discrimination, would be a society in which democracy had ceased to live.

Therefore, there is an important sense in which propaganda is anti-democratic in its very nature—*even when its content is pro-democratic.* Whoever or whatever muddies the stream is damaging democracy, regardless of the extent of sincerity or nobility of aims. Some of the chief enemies of democracy are those who teach people to hate blindly and love blindly, even though what they hate be bad and what they love, good. Ultimately the processes of democratic sharing of interest and opinion are of deeper importance than any commitment to a form of government or economy.

One of the greatest spokesmen of democratic freedom was John Stuart Mill. We perhaps cannot do better than to close with the summary on discussion taken from his essay, *On Liberty,* Ch. II.

.... We have now recognized the necessity to the mental well-being of mankind (on which all their other well-being depends) of freedom of opinion, and freedom of the expression of opinion, on four distinct grounds ...

First, if any opinion is compelled to silence, that opinion may, for aught we can certainly know, be true. To deny this is to assume our own infallibility.

Secondly, though the silenced opinion may be an error, it may, and very commonly does, contain a portion of truth; and since the general or prevailing opinion on any subject is rarely or never the whole truth, it is only by the collision of adverse opinions that the remainder of the truth has any chance of being supplied.

Thirdly, even if the received opinion be not only true, but the whole truth; unless it is suffered to be, and actually is, vigorously and earnestly contested, it will, by most of those who receive it, be held in the manner of a prejudice, with little comprehension or feeling of its rational grounds. And not only this, but, *fourthly,* the meaning of the doctrine itself will be in danger of being lost, or enfeebled, and deprived of its vital effect on the character and conduct: the dogma becoming a mere formal profession, inefficacious for good, but cumbering the ground, and preventing the growth of any real and heartfelt conviction, from reason or personal experience.

Before quitting the subject of freedom of opinion, it is fit to take some notice of those who say that the free expression of all opinions should be permitted, on condition that the manner be temperate, and do not pass the bounds of fair discussion. Much might be said on the impossibility of fixing where these supposed bounds are to be placed; for if the test be offense to those whose opinions are attacked, I think experience testifies that this offense is given whenever the attack is telling and powerful, and that every opponent who pushes them hard, and whom they find it difficult to answer, appears to them, if he shows any strong feeling on the subject, an intemperate opponent. But this, though an important consideration in a practical point of view, merges in a more fundamental objection. Undoubtedly the manner of asserting an opinion, even though it be a true one, may be very objectionable, and may justly incur severe censure. But the principal offenses of the kind are such as it is mostly impossible, unless by accidental self-betrayal, to bring home to conviction. The gravest of·them is, to argue sophistically, to suppress facts or arguments, to misstate the elements of the case, or misrepresent the opposite opinion. But all this, even to the most aggravated degree, is so continually done in perfect good faith, by persons who are not considered, and in many other respects may not deserve to be considered, ignorant or incompetent, that it is rarely possible, on adequate grounds, conscientiously to stamp the misrepresentation as morally culpable; and still less could law presume to interfere with this kind of controversial misconduct. With regard to what is commonly meant by intemperate discussion, namely invective, sarcasm, personality, and the like, the denunciation of these weapons would deserve more sympathy if it were ever proposed to interdict them equally to both sides; but it is only desired to restrain the employment of them against the prevailing opinion: against the unprevailing they may not only be used without general disapproval, but will be likely to obtain for him who uses them the praise of honest zeal and righteous indignation. Yet whatever mischief arises from their use is greatest when they are employed against the comparatively defenseless; and whatever unfair advantage can be derived by any opinion from this mode of asserting it, accrues almost exclusively to received opinions. The worst offense of this kind which can be committed by a polemic is to stigmatize those who hold the contrary opinion as bad and immoral men. To calumny of this sort, those who hold any unpopular opinion are peculiarly exposed, because they are in general few and uninfluential, and nobody but themselves feels much interested in seeing justice done them; but this weapon is, from the nature of the case, denied to those who attack a prevailing opinion: they can neither use it with safety to themselves, nor, if they could, would it do anything but recoil in their own cause. In general, opinions contrary to those commonly received can only obtain a hearing by studied moderation of language, and the most cautious avoidance of unnecessary offense, from which they hardly ever deviate even in a slight degree without losing ground; while unmeasured vituperation employed on the side of the prevailing opinion really does deter people from professing contrary opinions, and from listening to those who profess them. For the interest, therefore, of truth and justice, it is far more important to restrain this employment of vituperative language than the other; and, for example, if it were necessary to choose, there would be much more need to discourage offensive attacks on infidelity than on religion. It is, however, obvious that law and authority have no business with restraining either, while opinion ought, in every instance, to determine its verdict by the circumstances of the individual case; condemning everyone, on whichever side of the argument he places himself, in whose mode of advocacy either want of candor, or malignity, bigotry, or intolerance of feeling manifest themselves; but not inferring these vices from the side which a person takes, though it be the contrary side of the question of our own; and giving merited honor to everyone, whatever opinion he may hold, who has calmness to see and honesty to state what his opponents and their opinions really are, exaggerating nothing to their discredit, keeping nothing back which tells, or can be supposed to tell, in their favor. This is the real morality of public discussion; and if often violated, I am happy to think that there are many controversialists who to a great extent observe it, and a still greater number who conscientiously strive towards it.

It has been the purpose of this book to facilitate communication by affording better understanding of what communication is. No one ever becomes perfectly able to express himself and to understand others. Perfection in communication, like perfection in machines, government, art, or anything else, is an ever-elusive ideal. But the best of ideals beckon: the more invitingly the better they are perceived.

PROBLEMS FOR DISCUSSION

A. Read Mill's essay, *On Liberty,* Chapters II and III. Is his kind of individualism impracticable in our contemporary world?

B. Read the works of John Milton in respect to liberty. Are his theses alien to American tradition?

C. Argue that good literary style has a job to do in democracies.

D. On the whole do radio and television facilitate the communication of political and economic ideas, or not? Does it seem to you that the authority of the Federal Communications Commission extends or restricts freedom of speech?

E. It is sometimes argued that inevitably a very large percentage of the populace of any country, regardless of its literacy, will simply be insufficiently intelligent to make important use of their freedom of speech; consequently, except for the élite, such freedom is really meaningless. Evaluate this argument.

F. Carl Rogers (*op. cit.*, p. 30) has offered this rule for introducing real understanding into an argument: " 'Each person can speak up for himself only *after* he has first restated the ideas and feelings of the previous speaker accurately and to that speaker's satisfaction.' " Is this too much to ask for? Would it solve *all* problems?

G. Rogers further insists that to do this takes great courage. "If you really understand another person in this way, if you are willing to enter his private world and see the way life appears to him, . . . you run the risk of being changed yourself. You might see it his way; you might find yourself influenced in your attitudes or your personality." (*Op. cit.*, p. 30). Do you agree? Is this fear sometimes back of censorship drives?

EXERCISES

I. Write a 1000 word essay on the meaning of freedom to communicate ideas.

II. Develop the best argument you can think of against freedom of speech and press.

III. Read Zarathustra's Prologue to First Part, *Thus Spake Zarathustra,* by Friedrich Nietzsche. Analyze its meaning in writing.

IV. Consult several issues of *ETC.* and report on one article that interests you.

SOURCES AND ADVANCED READING

1. L. Susan Stebbing, *Thinking to Some Purpose.* Harmondsworth, Middlesex, England: Penguin Books Limited, 1939. Ch. XV.

2. John Dewey, *The Public and Its Problems*. New York: Henry Holt and Company, 1927. Especially "Search for the Great Community."

3. John Stuart Mill, *On Liberty*. Reprinted, New York: F. S. Crofts & Co., Inc., 1947.

4. Carl Becker, *Freedom and Responsibility in the American Way of Life*. New York: A. A. Knopf, 1945.

5. Clarence I. Lewis, *The Ground and Nature of the Right*. New York: Columbia University Press, 1955. Especially "Right Believing and Concluding."

INDEX